To Save a Nation

Geoffrey S. Smith was born in San Francisco and studied history at the University of California, both at Santa Barbara and at Berkeley. He has written widely on American foreign policy and on the internal security policies of the United States. At present he is Professor of History at Queen's University in Kingston, Ontario.

TO SAVE A NATION

American 'Extremism,' the New Deal, and the Coming of World War II

GEOFFREY S. SMITH

REVISED EDITION
WITH A NEW EPILOGUE BY THE AUTHOR

Elephant Paperbacks

IVAN R. DEE, PUBLISHER, CHICAGO

First ELEPHANT PAPERBACK edition published 1992 by Ivan R. Dee, Inc., 1332 North Halsted Street, Chicago 60622. Manufactured in the United States of America and printed on acid-free paper.

Library of Congress Cataloging-in-Publication Data:
Smith, Geoffrey S.
    To save a nation : American 'extremism,' the New Deal, and the coming of World War II / Geoffrey S. Smith ; with a new epilogue by the author. — Rev. ed.
        p.   cm.
    "Elephant paperbacks."
    Includes bibliographical references and index.
    ISBN 0-929587-97-9 (pbk.)
    1. United States—Politics and government—1933–1945.   2. Right and left (Political science).   3. New Deal, 1933–1939.   4. Radicalism—United States—History—20th century. I. Title.
E806.S684   1992
320.973—dc20   92-13773

For my parents,
Dorothy Tuck Smith
and Harry B. Smith, Jr.

Preface

★ ★ ★ Like many books by younger scholars, the first edition of *To Save a Nation* reflected considerable indecision—in this instance about the relationship between American political "extremism," the political establishment, and groups that challenged that order. Perceptive reviewers noted and criticized this ambivalence. Yet there seemed compelling reasons for my uncertainty. *To Save a Nation* sought to analyze, explain, and ultimately question the administration of Franklin D. Roosevelt for its treatment of Americans who sincerely and resolutely opposed FDR's attempts to bring the United States into war against Hitler. Although I was suspicious of the strategies and tactics employed by FDR against his adversaries, most notably Charles A. Lindbergh and America First, I concluded that the gravity of the European crisis justified the president's dubious methods, however problematic these were for civil liberties.

I believe now, nearly two decades later, that my earlier historical interpretation, though essentially correct, did not go far enough in following through on questions I raised about the consequences of presidential strategies and tactics. I could not see beyond the liberal historiographical consensus that dominated so much of my upbringing and education.

Although in my early years my father was a Hoover Republican, and my uncle several steps to the right of him, my mother imbued me with a skepticism that prevented me from embracing their politics. As a student at the University of California in the late 1950s and early 1960s I might as well have been at Columbia, so enamored was I by the work of such scholars as Richard Hofstadter, William Leuchtenburg, Daniel Bell, and Seymour Martin Lipset. Their writing and arguments were congenial to a student who had trouble questioning President Clark Kerr's prediction that, as the flower of liberal planning, the "multiversity" would become the font of the "knowledge industry" and the driving dynamic for the second half of this century. With the accession of John F. Kennedy, liberal assumptions and aspirations reached their zenith.

I shared these assumptions and aspirations. Living through the 1960s altered my views, but ever so slowly—despite war, assassinations, riots, and political scandal, events that were nothing if not destructive of my earlier optimism. Not until the mid-1970s did I move away from the comfortable certainties of consensus historiography. Gazing southward across the forty-ninth parallel while developing and teaching a course on "Conspiracy and Dissent in American History" at Queen's University in Kingston, Canada, I became convinced that consensus history, despite its insights, ended up as an *apologia* for the status quo. It said little about real conflicts in history, about legitimate dissent, and about the ongoing competition for power between defenders of the established political order and their adversaries. The cumulative impact of the Vietnam War and the bizarre executive skullduggery that became known as Watergate, together with my own modest participation in the civil rights and antiwar protest movements, produced for me a new and, I trust, more balanced view of history, certainly one less accepting of explanations by political and social elites.

Hence the epilogue to this revised edition of *To Save a Nation* attempts to do two things. First, I argue emphatically that conspiracy theories informed the arguments put forth by both noninterventionists and interventionists before and during the Great Debate on American foreign policy, and that these notions helped to give such deliberations their polemical character. For reasons that will become clear, I am less willing now than I was in 1973 to defend the Roosevelt administration's strategies and tactics, especially after 1939. Further research in the years after 1973, together with the suggestions and insights of colleagues, have increased my misgivings, as has the tangled course of American history itself.

Second, because liberal internationalists triumphed in their battle with isolationists and noninterventionists (and in the process institutionalized the pejorative descriptions of their old adversaries), I seek to draw connections between that victory and the corresponding primacy of liberal-pluralist historiography and social science during the first two decades of the Cold War. Like political elites before and after World War II, liberal-pluralists sought to mediate between the excesses of a powerful state such as Nazi Germany or the Soviet Union, and the perceived dangers of mass democracy—thereby staving off the dangerous fusion of authoritarian rule and totalitarian ideology. I argue as well that despite the apparent sea change in American political life since the 1960s, the neoconservative notion of a menacing New Class in the 1970s was similar in many essentials to the earlier liberal-pluralist image of a dangerous conspiracy of radical rightists. It is one of the great ironies in recent American history that the New Right, which emerged in the late 1970s and helped bring Ronald Reagan to the White House, used many of the old liberal-pluralist arguments with great effect. Where Reagan and many of his supporters might have been grouped with the "fringe" right of the late 1950s and the early 1960s, by 1980 Reagan's opponents were both accused—and indicted—extremists.

In reflecting upon the fate of the noninterventionists, the ensuing dominance of liberal internationalists and liberal pluralists, and the usefulness (and meaninglessness) of the term "extremism," I offer several tentative hypotheses. First, for historians and social scientists the terms "extremist" and "extremism" during the last half-century are most useful as clues to the fears, aspirations, and ideologies of the groups and individuals employing them, rather than as descriptions (and prescriptions) based on assumed reality. Second, though this point was also shrouded before the late 1960s, conspiracy fears and assertions have always been a feature of mainstream politics, not merely the fringes. If these fears and assertions have been used to greater effect by "ins" more than "outs," this does not mean that when the "outs" gain authority they will eschew conspiracy accusations. This power is not merely political but may suffuse the entire culture. Third, by polarizing conflict situations in abstract, often symbolic, terms, conspiracy theorists both within and outside government have shifted national debates away from real problems involving class, race, gender, and the national interest abroad to symbolic, often ephemeral issues. This process, in turn, has blurred definitions of difficult and complex policy questions and exacerbated their resolution. Conspiracy accusations make for fashionable theatre—the more theories the better, film producer Oliver Stone might say. Clearly, the current popularity and marketability of such theories and accusations—primarily within dominant communications media—reflect a national leadership undeniably cynical and a populace increasingly bewildered.

Many people, colleagues and friends, have helped me think and rethink my hypotheses about the place and meaning of conspiracies and "extremism" in American life since the 1930s. Since the original publication of *To Save a Nation* I have discussed and debated with—and learned more of these matters from—(among many others) Robert A. Divine, Gaddis Smith, Robert H. Ferrell, Leo P. Ribuffo, Justus Doenecke, Roger Daniels, Wayne S. Cole, Richard M. Fried, Richard Parry, William M. Tuttle, Jr., Myf Marshall, Jack Kurzweil, and Wilson Carey McWilliams. Alexander DeConde has been a source of continuing support, as have colleagues George Rawlyk, Klaus Hansen, and Sandra Taylor, as well as librarians and archivists at Queen's and many other universities, the National Archives, the Library of Congress, the Smithsonian Institution, and the Franklin D. Roosevelt Library. Finally, I am grateful to Ivan R. Dee for making this revised paperback edition possible. I, of course, remain responsible for errors and interpretations in this book.

Footnotes have been omitted from this new edition of *To Save a Nation*. Readers who wish to check them may refer to the original edition (1973); to two later articles, "Isolationism, the Devil, and the Advent of the Second World War: Variations on a Theme," *International History Review*, IV

(February 1982), 55–88, and "Racial Nativism and the Origins of Japanese American Relocation" in Roger Daniels, Sandra C. Taylor, and Harry H. L. Kitano, eds., *Japanese Americans: From Relocation to Redress* (Salt Lake City, 1986), 79–87 (2nd rev. ed., Seattle, 1991, same pp.); and to "The Strange Career of American Extremism: From McCarthy to Reagan," a paper presented at the 1991 meeting of the Organization of American Historians, Louisville, Ky. The Bibliographical Note to this new edition of *To Save a Nation* indicates those secondary sources to which I owe my greatest debt.

I also wish to thank the great numbers of Queen's undergraduates who have made my lecture course "Conspiracy and Dissent in American History" such an exciting challenge during the last twenty years. Roberta Hamilton, my partner in life and intellect (if not always in agreement), has offered constant stimulation and constructive criticism. My dog, Tuborg, by demanding his four daily walks, made certain that I would not become too stodgy during this revision. My children, David, Brian, and Kristin, have often wondered why their father became an historian. Now, I think, they know—and I dedicate this book to them.

G. S. S.

Kingston, Ontario
March 1992

Contents

7

To Save a Nation

Introduction:
The Alien as Nativist

★ ★ ★ At first glance Father Charles Coughlin, William Dudley
Pelley, and Fritz Kuhn strike the observer as waste products of the Great Depression. There is a good deal of evidence that sustains this view. Essentially
nonpolitical creatures, these men ignored normal channels for securing change
and reform and preached a gospel of hatred and despair. Failing to clarify
how they would lead their followers to power, the American countersubversives depended primarily upon self-avowed powers of charisma. Yet instead of galvanizing the faithful to action, their apocalyptic predictions and
negative symbolism served only to sink their supporters into deeper apathy
and alienation. For these men, protest became a matter of stylistic self-expression, not at all geared to the problem of persuading the masses. Indeed,
although they claimed to be agents of destiny, Coughlin, Pelley, and Kuhn
emerged as men who seemed to derive perverse delight from practicing the
most brutal form of character assassination, disdaining common courtesies,
and disregarding entirely the opinions of their adversaries.

Priding themselves upon their Americanism, the extremists should have
sensed that their anti-Semitism, the major theme that tied them together spiritually, was repugnant to most Americans during the 1930s. Indeed, since the
arrival of the Puritans at Massachusetts Bay, American and Jewish values
had exhibited a striking similarity. When Thomas Jefferson suggested as a
design for the seal of the infant United States "the children of Israel in the
wilderness, led by a cloud by day and a pillar by night," he emphasized the
resemblance between the Puritans who, considering themselves members of
an elect body, established a "City on a Hill" to exemplify righteousness in an
evil world and the Jews, a chosen people who were forced to flee from the

3

promised land. And Jews accommodated themselves well to the mores of the United States. Embracing the principles of voluntaryism and pluralism which characterized denominational Protestantism in the early nineteenth century, Jews also accepted the competitive values that dominated national business life—thrift, enterprise, and rational calculation in the marketplace. In addition, the Jewish community actually benefited from the xenophobia that characterized the 1920s, an intolerant era in which racial and religious minorities were excluded from high political and social office. With the advent of economic chaos in 1929, representatives of the established order were clearly exposed. The American people vented their anger not on any ethnic minority, as was the case in Germany, but upon individuals who were preponderantly white, Anglo-Saxon, and Protestant.

Even as the American Jew achieved political and social influence as a member of the New Deal coalition, several fortuitous circumstances prevented anti-Semitism from becoming popular. For one thing, the 1930s were marked by a spirit of ethnic liberalism. By developing new hypotheses derived not from biological but from environmental and relativistic frames of reference, reputable scholars laid to rest many of the racist assumptions that had previously dominated American life. Then too, immigration restrictions that had been placed on Jews during the 1920s had the ironic effect of accelerating the process of Jewish acculturation into middle-class America. Organized Jewish religion provided the sense of identity and community that had formerly been found in the ghetto. So complete was this process of cultural homogenization that by 1937 demographers discovered that Jewish migration within the United States had ceased almost entirely. But Jews were less visible than they might have been for yet another reason: with the possible exception of the candidacy of Alfred E. Smith in 1928, ethnic issues had never been a major divisive force in American politics. And the language spoken by such disparate critics of Roosevelt's programs as Herbert Hoover, Norman Thomas, and Communist Party leader Earl Browder, was culled from a political tradition that tended to de-emphasize religious and social conflict.

In seizing upon the Jews as the paramount menace to American values and traditions, the countersubversives committed a serious strategic blunder. Yet even if they lacked what historian Henry S. Commager has called "the dignity of intelligence or accuracy and a moral purpose," an assertion that will be contested later in this book, their irrational behavior and perfervid emotionalism may nevertheless be analyzed to suggest the kinds of tension that permeated American society during the 1930s. It was, in fact, the troubled milieu of 1929 that catapulted Father Coughlin from the obscurity of a rural pastorate in Royal Oak into millions of American living rooms as a microphone messiah. Through his masterful understanding of the potential of radio technology and his disarmingly simple analysis of the economic and social state of the nation, the priest suddenly found himself the wielder of great power.

During the years preceding Pearl Harbor, the cleric was labeled a populist, a democrat, a radical, a conservative, a Nazi, and a communist. And as a mirror image of the fears and aspirations of the American people, he indeed personified these political stances—and more. Although he preached a gospel that emphasized the necessity of restoring the old order (or of achieving a new order in which old values would be revived), his activities foreshadowed those of later clerics who correctly foresaw the stifling of individuality in an impersonal and industrial society. In addition, while he denounced big government consistently during his public career, the radio clergyman's inconsistent demands for reform in 1931 and 1932 actually prepared many citizens for the policy of state planning that was institutionalized by the New Deal.

If Coughlin's proposed solutions to existing ills were often naive, his rhetorical style was amazingly complex. He was, with the exception of President Roosevelt, probably the most eclectic thinker of the day, borrowing an idea here, modifying it there, citing, quoting, and adducing. The priest sought authorities to support his views, and in most cases the sources to which he turned—the Constitution, the papal encyclicals issued by Leo XIII and Pius XI, George Washington's Farewell Address—were employed not to develop a careful argument but to buttress his otherwise unsupportable assertions.

While anti-Semitism became a central theme in Coughlin's rhetoric only in 1938, and even then as a seeming last resort, anti-Jewish imagery was both a mania and a means of support for William Dudley Pelley. Somewhat scatterbrained and schemeful, but withal shrewd, Pelley spent the 1920s dissipating his energies as a writer in a futile attempt to secure fame and fortune. A mystical religious experience changed his outlook in 1928, however, and with the accession to power of Adolf Hitler five years later, he established his own countersubversive, paramilitary organization to solve the "Jewish problem" in the United States. For every problem, he believed, there was a Jewish cause. Yet despite this obsession he exhibited intellectual and technical ability. In his published works, especially *No More Hunger* and *Nations-In-Law*, he envisioned a good society ruled by a national "Christian Commonwealth" and a global "Aryan Federation." Although many of his ideas were as utopian as Father Coughlin's sixteen-point Union Party platform of 1936, Pelley's sources were somewhat more esoteric: German philosopher G. W. F. Hegel; Herbert Spencer, the father of Social Darwinism; and Edward Bellamy, the American reformer of the late nineteenth century.

Like Coughlin, who encountered trouble with his monetary theories, and Fritz Kuhn, who embezzled from his group's treasury on the excuse of the Nazi *Führerprinzip*, Pelley epitomized the tendency of countersubversive leaders during the depression to seek personal and financial aggrandizement at the expense of men and women who were starved for leadership. At the propaganda-for-profit game the Silver Shirts leader was, for several years, quite successful. Later, however, his luck ran out and he was revealed as a charlatan—a salesman of patent medicine disguised as ideology—and in the long run such types have fared poorly in American political life.

Less an offshoot of domestic troubles than a reaction to the appearance of a mighty force rising from the ashes of post-Versailles Germany, the German-American Bund attracted to its banners youthful immigrants, often unemployed, who were excited by Hitler's New Germany and who willingly surrendered their personal freedom to the *Führer's* American emulators. The organization's most publicized leader, Fritz Kuhn, fancied himself a sidewalk Sorel, but in truth he was more like a Manhattan version of Charles Chaplin's Bohemian corporal. Physically corpulent, spiritually lethargic, and oratorically ponderous, Kuhn could not match either Coughlin's ability to enchant his radio audiences or Pelley's curiously cerebral anti-Semitism. So he and his supporters adopted a more direct approach—confrontation politics. Yet this method did not terrorize the Yorkville populace into a state of helpless submission. On the contrary, the Bundists enraged American opponents of Hitler and, in one of the more humorous and often overlooked episodes of those dark days after 1937, proved a constant source of embarrassment to the professionals in the German Foreign Ministry.

Claiming to represent the Axis cause, which they had identified as America's own, the countersubversives impressed most citizens as traitors, or at best sadly misguided men with little constructive to say. Yet in a narrow sense, their emotional attacks upon a Jewish-communist global conspiracy constituted a restatement of historian George Bancroft's assertion that America was God's Israel on earth. Lamenting the passing of American innocence, albeit in different ways, Coughlin, Pelley, and Kuhn employed a kind of countersubversive rhetoric that enabled Americans who felt alienated from their own country to reconstruct symbolically a good society free from the bewildering changes occurring around them.

In their countersubversive persuasion, Coughlin, Pelley, and Kuhn had much in common with earlier nativists. But in one crucial respect the extremists of the 1930s departed from tradition, and this difference had significant implications for the evolving Great Debate on American diplomacy before Pearl Harbor. Like most Americans, nativists historically drew their inspiration and strength from a national consensus notable for its uniform political, social, and economic goals and values. Speaking in behalf of this consensus in relatively tranquil times—that is, when citizens exhibit little disagreement as to what constitutes a "good" American—xenophobes generally attacked ethnic and religious minorities, emphasizing their alien characteristics and criticizing their tendency to remain outside the mainstream of national life. But in eras marked by widespread economic distress or by real or imagined ideological or military threats from without, the consensus has ossified to a point where values are no longer held merely in common by the American people; instead, they must be shared. When this occurs, Alexis de Tocqueville's threatened "tyranny of the majority" evolves into a more portentous danger of unanimity; the capital "A" in "American" grows larger; and external threats become internalized.

This is essentially what happened during the depression. In order to exorcise alien ideas and conventions from the body politic, Coughlin, Pelley, and the Bundists became vigilantes of a peculiar sort. Rather than attacking actual alien groups on ethnic, economic, or religious grounds, the countersubversives purveyed a strangely transposed, or inverted, form of nativism. The radio priest, for example, did not attack identifiable foreigners at all. He decried treason by members of the establishment—Herbert Hoover, Andrew Mellon, WASP *rentiers,* government functionaries, and, finally, the entire Roosevelt administration. This approach allowed Coughlin's German-American, Italian-American, and Irish-American supporters—the traditional targets of American nativists—to retaliate against their former tormentors. Pelley's "Judeo-Bolshevik" conspiracy served a similar purpose for dispossessed agrarians, in fact and in belief, who were angered and befuddled by chaotic economic conditions, the seeming callousness of the emerging technological and urban nation, and the ethnic and religious heterogeneity of the New Deal political coalition. The Bund provided a similar outlet for the minority of German-Americans caught in the impossible position of reconciling their own Americanism with their admiration for Hitler's totalitarian leviathan.

Although the extremists generated most of their fire in contending that alien forces already controlled the nation's destiny, this allegation was in itself less important than the reasons for its use. By suggesting that the members of the legitimate political order were the real aliens in America, Coughlin and his fellow countersubversives in effect pinpointed those persons and groups whom they perceived to obstruct the main routes of access to affluence and political power. The symbolic statements of Americanism that emanated from these men thus allowed their followers, erstwhile aliens, to become American nativists in good standing.

The theme of aliens posing as nativists was a novelty in American history, and in the context of deepening global crises, a major cause of the declining influence of responsible isolationism after 1939. Having fought the administration's domestic policies, the inverted nativists now undertook the task of preventing Jewish and communist conspirators from landing the United States in war. Soon, however, like the boy who cried "wolf!" the countersubversives themselves had become victims of a subtle counterattack launched by interventionists and liberal Democrats who realized the potential uses to which an indigenous "fascist" fifth column might be put.

The mere existence of numerous organizations that loosely qualified as fascistic should not have implied that these groups were also well-organized or in any way professionally coordinated. But this is exactly what transpired: the menace posed by the superpatriots-turned-traitors was perceived as terrifyingly real by growing numbers of Americans. The popular fear of countersubversive strength and unity was undeniably overdrawn, but it was also a manifestation of a generalized fascist scare that began in 1933 and 1934 and accelerated in response to a milieu that was nearly as fearful as during the nadir of depression, and of the concomitant desire of nervous liberal Democrats to attack some variety of un-Americanism not connected with the Communist Party. The reason for this sensitivity is not difficult to isolate; it came from within the Democracy and ironically assumed the form of yet another, more potent movement of countersubversion, a movement that was sanctioned by the government and public opinion—the House Committee on Un-American Activities. Reacting angrily to Chairman Martin Dies's charge that certain New Dealers were abetting the cause of communism in the United States, ardent leftists attempted to link Dies with the Coughlins and Pelleys of the land to prove that the Committee was oriented toward fascism. It was, therefore, an historical accident that enabled the extremists to gain renewed attention just when it appeared that their star had slipped beneath the horizon.

Failing to realize that this publicity was the figurative tail fin on the black herring hooked by liberals to hurl at the Dies Committee, each of the countersubversive leaders made as much of his notoriety as possible and, in the years preceding Pearl Harbor, unwittingly allowed advocates of Roosevelt's foreign policy to posit the existence of a fascist menace where none in fact existed. Although the perverted patriots attempted to ride the surging tide of sincere isolationist sentiment, their cynical disregard for national security and the fate of Continental democracy tended to leave them perched upon the totalitarian wave of the future. With the advent of war in 1939, their position became completely untenable. The United States no longer faced a threat from international bankers, Judeo-Bolsheviks, or a secret cabal located in Washington. The enemy, in the minds of most Americans, was Nazi Germany.

In the activities and rhetoric of the countersubversives, interventionists discovered some effective arguments. Bundist rallies at Madison Square Garden and the "exercises" conducted by Pelley's Silver Legion seemed in fact to echo noises made by goose-stepping Nazi SS or by party faithful convening at Nuremberg, while Father Coughlin's excoriations of Judaism seemed to come directly from the throat of Propaganda Minister Joseph Paul Goebbels. The effect of such superficial resemblances was profound. In the eyes of many Americans, just as the extremists did not escape the implication of their mimicry of the Nazis, so also did Berlin fail to cleanse itself of the stigma left by the extremists.

The countersubversives actually facilitated President Roosevelt's education of the American people on the delicate subject of national security. Although disguised in red-white-and-blue bunting, extremist propaganda could only increase sympathy for Great Britain. Even more important, however, the emotionalism and irrationality of the yahoos made it nearly impossible for responsible noninterventionist spokesmen to discuss dispassionately the demerits of executive diplomacy. With each reorientation of American policy, the isolationist burden grew more onerous. By the middle of 1941, in fact, the Great Debate had itself become a symbolic discussion. The issue of national security seemed buried amid a welter of charge and countercharge. The impassioned remarks of interventionists and noninterventionists alike illustrated the power of the fear of conspiracies to turn sincere persons into persecutors, bent on impugning the motives and blackening the reputations of their adversaries.

Isolationism had been a comparatively respectable term during the 1920s and early 1930s, but as America drew closer to actual war it became an epithet. The failure of noninterventionists to free themselves from pejoratively imputed totalitarian sympathies provided incontrovertible evidence of this progression. In September 1941, following his ill-conceived address in Des Moines, Iowa, Charles A. Lindbergh and isolationists everywhere stood convicted of un-American conduct. Their culpability, to be sure, was in large measure a case of guilt by association. They had been victimized by the moral obtuseness, hysteria, malice, and prejudice of their extremist admirers.

1

Father Coughlin: The Radio Messiah

★ ★ ★ Between 1926 and 1936, the Reverend Charles E. Coughlin rose from obscurity as a parish priest in Royal Oak, Michigan, to become both a national hero and villain. A striking figure, he aroused devoted enthusiasm and strong criticism. Some Americans saw in his skillful use of the radio evidence of Christ's imminent Second Coming, while others labeled the cleric a fascist. The story of Coughlin's success provides an important chapter in the text of the American dream; but, unlike Horatio Alger's homilies of "Ragged Dick" and "Mark, the Match Boy," it illustrates the fact that the national mythos of rising from unimportance to fame need not necessarily end on a happy note.

Little in Coughlin's early life hinted at his excesses of later years. The only child of Thomas and Amelia Coughlin of Hamilton, Ontario, he was born into an environment of unpretentious, middle-class Catholicism on October 25, 1891. Inheriting more his mother's spirituality than his baker-father's passion for work, he became a robust youth who often escaped classroom drudgery by playing truant from St. Michael's Parochial School. At age twelve he entered St. Michael's College, affiliated with the University of Toronto. Here, guided by the Basilian Fathers, he studied Greek, Latin, and scholastic philosophy. He also enjoyed poetry, except Romantic works, which he disdained for their pagan qualities. He possessed a quick wit and a keen intellect and did not fear entering class unprepared. If called upon to recite, he would rise to his feet and with a confidence that belied his youth, extemporize brilliantly on subjects as diverse as religion, politics, and sociology.

As a student at St. Michael's, Coughlin practiced the strenuous life. A regular on the handball court, he also became a favorite of local rugby fans for

11

his inspired play. For the impressionable youth, manliness and athletic prowess were as important as the precepts of medieval scholasticism. Both as student and athlete, Coughlin revered authority, equating the primacy of teacher and athletic coach with the omniscience of God and Church. Leaders, he believed, were to be obeyed.

Following graduation and a subsequent tour of Europe, Coughlin returned to Canada, where a conversation with a former teacher convinced him that he possessed a religious vocation. Ordained a priest in the Basilian Order in June 1916, he subsequently joined the faculty of Assumption College in Sandwich, Ontario, where he taught English, Greek, history, philosophy, and theology. His students respected him as a stern disciplinarian. By 1920 his reputation had impressed the bishop of Detroit, Michael Gallagher. Beset by a shortage of priests to tend growing flocks in the greater Detroit area, Bishop Gallagher arranged a permanent transfer for Coughlin to the metropolitan diocese. After serving a Kalamazoo parish for three years, the cleric moved to North Branch and, two years later, took up a charge in suburban Royal Oak.

Located north of Detroit and described by one observer as "a raw, desolate, partially inhabited, suburban frontier," Royal Oak presented Father Coughlin with a severe test. Only twenty-five Catholic families inhabited the shingled, jerrybuilt homes that comprised his parish. More numerous than local faithful were members of the Ku Klux Klan, the nativist organization that considered Catholicism anathema to the nation's values and steadfastly opposed the encroachments of the automotive industry and the phenomenal growth of yet another "subversive" city.

Coughlin literally had time to make a hasty sign of the cross before the Klan welcomed him with a fiery cross planted in front of his church. This confrontation with local forces of intolerance had an immediate effect. The priest determined to oppose actively all manifestations of bigotry in the neighborhood. Possessing a church and steeple but lacking people, he decided to employ radio to attack the Klan and to discuss important moral issues. He had a commanding voice, and listeners might drive to Royal Oak to hear him. He could build up a larger audience for his Sunday sermons.

Ignoring the pleas of parishioners to avoid controversy, Coughlin discussed his plan with a sympathetic friend and fellow Irish-Catholic, Leo J. Fitzpatrick, who agreed with the cleric's idea. The owner of radio station WJR in Detroit, Fitzpatrick launched Coughlin's radio career on Sunday afternoon, October 26. For the next four years, the "Golden Hour from the Shrine of the Little Flower" apprised listeners, mostly children, of the importance of the Golden Rule and other moral precepts. Soon, attendance at the priest's Sunday masses increased notably. Americans of all creeds wrote appreciative letters, often including voluntary contributions.

Undeniably, Father Coughlin's greatest asset was his unforgettable speaking voice. Despite primitive radio technology, the cleric's rich, mellow, and musical tone, highlighted by an engaging brogue, caught the ear. To hear the priest, according to one listener, was to understand him. Coughlin's was a voice made for fervent hopes.

The Wall Street crash of October 1929 and ensuing economic chaos allowed the Royal Oak pastor to tap the potential power from his church of the air. Although many Americans initially believed that they could explain the reasons for their distress, their temple of optimism was soon shaken. There were no simple answers to solve the riddle of economic collapse. Men and women lost their savings, their homes, and their farms. The long lines of unemployed grew longer—5 million in 1930, 9 million in 1931, and nearly 13 million in 1932. Historically a wandering people, Americans were transformed into legions of dispirited nomads. By November 1932, according to statistics released by the United States' Children's Bureau and the National Association of Travelers' Aid Societies, more than 25,000 families and 200,000 young men and women had become vagabonds, inhabiting boxcars and hobo jungles, traveling by freight, and depending upon their wits for food and clothing.

Only occasionally during 1927 and 1928 had Father Coughlin commented upon nonreligious matters. With the onslaught of the depression, however, he became a full-fledged political analyst. On January 12, 1930, the priest told listeners on an enlarged CBS network that after careful research he had discovered an active communist conspiracy within the United States. Hitting hard at "Russia and the Red Serpent," he traced the source of Soviet subversion to the font of eighteenth-century Bavarian Illuminatism. A barrage of letters criticizing his performance as unbecoming a Catholic priest only succeeded in furthering his determination to wage war against the internal Bolshevik menace. Strengthened by the creation of the Radio League of the Little Flower, through which he financed his broadcasts, the cleric stepped up his attack. He directed his harshest words at contemporary social evils—divorce, birth control, free love—all of which he linked to communism. "Christian parents," he asked, "do you want your daughter to be the breeder of some lustful person's desire, and when the rose of her youth has withered, to be thrown upon the highway of Socialism? It is either the marriage feast of Cana or the brothel of Lenin!"

Testifying in July before Representative Hamilton Fish's House Committee to Investigate Communist Activities, Coughlin predicted that unless stern measures were taken, a revolution would sweep the country. The rebellion would not be led by a dispossessed proletariat, he warned. Rather, the uprising would result from the failure of the rich to work for social justice. Henry Ford, and not the hungry worker, epitomized the force that could produce an American Bolshevism. Having recently signed a 13-million-dollar contract with the Soviet Government, Ford had become, in Coughlin's words, an unwitting agent of the communist conspiracy and "the greatest force in the movement to internationalize labor throughout the world."

The symbol of social justice provided Coughlin with a catch phrase and program of action. Although he never advocated the destruction of the capitalist system, the priest stressed the necessity of state intervention to restrict the use of private property. Like St. Thomas Aquinas, he believed that in the divine nature of things private ownership entailed wise stewardship. If the property owner failed to meet his social responsibility, then the state should intervene to enforce a program of Christian socialism.

Coughlin's Thomistic views were buttressed by encyclicals issued by Popes Leo XIII in 1891 and Pius XI forty years later. Pope Leo's *Rerum Novarum* sought to avoid class warfare by diverting Catholic laborers from the charms of Marxian socialism. In treating their workers as chattel, the document charged, employers had undermined the dignity of labor and forced many Catholics to embrace socialism. The future of European Catholicism could be saved only by a rapprochement between labor and capital for the greater glory of God.

The onset of the depression produced another official statement on social issues. In his *Quadregesimo Anno,* Pius XI decried the failure of capitalism and sharply criticized American rugged individualism. Capitalist domination having injured the general community, he argued, a just wage for all workers and the public ownership of property would provide the sole means to prevent the tyranny of one class over another.

Thomistic doctrine and the papal encyclicals heavily influenced Coughlin's social thought, but it was Bishop Gallagher who provided the cleric with his greatest support. His career grounded in the traditions of Austrian Social Catholicism, Gallagher had studied at Innsbruck during the 1890s and became an admirer of Monsignor Seipal, the Austrian premier following the First World War. A close friend of Engelbert Dollfuss, elected premier in 1932, the Detroit prelate would march in the latter's funeral cortege two years later. A staunch champion of clerical corporatism, Gallagher emerged as his subordinate's first line of defense. In fact, had the Detroit bishop possessed a good radio voice, Coughlin might never have left the pulpit of his Church of St. Therese of the Little Flower and the Child Jesus.

In October 1930, hoping to convert American business leaders to a policy of social justice, Father Coughlin initiated a new season of radio broadcasts. The priest could not accept the prevailing philosophy of rugged individualism, which told Americans that their misfortune resulted from personal failures to practice the virtues of hard work, frugality, and self-reliance. The problem, Coughlin reasoned, lay not with the people but with the men who controlled the capitalist system. Most likely, although some observers argued to the contrary, the priest's first economic sermon, "Charity—the Policy of Christ," reflected his profound distress at social and economic conditions.

Coughlin's motives may have been uncertain, but there can be no doubt that his early prominence resulted less from the veracity of his own arguments than from the frustrations of his unseen audience. Most listeners ignored the priest's failure to document his charges and heard only an honest Catholic cleric attempting to unravel the mysteries of the depression. This Coughlin did beautifully. By constructing his plot around a single villain or group of villains, he reduced abstract social and moral questions to a mundane common denominator and thus enabled lower-middle-class Americans to project a sense of personal guilt onto an easily identifiable external group. In other words, Coughlin offered his listeners—Jew and Gentile alike—absolution for their sins. His soothing voice, spiced with jeremiad and vivid metaphor, revealed to them their spiritual and financial betrayal by international bankers and American capitalists who had controlled national currency at the time of the Great Crash.

In January 1931, following a conversation with Representative Louis T. McFadden of Pennsylvania, a Jew-baiter and acrid critic of the Treaty of Versailles, Father Coughlin became a center of national controversy. According to statistics produced by McFadden, only a revision of the treaty would prevent another war and at the same time rescue the world from the ravages of the depression. The Royal Oak cleric, who had already criticized President Woodrow Wilson for shielding the machinations of international financiers, realized that the controversial Versailles pact was a timely issue and hoped to profit from its discussion. But officials of the Columbia Broadcasting System, worried by complaints concerning Coughlin's discussion of Bolshevism, attempted to persuade him to change his subject. This the priest did, but on January 4, 1931, he spoke critically of the attempt by CBS to censor him. The results of the broadcast were astonishing: approximately 1,250,000 letters arrived at CBS affiliates across the nation. The voluminous mail contained a singular and unequivocal demand: Coughlin must be allowed to express freely his own thoughts.

Strengthened by this manifestation of public support, the priest devoted his next radio sermon to the problems of unemployment. Claiming to possess facts and figures to support his allegations, he charged that "Shylocks" in London and Wall Street remained interested only in returns on their heavy European investments despite the terrible suffering around them. Terming unjust the reparations settlements saddled upon Germany at the end of the war, he also criticized the Dawes and Young Plans, through which the United States Government had attempted to revive European economies during the 1920s. These plans, he argued, were unnecessary attempts to salvage a treaty that had failed to produce peace either in Europe or America. The radio sermon produced another flood of letters, most of them positive, although some writers questioned the priest's competency to discuss matters of national importance.

Coughlin's success in condemning the Versailles Treaty became a Pyrrhic victory when CBS soon afterwards discontinued sponsoring his radio sermons. Unable to secure another outlet through the NBC network, the cleric organized his own string of stations, and by late spring the "Golden Hour" reached twenty-six states from Colorado to Maine. Although by depression standards the weekly cost of the program ($14,000) was astronomical, Coughlin's drawing power was even greater. Twenty thousand dollars a week enabled him to meet his bills and to bank substantial sums. Ironically, while most Americans were forced to eke out a living, the radio shepherd of discontent entered a period of prosperity and power.

Coughlin's proclivity for argument quickly earned him the title of "a religious Walter Winchell." Undaunted, the clergyman next directed his fire at President Herbert Hoover. The Chief Executive, Coughlin reasoned, shared with the communists and international bankers guilt for America's misfortunes. In fact, however, Hoover's greatest sin was that he occupied the White House when the depression struck. An outstanding civil engineer in happier days, the President insisted that if federal funds were employed to combat the depression, the proper place to expend the money would be in strategic banks, railroads, and other corporations. Fearing the creation of a burdensome bureaucracy which would sap the initiative and self-reliance of the American people, Hoover also opposed the direct expenditure of federal credit to relieve the unemployed or the farmers.

Using as a contrast Hoover's commendable role in helping feed hungry Europeans following the First World War, Coughlin ridiculed the President's policy of leaving relief measures to local agencies. In a radio sermon entitled "Hoover Prosperity Means Another War," the cleric announced that the administration's "airy platitudes" provided Americans a poor means of sustenance. Coughlin's own charitable society had already raised half the required $15,000 to provide milk for destitute Detroit children, while the rest of the county had scraped together a meager $3,500. If this was an example of Hoover's answer to the depression, the priest reasoned, then almighty God Himself should be condemned for aiding the Jews in the desert, when that hardy people found it impossible to sustain life.

Probably nothing that Hoover could have done would have protected him from Coughlin's attacks. But the manner in which the President operated was especially vexing. When Hoover employed federal funds, as in the establishment of the Reconstruction Finance Corporation, the clergyman charged that by operating on a Hamiltonian theory of aid, the agency would benefit only the capitalists. Hoover had become "the banker's friend, the Holy Ghost of the Rich, the protective angel of Wall Street." In all of his attacks upon the Republican relief program, Coughlin did not specify weaknesses but satisfied his listeners with broad charges. In this spirit the cleric termed the Federal Farm Loan Administration "an agent of torture and destruction and confiscation," and the Agricultural Marketing Act "financial socialism."

Concerned that many spiritual shepherds were neglecting their hungry flocks, the Royal Oak pastor engaged in a vituperative debate over prohibition with Dr. Clarence True Wilson, executive secretary of the Board of Temperance, Prohibition, and Public Morals of the Methodist Episcopal Church. The quarrel stemmed from a meeting held in Detroit on September 21, where President Hoover appealed to American Legion conventioneers "to enlist in a war to bring back business stability and prosperity." Apparently the Chief Executive's plea had no effect, for when he finished, the assemblage chanted in unison, "We want beer! We want beer!"

The impassioned outburst shocked Dr. Wilson, who announced that the veterans had behaved like "perjured scoundrels" at a drunken orgy. Under no circumstances, he argued, should the men hide under the aegis of the American flag. Old Glory was too good for them.

Coughlin seized the issue to defend the soldiers and professed shock at what he termed Wilson's sacrilegious infamy. "These dead soldiers," he cried, "whose lips no longer can themselves defend; their old mothers and broken-hearted wives and little boys and girls whose voices are too inarticulate to shield themselves—these have become the latest targets of attack in defense of Prohibition!" Offering cold consolation to the survivors of these heroes, Coughlin continued, Wilson had "sneered into the ears of their children and wives and gray-haired mothers. . . ." Referring directly to Wilson, the priest concluded that not all radicals wore overalls. On the contrary, conservatives were often "the worst of radicals." Paradoxically, then, by the end of 1931, Coughlin's ship of subversion was manned by communists, socialists, international capitalists, and a Methodist clergyman.

Early in 1932 Coughlin again answered the call of American veterans when he offered his support to a controversial bonus plan. In addition to helping veterans and their families, the priest reasoned, the bonus would also revalue the dollar to its 1929 level and force the United States off the gold standard. By increasing the value of farm products and the honest work of labor, passage of the bonus proposal would result in "a mighty victory . . . over the massed armies of depression and growing discontent," and avert an internal revolution of immense proportion. The cleric did not hesitate to remind listeners of the bloody excesses of the French and Russian uprisings.

Coughlin's position conflicted directly with the views of Andrew Mellon, Secretary of the Treasury, who believed that the bonus plan would bankrupt America. In the midst of depression, Mellon argued, it was a time to retrench —not to spend. Expecting such an answer from the administration, the priest considered Mellon a partner in the unholy alliance of the Four M's— including J. P. Morgan, Ogden Mills, and Eugene Myer—Coughlin's modern version of the Four Horsemen of the Apocalypse. Paraphrasing a statement reputed to have been made by American diplomat Charles Cotesworth Pinckney in 1798, the cleric retorted for Mellon's benefit: "Billions for the international bankers who never fought! But none to the soldier who risked life and limb!"

The Bonus Expeditionary Force that marched to the outskirts of Washington, D.C., in the late spring hoped to convince Capitol Hill legislators of the righteousness of its cause. On July 16, however, Congress adjourned without considering the measure. By July 28 a pitiful group of 5,000 men, women, and children remained encamped on Anacostia flats. That evening, following two incidents involving District police, the United States Army forced the veterans to flee. Acting on orders from President Hoover, who failed to understand that the Bonus Army had become a "whipped, melancholy group of men trying to hold themselves together when their spirit was gone," General

Douglas MacArthur employed cavalry, infantry, machine gunners, and six tanks in the operation. Subsequently, the campsites were razed. Hoover and his advisers assumed that the Anacostian army presented a lawless, communistic threat to the nation's welfare. The savage treatment accorded the Bonus Force shocked Father Coughlin, who had endorsed the march and contributed $5,000 to its leaders. In an emotional radio sermon, he lauded their "sweat and blood," and "great sacrifice in defense of Christian ethics." The priest also approved the policy of District Police Chief Pelham D. Glassford, who displayed composure in controlling the situation until the issuance of Hoover's fateful order.

The controversial radio priest engaged in another battle during the last year of Hoover's administration, bringing him his first contact with Franklin D. Roosevelt. By midsummer political and personal enemies finally cornered the colorful mayor of New York City, James Walker, who faced an investigation for alleged fraud. His opponents, including Rabbis Sidney Goldstein and Stephen Wise, socialist Norman Thomas, left-wing columnist Heywood Broun, and the liberal leader of the Park Avenue Community Church, the Reverend John Heynes Holmes, hoped to destroy him, thereby embarrassing Tammany Hall and Governor Roosevelt, now Democratic candidate for president.

An Irish-Catholic, Walker received Father Coughlin's support. Convinced of the mayor's innocence, the clergyman wrote Roosevelt, charging that "communists" like Wise and Holmes had used Walker in a plot to undermine the confidence of the American people in local, state, and national government. Certain clever Republicans, furthermore, had utilized the conspiracy to defeat Walker in November. Thus the governor ought to give Walker his day in court. Aware of Coughlin's reputation, Roosevelt also recognized the priest's potential power. Desirous of the cleric's support in the coming election, he agreed to let Walker answer the charges against him. Happily for Roosevelt, however, Walker resigned following open hearings held in Albany and the New York governor was never forced to reveal publicly his feelings on the case.

As Father Coughlin attracted increased national attention, a conservative Bostonian, William Cardinal O'Connell, stepped forward as the sole member of the Church hierarchy to voice opposition to the Royal Oak cleric. Though not mentioning the priest by name, Cardinal O'Connell feared that his activities would divide congregations and rekindle the historic American suspicion of clerical meddling in politics. "You can't begin speaking about the rich or making sensational accusations against banks or bankers or uttering demagogic stuff to the poor," he warned members of the Guild of St. Appalonia. "The Church does not take sides, rich or poor, Republican or Democrat."

The lack of genuine opposition to Coughlin from within the Church hierarchy may be explained partly by the fact that the cleric's attack upon American capitalists remained consistent with the Catholic tradition of only condemning movements and doctrines felt to be inimical to the faith. Yet the silence of Catholic leaders suggested less their approval of the priest than their recognition of his strength. Considering Coughlin's wide popularity and Bishop Gallagher's unflagging support of his ambitious charge, an open row would have risked serious internecine warfare. Thus by the end of 1932, it appeared that nothing could curb him.

Even more than his xenophobic nationalism, his Anglophobia, and his neo-Populist monetary theories, it was the radio that enabled Coughlin to establish his special relationship with discontented Americans. His sophisticated approach to radio technology signaled a new departure in the style of American dissent. Where earlier dissidents such as Tom Watson, "sockless" Jerry Simpson, and Mary Lease mounted hay wagons, park bandstands, and soapboxes to reach their public, Coughlin eschewed direct confrontation and influenced public opinion by remote control, thereby escaping possible hecklers.

And there were many indications to substantiate the priest's claim that he understood public opinion better than any other man. A listening audience estimated at from 30 to 45 million persons placed him ahead of such established performers as Gracie Allen, Ed Wynne, and Amos 'n Andy. Plans were underway to construct a larger church, which would not only house a circular altar to allow added contact with parishioners during Mass, but would also include a massive crucifixion tower in which Coughlin could take refuge from the throng of faithful followers and curiosity seekers that threatened to engulf him. Four new secretaries helped sort through voluminous correspondence. Researchers analyzed the complexities of the money question. And finally, the priest's parents joined their son in Royal Oak. Thomas Coughlin did gardening chores around the church, and Amelia served as a receptionist.

Visitors meeting Father Coughlin in person noted the priest's surprising shyness as well as his great personal charm. They were also struck by his size —a shade under six feet and nearly 200 pounds—and perhaps concluded from his ruddy complexion that the cleric was athletic. Coughlin's cobalt-blue eyes looked out calmly through ascetic, steel-rimmed glasses. But as he discussed religion, the theatre, baseball, or sex, he often smoked and enlivened his conversation with emphatic gestures or unsaintly expletives. After dismissing guests, the priest might turn to handball or bridge or walk the grounds of his church, accompanied by his Great Dane. Though he was not a recluse, Coughlin preferred to keep to the background.

His sonorous voice and persuasive charm having made him a Pied Piper of discontent, the radio priest enjoyed the support of a sympathetic bishop and stood in apparent agreement with the social teachings of the Catholic Church. Although he oversimplified the causes of the depression, the widely heralded Senate Banking Investigations of 1934 and 1935 reached similar conclusions. However, it was also clear that Coughlin achieved much early success by beating dead horses, President Hoover and the financiers having been unable to fight back. As Americans looked ahead to the inauguration of Franklin D. Roosevelt, that situation was subject to change.

2

An Uncertain Alliance

★ ★ ★ Franklin Delano Roosevelt may have lacked a clear notion of the methods needed to end the depression, but his inauguration clearly revived the spirit of the American people. The event also excited Father Coughlin, who had warmly endorsed the Democratic candidate and now, because of Roosevelt's failure to disavow this support, believed that he might become an unofficial spokesman for the new administration. But the impetuous cleric soon learned otherwise. In fact, the incoming President valued Coughlin's aid for political, not personal reasons. The Democratic Party had broken completely in 1928 over the candidacy of Alfred E. Smith, a wealthy New York Catholic, and Roosevelt believed that by indulging the priest he might heal the rift between rural, fundamentalist Protestants and urban Catholics.

The White House continued to treat the Royal Oak pastor carefully in the months after the inauguration, a fact which led many Americans to believe that Coughlin did indeed speak for the New Deal. The issue that ostensibly united the cleric with Roosevelt stemmed from the dire condition of American banking, particularly in Detroit. In February 1933 Union Guardian Trust closed its doors, thus endangering the city's entire financial structure. Executives of Guardian Trust and of the defunct Detroit First National Bank then sought a Reconstruction Finance Corporation loan to remedy the situation, but President Hoover, acting on the advice of Henry Ford, refused the request.

Because the banking crisis provided Coughlin with evidence that local "agents of Mellonism" soon would atone for their financial transgressions, the priest opposed all federal loans to banks that remained solvent. Charging that Detroit bankers had conspired to make exorbitant loans to themselves to save personal investments made after the stock market crash, he wholeheartedly approved an order by Roosevelt's Treasury Secretary, William H. Woodin, to federal offices to garnishee the resources of Guardian Trust and First National. This directive, which produced understandable cries of anguish from the bankers involved, convinced the cleric that the time had arrived to defend administration policy.

On March 27, after seeking permission from the White House and evidently securing assurance that he had the President's approval, Coughlin delivered a vindictive radio sermon in which he accused Detroit bankers of outright criminal behavior. Noting that Roosevelt's appointments secretary, Marvin H. McIntyre, had asked him to speak, he staunchly defended Secretary Woodin's refusal to reopen First National and Guardian Trust and charged directors of the former institution with absconding with 3 million dollars. Through the offices of the Roosevelt administration, Coughlin predicted, these villains would be prosecuted and convicted.

Public reaction to the cleric's role as New Deal spokesman came quickly. The banking sermon evoked more than 300,000 responses, most of them favorable. Only a few writers wondered whether Coughlin's lack of training enabled him to know much about economics. One of these was an editorial writer for the *Detroit Free Press,* who labeled the Royal Oak pastor "an ecclesiastical Huey Long" and argued that Coughlin had overstepped all boundaries of decency in charging that the sole aim of Guardian Trust was "to cheat the widow, rob the orphan, and oppress the poor." Even more incensed was the publisher of the *Free Press,* E. D. Stair, who threatened to file suit for slander.

Other local residents, including the rector of St. Joseph's Episcopal Church, joined in the outcry against the contemporary Savonarola. The presidents of the Detroit Mathews Company and Detroit Aerocar called upon the administration to disavow any connection with the priest, as did a member of the Detroit Board of Education, who warned: "Whenever several Irishmen get together in one cause—By-law No. One—no one Irishman must do all the talking or monopolize the radio!" An anonymous correspondent was no less irate: "A Catholic priest the mouthpiece of the Administration down at Washington! Ye Gods! O Tempora! O Mores! The most stupendous, bone-headed, asinine, stupid, crass blunder that could possibly be made!"

But Coughlin did not lack defenders. A Minnesotan epitomized the widespread belief that the cleric and Roosevelt labored in holy partnership for the benefit of mankind. "Father Coughlin certainly has a way of expressing the wide-open American opinion," he wrote. "It seems he is part of the New Deal that the common American people are getting. . . . Let's pray that no more money powers can snuff out his voice." A Pennsylvanian, meanwhile, evidenced deep admiration for "the man in Detroit who has the courage to tell the people of the United States about the true conditions of the financial structure." To a Brooklyn variety-store owner, Coughlin was "one of the great orators of our time."

Continuing through the Senate Banking Investigations in June, the priest's attacks upon Detroit financiers convinced the Roosevelt administration, already embarrassed by the cleric's advocacy, to disavow his support. Yet rather than jeopardize their legislative program by an open break with the Royal Oak clergyman, the President and his advisers adopted a policy of delicate disengagement. After March secretaries McIntyre and Marguerite Le Hand either ignored the priest's missives or answered them perfunctorily. Because of the administration's policy of finesse, many Americans, some of whom never lost the belief, still thought Coughlin an economic adviser to the President.

In early June, as Roosevelt continued to treat the priest cautiously, six senators and fifty-nine representatives petitioned the Chief Executive to name Coughlin an adviser to the American delegation at the forthcoming world monetary and economic conference in London. Impressed by the cleric's advocacy of inflation and silver and his criticism of the gold standard, the lawmakers informed the President that Coughlin was sufficiently interested in the conference to pay his own way in lieu of governmental support. Although Roosevelt refused this request and instead named James P. Warburg, a New York banker and student of international affairs, to head the American mission, the petition clearly underlined Coughlin's potential political power.

Convened to stabilize currency exchange, restore international trade, and return to the international gold standard, the London Economic Conference accomplished none of these goals. To the surprise of European delegates and a number of American representatives, Roosevelt denounced the conference as a failure to define the truly significant economic issues of the day and announced that the United States would not submit the dollar to the fate of foreign currencies until the other nations, especially France, balanced their respective budgets. Privately, as Coughlin had publicly, the President lambasted the international bankers—"the fellows in Amsterdam and Antwerp etc."—whose practices he felt had undermined the American economy.

Amid charges that Roosevelt had helped plan and then sabotaged the London conclave, Father Coughlin moved to defend the Chief Executive. His hatred of international financiers stimulated and his hopes for monetary reform increased, the priest forwarded congratulations to the President for his "bombshell" dispatch. And, ignoring for the moment his earlier decision to disdain the cleric, Roosevelt replied by thanking him for his "nice telegram about my message."

But the uneasy, unofficial alliance between priest and President did not endure. The first evidence of a public split became noticeable during the fall of 1933, widened in the winter months, and became irrevocable by the end of 1934. As long as Roosevelt appeared to follow the path Coughlin approved, the clergyman compared the Chief Executive's ideas with "principles which centuries ago were sounded on Sinai's mountaintop, and of old were echoed on the hillsides where Christ preached the gospel of brotherhood." This did not mean, however, that Coughlin would extend his imprimatur to New Deal policies. Indeed, until the administration increased the amount of money in circulation, "want in the midst of plenty" would remain the great paradox of the depression, and the priest would continue in his endeavor to "inject Christianity into the fabric of an economic system woven together upon the loom of greed, by the cunning fingers of those who manipulated the shuttles of human lives and human happiness for their own selfish purposes."

Styling himself a "Christian radical" who supported the precepts of Christ in the official writings of Pius XI, the cleric partly approved of the National Recovery Act because it eliminated child labor, established a minimum wage, and gave laborers "the right to organize independently of their employers and independently of any existent labor unions." The NRA, he believed, heralded "an immortal step backward to the principles of our being our brother's keeper," and its author deserved a place in "the American Hall of Fame."

But because the NRA had failed "to break the back of the depression," Coughlin likened the measure to "a fine motor car . . . equipped with flat tires." The flat tires being the American dollar, only sound money could enable Americans to "travel along the highway of Christian-American prosperity." "It is," he told listeners, "the Morgans, Mellons, Baruchs, Achesons, Douglasses, and Wallaces who want unsound money, and by wanting it, also want your farm, your business, your job, your cheap wheat, and your high debts." Unless Roosevelt convinced Congress to enact reform measures immediately, the NRA would become, finally, a tremendous failure.

If the money question constituted for Coughlin "the very heart and soul of the New Deal," it is not surprising that his version of economic salvation rested upon the freeing of national wealth from control by "the protectors of privately manufactured money." The American people would gain deliverance from these "grinning devils" when Congress destroyed Federal Reserve Banks; supplanted interest-bearing government notes with non-interest-bearing notes; and, most important, increased the amount of circulating currency.

The latter task, argued Coughlin, would be accomplished when the administration ordered the remonetization of silver and began to issue greenbacks. Proceeding upon the assumption that national economic· ills could be cured only by an abundant supply of money, the radio priest supported the desire of the Agricultural Adjustment Administration to raise farm prices but decried the agency's method. Agriculture Secretary Henry Wallace's program of crop destruction and the wholesale slaughter of livestock rested upon a philosophy that was as logical "as pouring water into a sieve." For the cleric there could be "no superfluity of either cotton or wheat until every naked back has been clothed, until every empty stomach has been filled."

On November 11, the fifteenth anniversary of Armistice Day, Coughlin related his views on the current financial crisis to world history. Undertaking to explain the causes of the Great War, he emphasized that he did not mean "the causes—so-called, which are taught the children—the murder of a Grand Duke, the violation of Belgian neutrality, the sinking of the *Lusitania*." "I have grown old enough," he continued, "and so have you—to distinguish the rouge from the flesh, the propaganda from the truth. A war to end war, a war to make the world safe for democracy—these motives for the mad slaughter are as truthful as the advertised causes."

How had the war come about? What lessons were to be learned from the conflict? Coughlin argued that the road to war had been paved much earlier by a general revolt against authority. The devils that lurked behind the priest's conspiratorial understanding of history were numerous: "Voltaire and his deification of reason; John Stuart Mill and his philosophy that morals have no part in economics. To these add the elements of industrial slavery; of the Rothschilds' gold control; of the central banks where wealth was concentrated in the hands of a very few—compound all these together—and perforce, this strange mixture forms a social chemical which by its very nature was destined to explode—to shatter the presumptions of its makers and of the whole world upon the battlefields of Europe. The war was the inevitable sequence of this philosophy and of those practices. It was nature's only method of purification."

The Royal Oak pastor also believed that no nation had won the war. Rather, the forces of gold and international finance, "devoid of all allegiance to either God, country, or humanity," had emerged as the true victors. During the 1920s, continued Coughlin, these interests sought to control the human race by imposing upon it a cross of gold, and by "crucifying it between the thieves of poverty and greed, forgetful that their Good Friday of Oppression must give way to the sunshine of Easter morning."

Stressing the need for silver restoration, Father Coughlin awaited the expulsion of the money changers from the temple of the American economy. Despite President Roosevelt's currency devaluation in the fall of 1933, the priest still believed that the nation faced a money shortage. Excusing the Chief Executive's caution in "trying to convert the international bankers," Coughlin explained that "for more than two and one-half years Christ attempted to convert the money changers of Jerusalem. Eventually He was forced to drive them from the temple after upsetting their tables. I am confident that this very day, Mr. Roosevelt is prepared to do likewise."

In late November the priest's commitment to revaluation led him to attack Alfred E. Smith of New York. Four times governor of the Empire State, Smith took a Hamiltonian view of human nature, was sympathetic to Wall Street interests, and disdained the oratory of the Midwestern farmer. In addition, the wealthy Democrat begrudged FDR his presidential victory. Charging the President with demagoguery in the agrarian tradition of William Jennings Bryan, Smith argued that in his inaugural address the Chief Executive set class against class with his reference to the "forgotten man" of America. In fact, however, this accusation veiled Smith's fear that the government's monetary policy was heresy, that it had become infected with the virus of Populism. "I am for gold dollars as against Baloney dollars," Smith wrote the New York Chamber of Commerce. "I am for experience against experiment."

Smith's attack upon the fiscal policy of the New Deal amounted to a criti-

cism of Coughlin's personal views. That the New York leader was a prominent Catholic layman did not divert the priest from quickly linking his financial ideas with those of the stigmatized international banker. Citing as
evidence an alleged visit made in 1929 by Smith, Bishop Gallagher, and
Bishop Dunne of New York to the offices of J. P. Morgan, the radio cleric
labeled the former governor "a puppet of Wall Street" who "moved in Morgan's circles" and made at least "part of his living from the County Bank of
New York."

As the *Christian Century* suggested, perhaps the controversy did not de-
serve the coverage accorded it by the press. Nonetheless, the intramural battle
allowed the American Catholic community to express itself on the subject of
Father Coughlin. Monsignor Thomas G. Carroll of New York pointed out
that the priest had committed a serious ecclesiastical blunder by failing to secure prior approval to speak from Cardinal Hayes. Monsignor John Belford
of Brooklyn, pastor of the Church of the Nativity, employed picturesque ter-
minology in denouncing Coughlin as a public nuisance who throve on "the
applause of morons and the rabble." And, although the Royal Oak clergyman
emerged relatively unscathed from the affair, it was clear that Catholic opposition was increasing and that his penchant for controversy and his advocacy
of the New Deal were spawning enemies.

In the early months of 1934, Coughlin remained an important spokesman
for agrarian Americans who as yet had not embraced modern capitalism and
for urban groups that received little solace from the New Deal. Directing his
rhetoric at these bewildered people, the priest continued to attack the international banker, the cadaverous economy, and the gold standard. On March 11,
after suggesting symmetalism as an answer to national ills, he announced a
six-point program to revive the economy. The plan included nationalization
and revaluation of all gold; the restoration of silver coinage and nationalization of silver; the establishment of a government bank to control currency
and credit; the complete nationalization of all forms of credit; the extension
of credit to consumers as well as to producers; and the complete elimination
of interest-bearing, national government bonds.

This announcement heralded Father Coughlin's own "New Deal," and it
appears, moreover, that the priest had deemed the time appropriate to test his
strength against the President's. Two months before the cleric enunciated his
program, in fact, he had conferred privately with Roosevelt in Washington.
Although impressed by what he termed the Chief Executive's "advanced sociological thought," Coughlin emerged from the meeting less than overawed.
Two days later he forwarded an open letter to one of his ardent supporters,
Representative Martin Sweeney of Ohio. Counting on Congress to assume a
crucial role in gaining control of national currency and credit, and realizing
the historic importance of the congressional legislative prerogative, the priest
used the letter to entreat American legislators to resist executive usurpation.
While Roosevelt had by no means become a dictator, Coughlin reasoned, the

"preservation of the American Constitution" depended upon "the integrity of our Senators and Congressmen" who could not let themselves become "sublimated rubber stamps."

In April the priest's relationship with the administration underwent severe strain when the President, hoping to embarrass congressional advocates of a silver-coinage plan that he opposed, ordered Treasury Secretary Henry Morgenthau to publish a list of individuals and groups that had invested heavily in silver. Although the list became tactically insignificant when Roosevelt subsequently abandoned his opposition to the remonetization of silver, it did include a curious name—Father Coughlin's Radio League of the Little Flower.

Having been briefed on the subject of silver in November 1933 by George LeBlanc, a Canadian gold trader, and Robert M. Harriss of the New York Cotton Exchange, Coughlin nonetheless denied involvement in any silver transactions. Refusing to criticize Roosevelt for ordering the Treasury Department publication, the cleric instead lashed out at an alleged conspiracy headed by Morgenthau and "Jewish cohorts" who had acted "like Dillingers" in plotting against him and the downtrodden American people. As a spokesman for the international bankers, furthermore, Morgenthau sought to prevent silver legislation for "the ultimate benefit of one billion Orientals." These angry words notwithstanding, the fact remains that Father Coughlin advocated free silver in substance as well as theory, and that he undoubtedly hoped to reap a large profit from his holdings of nearly 500,000 ounces should the government adopt monetary reform.

Despite the pleas of the secretary of the Radio League that she had purchased the silver without the priest's knowledge, the administration's revelation tarnished his image. Although Coughlin did not lose much of his radio audience, many listeners questioned the advisability of his attack on Morgenthau. Others concurred with the Nation's conclusion that the clergyman had become "perhaps the most vicious single propagandist in the United States." In any event the silver episode marked the first public confrontation between Coughlin and the New Deal. What had formerly been a staunch alliance became lukewarm as the cleric began to reassess his relationship with the legitimate political order.

Father Coughlin chose an advantageous time to make his move. A climate of violence and uncertainty during 1934 had left many Americans, in the words of playwright Clifford Odets, "waiting for Lefty." A token improvement in living conditions had only increased general feelings of anxiety. Perhaps, as the priest believed, a revolt would soon occur if the administration did not answer the sphinxian riddle of the depression.

With the Roosevelt magic seemingly dispersed, a number of people came forth offering panaceas to an anxious citizenry. Former muckraker Upton Sinclair captured the California Democratic Party and nearly won the 1934 gubernatorial race on a platform dedicated to "End Poverty in California." Dr. Francis Townsend, a gaunt South Dakotan, initiated an "Old Age Revolving Pension Fund" in southern California. Louisiana demagogue Huey Long, a former elixir salesman, was elected to the United States Senate, where he launched a "Share-Our-Wealth" program aimed at the redistribution of vast fortunes to provide each American family with a home, radio, and car. The New Deal, with its myriad of agencies, had promised better things; but its pledge of recovery seemed empty.

Thus, to consolidate his followers and maintain primacy as a national spokesman of discontent, Coughlin announced the formation of the National Union for Social Justice in an emotional radio sermon delivered on Armistice Day. Forged on an anvil of Christian socialism and agrarian radicalism, the new organization was to be consecrated to ending the depression. Again emphasizing that he was neither Republican, Democrat, nor Socialist, the cleric indicated that the National Union was just a popular lobby to which persons of all creeds might belong. This disclaimer was misleading, however, as the priest undoubtedly hoped that his organization would move Republicans and Democrats in the direction of his version of social justice. The first of the two major parties to adopt the National Union platform, he reasoned, would profit at the polls.

The most radical provisions of the organization's sixteen-point platform dealt with financial issues, including the abolition of the Federal Reserve System and the establishment of a government-owned central bank; the restoration of the right of Congress to coin and regulate the value of money; and the maintenance of the cost of living by the proposed central bank.

But the majority of the planks combined traditional agrarian appeals with the essence of the social encyclicals of Popes Leo XIII and Pius XI. Such measures as a "just, living annual wage for all citizens"; the nationalization of all public resources "too important to be held in the control of private individuals"; the "cost of production plus a fair profit for the farmer"; and the alleviation of taxation might easily have appeared in the platform of the Farmer-Labor Party in Minnesota, or, for that matter, in the program of the Social Credit movement in Alberta, with which the priest had had substantial contact.

His uncertainty concerning the means through which his program might be implemented, combined with an absence in the National Union platform of any mention of democracy, indicated to some critics that Coughlin had become a fascist. As shall be seen in subsequent chapters, however, this term was employed by Americans in such diverse ways during the 1930s that it became less a term of clarification than a vehicle of confusion. Coughlin did indeed share some of the characteristics of the Continental dictators—xenophobia, anticommunism, scorn for political parties, use of scapegoats, and intolerance. However, it is probably safe to say that Coughlin did not quite know what he wanted. He had written no equivalent of *Mein Kampf* and lacked a systematic, positive approach to the problem of establishing a corporatist state. Like many reformers in American history, the cleric was cursed by want and doubly cursed by not knowing what he wanted.

Placing Father Coughlin in the fascist camp may have proved emotionally satisfying to his adversaries, but to so categorize him was to ignore the fact that the priest's inconsistency provided him with his basic strength. As columnist Raymond Gram Swing observed, Coughlin's "advanced sense of stage movement" allowed him to play several roles simultaneously. As church builder, misinterpreted martyr, social philosopher, or saintly politician, he was a clerical chameleon, whose cassock changed color as the situation warranted. Perhaps, Swing concluded, "there was no real Father Coughlin, but just a succession of contiguous parts."

However, by the end of 1934, as membership in the National Union swelled to 5 million, there remained little doubt that the priest could generate substantial political power. Future relations with the Roosevelt administration promised to be turbulent.

3

The Emergence of an Extremist

■■■
★ ★ ★   Despite many warnings that in his attacks on the administra-
■■■
tion he had overstepped the boundaries of decency, Father Coughlin accelerated his crusade against the many evils of American life during his second
broadcast in December. Denouncing Al Smith, financier John J. Raskob,
and the ultraconservative American Liberty League for failing to appreciate
the intense suffering around them, the priest directed his harshest remarks at
Cardinal O'Connell, who had become "more notorious for his silence on social justice than for any contribution . . . towards the elimination of those
glaring injustices which permitted the plutocrats of the nation to wax fat at
the expense of the poor."

The Michigan pastor also found time to lend moral support to a Senate investigating committee headed by Republican Gerald P. Nye of North Dakota
that had undertaken an examination of the American munitions industry.
Adopting the "revisionist" hypothesis that the United States went to war in
1917 not for humanitarian reasons but at the behest of Allied propagandists,
international bankers, and American munitions firms, the Nye Committee
reinforced national isolationist sentiment. With Germany, Italy, and Japan
threatening to upset the uneasy equilibrium in Europe and the Far East, the
Senate group seemed to provide a formula for avoiding future wars. If munitions makers and international bankers, the alleged cause of all conflict, were
checked, the United States could preserve its peacetime status.

Coughlin incorporated the widely approved conclusions of the Nye Committee into his devil theory of history, and the munitions makers were added
to his lists of the damned. Christening the DuPonts "Merchandisers of Murder," the priest decried the alleged nexus between the chemical empire, the

State Department, and the armed services. Although he later championed Japanese expansion in the Far East, the cleric now wore the mantle of peacemaker, pleading for the cessation of arms sales to Tokyo.

Enlarging his repertoire of attacks, Coughlin next criticized the Latin American policy of the United States. Aghast at Roosevelt's recognition of the Soviet Union two years earlier, he now charged that the President and Woodrow Wilson were to blame for "aiding and abetting the rape of Mexico." Wilson's desire to secure Mexican oil leases for the United States, together with his failure to recognize the government of Victoriano Huerta, initiated the trend toward Bolshevism. Roosevelt's Good Neighbor Policy continued it. Coughlin was especially critical of the American Ambassador to Mexico, Josephus Daniels, who as Wilson's Secretary of the Navy, had helped plan the Veracruz invasion. Now, asserted the priest, Daniels possessed the temerity to praise the "atheistic" Mexican system of education, with its curriculum featuring sexual perversion.

Early in January 1935 the radio clergyman became involved in a controversy concerning possible American membership in the World Court. Recognizing the peril to world peace posed by Adolf Hitler, President Roosevelt offered the Senate a chance "to throw its weight into the scale of peace" when he submitted to that body the "Root Formula," a means for American adherence to the Court devised six years earlier by then Secretary of State Elihu Root. After informal newspaper polls indicated that the sixty-eight Democratic votes in the Senate would prove sufficient to pass the measure, the administration waited confidently. But Roosevelt did not count on the blitz of telegrams that struck Washington on January 28. A result of emotional attacks upon the Court by Huey Long, publisher William Randolph Hearst, and Coughlin, the messages foreshadowed the success of anti-Court forces in transferring the Senate's attention from the specific Root Formula to the more general and emotion-laden question of American responsibility in world affairs.

In stimulating latent opposition to the Court plan, Father Coughlin's role was decisive. On January 27, with the vote two days off, he implored "every solid American who loves democracy, who loves the truth, to stand foresquare [sic] back of those tried and true Senators of long experience in their hopeless yet honest fight to keep America safe for Americans and not the hunting ground for international plutocrats." The priest was, he told listeners, "old-fashioned enough to prefer Washington and his logic and principles to Wilson and those fellows who follow him with their crude internationalism and their unsound love of minorities." Because "95% of the distress suffered by Americans" was "absolutely national in cause and action," he added, Roosevelt should attempt to solve domestic problems before making himself savior of the world. Stressing the theme of fiscal irresponsibility within the internationalist camp, the radio priest expressed worry lest American adherence to the Court result "in the pilfering of twelve million dollars" in war debts from the American people. "The League of Nations and its perverted brain, the

World Court," he intoned, "is nothing more than a Frankenstein, raised by
the international bankers and the plutocrats of the world for the purpose of
preserving by force of arms that plutocratic system against the onslaught of
communism."

That the clerical anticommunist seemed to embrace Bolshevism as a
quasi-ally against Court membership was of course academic. What counted
was the cumulative effect of his words, and this was cataclysmic. Forty thousand telegrams overtaxed lines into Washington; many had to be rerouted
through Baltimore. And on January 28 visitors to Senate offices were astonished to see messengers pushing wheelbarrows of telegrams. The Democratic
majority in the Senate notwithstanding, the people had clearly rejected the
Court proposal. On the evening of January 28 administration forces used a
radio program to counter Coughlin's eleventh-hour appeal. While most listeners probably agreed with the opinions expressed by Mrs. Eleanor Roosevelt,
Father John A. Ryan, Newton Baker, and Senator Joseph Robinson of Arkan-
sas, few bothered to send telegrams to Washington.

With the Senate's defeat of the Court bill on January 29 by a 52–36 margin, the Royal Oak cleric assumed that his own position had been vindicated
and strengthened. In interpreting the vote as a personal referendum, however,
Coughlin ignored Roosevelt's decision not to stress the issue during one of
his fireside chats, or to resort to the "arm-twisting" technique he so often employed to secure legislation. Most Americans, furthermore, were strongly isolationist before the priest's emotional sermon. Coughlin might have galvanized existing public sentiment, but he clearly did not create the huge
response.

That the priest did not comprehend these qualifying factors became apparent as he renewed his attack on the administration, criticizing Roosevelt for
failing to nationalize the banks and for "Bolshevizing" the economy. The
President and his advisers, "still in love with the international bankers," were
unabashedly keeping America "safe for the plutocrats." A month later, as he
recapitulated the accomplishments of the administration, Coughlin explained
that the New Deal amounted to "two years of compromise and surrender
. . . two years of matching puerile, puny brains of idealists against the virile
viciousness of business and finance."

In criticizing the intelligentsia of the New Deal, the radio priest joined
many other Americans in expressing a vehemence rarely matched in national
politics. These critics, accustomed to years of nonacademic normalcy,
viewed the abrupt ascent of scholars such as Rexford G. Tugwell, Raymond
Moley, and Adolf Berle as an indication that control of the government had
fallen into the hands of an arrogant, irresponsible, and immoral elite.

By March the anti-intellectual thrust led by Coughlin and Huey Long had
created a climate of uncertainty on Capitol Hill. Either because of fear or
their desire not to endow their adversaries' charges with a semblance of dignity, spokesmen for the administration hesitated to respond to the demagogues. But General Hugh S. Johnson, the proud former administrator of the

NRA, was not so reticent and, despite warnings from friends, determined "to crawl down into the sawdust and wrestle with them." If demagoguery had "reached the point where a man must risk his standing by attacking it," he pointed out, "it is time for someone to get up on his hind legs and howl."

And he did. At a dinner given him by *Redbook* magazine on March 4, Johnson reviewed the accomplishments of Roosevelt's first two years in office and claimed that the New Deal had lifted the country "at least one-third of the way out of the depression." But the great push had ended, and politics had degenerated into warfare between selfish interest groups, the worst of these being the "emotional fringes." Turning his attention to the priest, Johnson characterized the radio sermons as "musical blatant bunk [that] goes straight home to simple souls weary in distress and defrauded in delay. We can neither respect nor revere what appears to be a priest in Holy Orders entering our homes with the Open Sesame of his high calling and there, in the name of Jesus Christ, demanding that we ditch the President. . . . People should tell the Huey Longs and Father Coughlins that they are not in the market for financial, magic hair tonic put up by the partnership of a Priest and a Pucinello, guaranteed to grow economic whiskers on a billiard ball overnight."

Reacting to Johnson's address, the *New York World-Telegram* labeled him "a D'Artagnan with a Dictionary." As did most American newspapers, the *Milwaukee Journal* approved the speech. "We need some kind of plain talk in these times," it editorialized. "We need men willing to refute the plans of the Longs, Coughlins, Sinclairs, and Townsends, well meaning as some or all of them may be." Writing in the *New York Times,* Arthur Krock suggested that Johnson's statements would give courage to legislators who had been intimidated by the extremists. Conversely, *Business Week* proposed that the administration seek an accommodation with the financial community to protect the United States from demagoguery.

Other publications, such as the *Detroit News* and the *Chicago Journal of Commerce,* questioned the propriety of the attack. *Commonweal,* the liberal Catholic journal, defended outright Coughlin's right to dissent, while the *Kansas City Star* termed Johnson's fear of the lunatic fringe "just a bit overdrawn and premature."

Coughlin, who was ill with a cold at the time of Johnson's speech, refuted the Blue Eagle's charges a week later. Because Johnson had questioned his citizenship, the cleric replied that the general's parents were "but one generation removed from Ireland," while his own grandfather's remains were buried in Lackawanna, New York. Defending his fight for the "preservation of our commonwealth," Coughlin added that his silver investments merely demonstrated his confidence in President Roosevelt.

Then the priest directed his fire at Johnson personally, condemning him as "a cracked gramophone record squawking the message of his master's voice." Johnson was, among other things, "the great casualty of the New Deal experiment . . . a political corpse whose ghost has returned to haunt us . . .

the genial General of generalities . . . a chocolate soldier . . . the sweet prince of bombast . . . a red herring (even though it chances to be a dead one)." Finally, the cleric turned on Johnson's alleged "master," Bernard M. Baruch. Referring erroneously to Baruch's middle name as "Mannases" (it was Mannes), he cried: "Another Mannases, like his Biblical namesake who sawed in twain the body of the prophet of Isaiah when the latter criticized him . . . like the Kuhn-Loebs, the Rothschilds, and the Morgans who devour the houses of widows . . . as did the scribes and Pharisees. I shall doubly bend my efforts to the task of handing back America to the Americans and of rescuing our beloved country from the hands of the Baruchs, your master."

Surprisingly, however, the priest's hopes still lay with the President. As he remarked at the end of his broadcast, the choice remained between "Roosevelt or Ruin!"

Upset by Coughlin's tirade, Johnson retorted that the priest and Long were more dangerous than the country's "100 worst gunmen," a company that included Dillinger, Capone, and "Mad Dog" Coll. The former director of the NRA promised to answer the cleric, but despite a prompt offer of sponsorship from the Post Toasties Corporation, he never did. Baruch meanwhile issued a dignified rejoinder in the *New York Times,* denying that he had ever been a banker, and repeating for Coughlin's benefit his real middle name.

Franklin Roosevelt, aware of the pitfalls of America's "free and sensational press," did not participate in the exchange. The President believed that people would soon tire "of seeing the same name day after day in the important headlines of the papers, and hearing the same voices, night after night, over the radio." By remaining silent in the face of demagoguery, he thought that the "inevitable histrionics" of the extremists would be self-defeating. Two weeks later, in fact, as he looked toward the 1936 presidential election, he remarked that he was quite satisfied with the political situation. "It was," he wrote Colonel Edward M. House, "vastly better to have this free side show presented to the public at this time than later on when the main performance starts."

Fearing growing divisions within the country should his associates engage the priest in open combat, the Chief Executive termed "very unwise" a subsequent attack upon Coughlin by Interior Secretary Harold L. Ickes. In an address to an Associated Press luncheon on April 23, Ickes had digressed from his topic of the Bill of Rights to label the clergyman "a cloistered individual whose rich but undisciplined imagination has reduced politics, sociology, and banking to charming poetry which he distills mellifluously into the ether for the entrancement of mankind."

On occasion Coughlin conferred with Huey Long, but no political agreement existed between them. Nevertheless, statements like those made by Johnson and Ickes strengthened rumors of an alliance, and many Americans consequently believed that the two men posed a unified threat to the democratic system. Elzey Roberts, the publisher of the *St. Louis Star-Times,* mentioned this possibility when he informed the President that his paper had been forced to suppress an editorial criticizing Coughlin because "thousands of his followers among our readers were so emotionally worked up that an appeal to reason seemed vain." It seemed, in fact, not to matter that the demagogues lacked a consistent program of reform. Their putative threat became the center of debate in American living rooms and recently opened beer parlors.

Characterized by Arthur Krock as "brilliant and dangerous," Long never constructed a complete political platform. Yet had he lived, he might have encompassed the priest within his "Share-Our-Wealth" movement. This possibility troubled Raymond Swing, who wrote that Johnson's polemic had "joined in holy matrimony two movements which had only reached the stage of flirtation." Swing, like the cynical H. L. Mencken, considered Long less dangerous than the radio priest. Writing in the *Nation,* Swing cited the results of a poll conducted by station WCAU in Philadelphia. At issue was whether the station should carry Coughlin or the New York Philharmonic on Sunday afternoons. Although the vote was taken at 11 P.M., while most music lovers were probably asleep, the cleric won by a margin of 187,000 to 12,000. Swing might also have been aware of a poll conducted a year earlier by station WOR in New York. In that contest to name the most important American public figure, Roosevelt excepted, Coughlin received 8,000 more votes than runner-up Hugh Johnson.

The priest's appeal troubled the liberal press, and the latter's reaction served to darken his image in the minds of many Americans. While the *New Republic* questioned Coughlin's means to implement his program, journalist Hamilton Basso termed him a "confused and confusing man." If the social justice movement ended in fascism, it would not be because the cleric was wicked or malicious, but because he "did not know how to get from one stage of society to another." Perhaps, warned Basso, the clergyman's organization might be captured by men who "also want a more abundant way of life—for themselves."

A writer in the *Christian Century* believed Coughlin's program to portend "roughly, but not inaccurately, the threat of fascism," and concluded that it was "probably too late to save a good part of the American church world from fascistic influence." Another *Century* journalist suggested that the priest had aligned himself with William Randolph Hearst, who was "under as deep obligation to the present banking system as any man in America." An Episcopal minister, the Reverend David C. Colony, displayed similar trepidation. "So far," he wrote in the *Forum and Century,* Coughlin's development was "ominously regular." Comparing the priest to Hitler, Mussolini, and Nazi theoretician Alfred Rosenberg, and the National Union for Social Justice to the Nazi SS, Colony also wondered whether the Church's silence indicated its approval of the cleric's activities. Agreeing with this estimate, Forrest Davis argued in the *Atlantic Monthly* that "Coughlin's is the most incisively fascist voice in America."

These comments, which reflected the concern of American liberals with events in Germany and Italy, attributed to Coughlin a singularity of purpose he did not possess. In reality the priest remained more an enigma than a budding fascist. After interviewing him in May, in fact, Walter Davenport of *Collier's* predicted that the clergyman would support Roosevelt in 1936 and might even formulate a portion of the Democratic platform. "After all," wrote Davenport, "FDR is a shrewd politician."

Nevertheless, Coughlin's stature as an opponent of the liberal establishment resulted from the fact that by 1935 the nation had yet to recover from the depression. "The New Deal has not gone far enough and fast enough," wrote Briton H. G. Wells, "and that is what all the shouting is about." Indeed, while economic and social conditions had improved, millions of people remained without jobs and millions more failed to qualify for relief. Letters sent the President by these alienated citizens illustrated the intense bitterness of persons prone to Father Coughlin's appeal.

Roosevelt manifested concern over the clergyman's activities by sending an envoy to Royal Oak to placate Coughlin. But the Chief Executive determined to remain in the background. He had not participated in the Johnson affair and would not do so now. "Individual psychology," he wrote Ray Stannard Baker, "cannot, because of human weakness, be attuned for long periods of time to a constant repetition of the highest notes of the scale." The President also realized that it would be difficult for the administration to move rapidly toward new programs of reform, since the New Deal faced both a growing conservative coalition in Congress and a hostile Supreme Court. But his procrastination made him a prime target for Coughlin's attacks.

As Roosevelt and his advisers turned their attention to the labor movement and to social security, the priest scheduled a series of rallies to make the National Union a more effective popular lobby. On April 21 at Detroit, he promised 15,000 onlookers that he intended "to drive out of public life the men who have promised us redress . . . and then having broken their promises, [have] practiced the philosophy of plutocracy." Attempting to squelch reports of his unpatriotic conduct, he also disavowed support for any type of "racial Hitlerism" and industrial fascism.

On May 8, before 24,000 spectators in Cleveland, the cleric criticized a bank-reform bill sponsored by the administration because the measure would make FDR "the financial dictator of the United States." The bill, authored by Marriner Eccles, sought to divest private banks of control over the currency, placing it in the hands of the Federal Government. Though Coughlin himself had desired such a measure, he quarreled with Eccles's belief that any reform should occur within the Federal Reserve System. Seeking to demolish the System, the priest characterized it as "a marriage license between a prostitute who has wrecked our home, and the government who has deserted his wife, the American people."

The highlight of the tour occurred on May 22 at Madison Square Garden. The deafening roar emanating from 22,000 spectators might have suggested that a heavyweight title match was in progress, but as journalist Hamilton Basso pointed out, the foul language, battered faces, and sharp accents of the boxing crowd were missing, supplanted by "plain men and women wearing their best clothes." These persons had come to the arena for political enlightenment, and they kept vendors busy selling rosary beads, religious medals, and buttons welcoming Coughlin to Manhattan.

Flanked by an escort of war veterans, the radio priest strode past flags and patriotic symbols on his way to the podium. After a noisy demonstration he began, as always, by establishing his credentials. A hater of fascism and Nazism, he was an American, a democrat, a simple Catholic priest—but above all fighting mad—at capitalism. As he enumerated the "enemies" of the people—J. P. Morgan, Bernard Baruch, James Warburg, and the President —tumultuous Bronx cheers greeted each name. Tension reached an apex when Coughlin decried Roosevelt's veto of a veterans' pension plan, and his lack of compassion in allowing relief workers to starve. "If we are forced to see $19 or even $50 a month paid for such relief work in what we call the New Deal," he bellowed, "then this plutocratic system must be constitutionally voted out of existence." Half a moment's silence passed, followed by a roar lasting a full minute.

On the surface, this was something new in American politics: 20,000 working- and lower-middle-class citizens apparently had voted to bury capitalism. Observers who covered the event emphasized this theme and its gloomy portent. Yet like many of the priest's critics, they imbued his comments with a consistency that did not exist. Father Coughlin had not broken completely with the President; nor had the cleric seriously considered destroying capitalism. That the Catholic protestant once more had varied his rhetoric to sustain a high level of emotional tension within his followers, however, cannot be denied.

Coughlin's remarks generated criticism from within the Church, but he continued his crusade. He ceased his attacks on labor and adopted as his own the cause of Detroit's Automotive Independent Workers' Association. Twice he promised the organization full support from the National Union in attempting to raise prices and procure steady employment for members. At the same time the priest derided the Supreme Court for declaring the NRA unconstitutional in the case of *Schechter v. U.S.* Pledging support for the Wheeler-Rayburn Bill, which sought to eliminate financial holding companies he considered unnecessary, the cleric also stumped, albeit unsuccessfully, for his pet project, the Nye-Sweeney Bill, which promised financial reform through creation of a new national bank that would control the nation's money supply and be directly responsible to Congress.

Following the defeat of the Nye-Sweeney measure in late July, Coughlin's angry voice was momentarily still. Whether this quiescence indicated his desire to reconcile differences with the President, or whether it merely reflected the cleric's concern with National Union issues, is uncertain. In any event, the assassination of Huey Long on September 10 further obscured the priest's position. Coughlin, who had feared such an eventuality and termed it "a most regrettable thing," confounded observers by conferring with Roosevelt at the White House immediately after the assassination. Although details of the meeting, which had been planned by a mutual friend, were not made public, subsequent reports indicated that the clergyman stood ready to embrace once again the slogan of "Roosevelt or Ruin!" Perhaps he would throw his support fully to the Chief Executive.

Rumors of an impending rapprochement evaporated on November 3 when, without warning, the priest declared war upon the President and Congress. The American people no longer faced a choice between Roosevelt and disaster. Now a new battle cry sounded: "Roosevelt and Ruin!" The time had come to take a strong stand. Congress had too long postponed the urgent business at hand. If the Senate and House did not swiftly enact legislation paralleling Coughlin's own program, the powerful National Union would vote recalcitrant solons out of office.

Coughlin also warned that another world war was imminent. He claimed to have information proving that the United States, acting through roving Ambassador Norman Davis, had secretly approved League of Nations' sanctions against Italy following her invasion of Ethiopia. The priest charged that Washington had readied its military might to wage another war on the side of the dreaded British financiers.

Less a fascist sympathizer than a passionate Anglophobe at this point, Coughlin championed the Italian cause. "After all," he explained, "Italy has at least some slight justification for her movement into Ethiopia. At least Italy can truthfully charge that her territory already existing in Algeria has been invaded at least ninety times by the Ethiopians." To the charge that the Italians were using brutal dum-dum bullets against the spear-throwing cadres of Haile Selassie, the priest retorted: "The only dum-dum bullets found in Ethiopia are those manufactured by the British."

The final blast came a fortnight later. In simple language the Royal Oak pastor announced that the National Union could not support a President who coddled communists with one hand and glorified plutocrats with the other. The accusation lacked a sound basis, but it clearly proved that the pragmatism of the New Deal had no place in the cleric's political lexicon.

4

The Union Campaign of 1936

★ ★ ★ If by the end of 1934 Father Coughlin had begun acting like a politician with definite plans, his scathing denunciation of the President did not necessarily denote a consistent opposition. On December 1, in fact, listeners heard him declare that far from advocating the demolition of the New Deal, he sought only its "perfection." A week later, moreover, the Royal Oak pastor traveled to the White House to confer with Roosevelt. These gestures of accommodation, however, were offset by the cleric's subsequent announcement that units of the National Union for Social Justice were prepared for action in more than 300 of the nation's 435 legislative districts. And, with the appearance in January 1936 of a news organ, appropriately titled *Social Justice,* it became clear that the priest hoped at least to influence upcoming congressional elections.

In the interim, events on Capitol Hill presented new hope to Coughlin. Senator Lynn Frazier and Representative William Lemke, both of North Dakota, had prepared a farm-mortgage bill to provide refinancing through government issuance of 3 billion dollars in silver certificates, or "greenbacks." The measure provided many agrarians a vision of economic salvation and offered the priest a chance to employ his monetary theories to attract Midwestern, rural Protestants who objected strongly to his Catholicism.

Thirty-three state legislatures had approved the Frazier-Lemke Bill, but the proposal still remained in committee. Blocking its passage was Representative John O'Connor of New York, chairman of the formidable House Rules Committee, who construed the measure as merely another of a long line of soft-headed recommendations for soft money. Recognizing the possibility of a defeat for the administration if the bill reached Congress, the New Yorker hesitated to report it.

O'Connor's delaying tactics enraged Coughlin, who immediately sent his Washington lobbyist, Louis B. Ward, to the White House to see what could be done to withdraw the bill. Informing presidential secretary Marvin H. McIntyre that Coughlin had evidence that Roosevelt had promised to support such farm legislation as early as 1932, Ward warned that if the measure were not reported, Coughlin would make public his information. McIntyre correctly interpreted Ward's threat as attempted blackmail and dismissed the request, denying that his chief had ever made such a pledge. To this rebuttal the radio priest reacted angrily, and on February 16, with the President among his listeners, he criticized Roosevelt and called for O'Connor's resignation. As a "servant of the money changers," the cleric argued, the latter had "forced" members of the House to withdraw their names from a petition circulated by supporters of the Frazier-Lemke Bill to rescue it from committee.

Upon reading Coughlin's intemperate remarks in the *New York Times,* O'Connor, also an Irish-Catholic, offered to kick the priest "all the way from the Capitol to the White House with clerical garb and all the silver in your pockets which you got from speculating on Wall Street—Come on!" It appeared for the moment that Washington might provide the scene for a most unusual battle, for on the following morning a friend of Coughlin's, Representative Sweeney of Ohio, shouted across the House floor to O'Connor: "He accepts your challenge and will be here at ten tomorrow morning!"

But Father Coughlin never appeared for the confrontation. No matter how robust, a Catholic priest could not engage in such primitive physical combat, and although Bishop Gallagher supported him completely, he was not prepared to become a second in Coughlin's corner. Yet the Detroit bishop did see humor in the verbal exchange. Defending his ambitious underling, he termed O'Connor puerile and quite presumptuous "to assume that he could kick Father Coughlin all the way down Pennsylvania Avenue."

The defeat of the Frazier-Lemke Bill two months later marked for Father Coughlin "the last hope for financial reform under the New Deal." Having strengthened the National Union and watched Union-endorsed candidates score impressive victories in Pennsylvania and Ohio primaries, the priest lent credence to reports that he planned to join the Townsendites and Share-Our-Wealthers when he announced that "within two or three weeks, I shall be able to disclose the first chapter of a plan, which, if followed out, will discomfort the erstwhile sham-battlers, both Republican and Democrat. We must go on to victory from the primaries."

During the first week of June, Louis Ward conferred with William Lemke, evidently informing him that Coughlin hoped to build a new party with the North Dakotan as its presidential candidate. On June 12, without revealing its substance, the Royal Oak pastor spoke of a great revelation in the offing. But before he could make his announcement, the secret had been revealed.

Two weeks earlier, Gerald L. K. Smith, once Huey Long's lieutenant and now a leading Townsendite, stood with his new leader under the historic arch at Valley Forge and, in Smith's words, "vowed to take over the government." On June 16 he announced formation of a Coughlin-Townsend-Smith-Lemke coalition, opposed to "the communistic philosophy of Frankfurter, Ickes, Hopkins, and Wallace."

In an impassioned radio sermon three days later, Coughlin announced his endorsement of Lemke and asked members of the National Union to do likewise. "I am constrained to admit," he cried, "that Roosevelt *and* ruin is the order of the day because the money changers have not been driven from the temple." The priest directed similar criticism at the "Punch-and-Judy Republicans, so blind that they do not recognize, even in this perilous hour, that their gold basis and their private coinage of money have bred more radicals than did Karl Marx or Lenin. To their system of ox-cart financialism we must never return."

Amiable, fond of chihuahuas and gladioli, his face freckled by the Dakota sun and pitted by smallpox, William Lemke left the desolate northern prairie to work his way through the state university, and later, Yale Law School. In a book entitled *Crimes Against Mexico* (1915), he vilified President Wilson for not according diplomatic recognition to the Huerta government. Thereafter he became a strong force in the North Dakota Nonpartisan League and then state attorney general. Removed from office in 1921 during a banking scandal, he soon rebuilt his reputation and was elected to the House in 1932 as a Republican. Although he supported most New Deal legislation, his heart belonged to the Western farmer. With Lynn Frazier he co-sponsored three bills to ameliorate agrarian problems. Two of these measures became law, while the third, the farm-mortgage plan, failed miserably.

Lemke also looked and acted the part of a farmer. He often wore unpressed suits in Congress, and his twangy voice emerged through a day or two's growth of beard stubble. A devout Lutheran who neither drank nor smoked, he hid his political inexperience behind the "somber ferocity" with which he supported rural welfare.

For vice-president Coughlin endorsed Thomas C. O'Brien of Boston, a rotund, slow-speaking railroad attorney, who had worked as a ticket agent and brakeman for the Boston and Albany Railroad while attending Boston Latin School and Harvard Law School. A Democrat, he turned his talents to labor law before becoming a barrister for the railroad brotherhood. Inasmuch as he was of New England, Irish-Catholic stock, he could balance the ticket with Lemke. The priest emphasized this fact in boosting his candidates: "Lemke and Yale, Agriculture and Republican! O'Brien and Harvard, Labor and Democrat! East and West, Protestant and Catholic, possessing one program of driving the money changers from the temple, of permitting the wealth of America to flow freely into every home!"

The inner history of the inception of the new party has not been written and, until Father Coughlin's files are opened to scholars, must remain obscure.

Yet it may safely be asserted that in Union there was weakness. The party platform, heralding the creation of a common man's utopia, appealed to every malcontent and crackpot in the United States. To satisfy the inflationists the cleric proposed creating a central government bank with complete control over money and credit. The Townsendites were offered "reasonable and decent security for the aged." To please Share-Our-Wealthers the Unionists planned to limit individual income and inheritances. For those not entirely enchanted with these promises, the platform also called Congress to guarantee a living wage to every laborer, a productive profit to every farmer, and prosperity to every small businessman. Finally, the Union program was bluntly isolationist, demanding that "America shall be self-contained and self-sustained."

If Union promises were grandiose, party leadership was incredible. Clearly directing the team of "Coughlin, Townsend, and Smith," the priest wrote the party platform, which endorsed neither the Townsend Plan nor the Share-Our-Wealth movement. He also named the presidential and vice-presidential candidates without consulting his associates or the membership of the National Union and seemed, in fact, to have assumed dictatorial powers to oust an alleged dictator from the White House. Lacking faith in his compatriots, Coughlin endowed Lemke with the nickname "Liberty Bill," although it was common knowledge that the "Liberty Bell" was cracked. The Royal Oak pastor had even less use for Townsend, who had been stripped of much prestige by a congressional investigation of his finances in 1935 and to whom the Union Party was insignificant compared to his own work. Nonetheless, the fact that Townsend commanded 5 million followers and claimed the ability to influence the votes of 20 million more Americans necessitated his presence.

Gerald L. K. Smith, meanwhile, had attempted to take over Share-Our-Wealth after Long's assassination but received the cold shoulder from his associates. Joining Townsend, Smith brought new fire to the old-age movement, and even attempted to organize youth battalions. "They're going to be green boys," he told a reporter, "none of your drugstore cowboys, your sophisticates, your parlor pinks, your campus intellectuals, but nice clean boys from the farms—simple and Christian—with courage that seems to be disappearing nowadays."

The roughhewn evangelist impressed reporters with his unabashed cynicism and the happiness he derived from stirring hatred against labor unions, foreigners, "lying northern newspapers," Negroes, Jews, atheists, and "communists in the Roosevelt administration." In a memorable remark delivered at a rally of Georgia rebels early in 1936, he stated: "We're going to drive that cripple out of the White House—and we're going to do it in 1936!"

The appearance of the Union Party evoked derision from the press, but on the question of the party's potential opinion was split. A writer in the *New Republic* considered the new group a threat to Democratic strength and warned that if Father Coughlin acted recklessly he risked "landing his followers just where Hitler landed his in Germany." The same journal's regular columnist, T.R.B., meanwhile, dismissed the Unionists as part of a Vatican plan to strengthen dwindling Catholic prestige throughout the world. Evincing less concern, Paul Ward predicted in the *Nation* that Lemke's vote would be inconsequential and that the priest, his power declining, could never determine the outcome of the election. H. L. Mencken, finally, thought all the worriers woodenheaded. Coughlin, he wrote, had "blown up with a bang a year ago." But, he cynically added, "politicians are too stupid to detect great shifts in public opinion."

While some politicians joked about the Union Party, others showed signs of distress. Republican presidential candidate Alfred M. Landon of Kansas soberly welcomed "all sincere persons and all sincere parties to the great political debate." Yet within Democratic Party circles there was concern. Party Chairman James Farley declined comment on the new development but immediately forwarded a copy of *Social Justice* to Roosevelt, then on a fishing trip. Farley asked the President to note especially a cartoon and the priest's accompanying explanation: "Why must there be war in the streets of a country at peace? Why should innocent children have to share in strike agony? Why should violence grip a nation? Why must hate divide us? GOP CONCEDES NORTH DAKOTA TO LEMKE!"

The President never considered Lemke an obstacle. In fact, disillusioned by earlier battles with wealthy Democrats, conservative newspaper publishers, and Liberty League liegelords, Roosevelt had determined to confront Landon and the "economic royalists" who "took other people's money" to impose "a new industrial dictatorship" directly. Ignoring the Union Party, he and his advisers turned their attention to perfecting a new coalition that included such previously dispossessed groups as the small businessman, the Negro, and the American laborer.

Yet this apparent lack of official concern was misleading because state and local Democratic officials moved promptly to counter Coughlin's challenge. California party faithful, for example, infiltrated Townsendite ranks to prevent that organization from endorsing its leader's new political venture, while Democratic Chairman David Lawrence of Pennsylvania changed the name of the state organization to the "Union Party" and suggested that other Democratic leaders do the same.

Father Coughlin's campaign began on Independence Day before a cheering throng of 10,000 people in Brockton, Massachusetts. Seeking a place for the Union Party on as many state ballots as possible, he also visited Trenton, Philadelphia, and Chicago. The priest's tour culminated two weeks later at the National Townsend Convention in Cleveland. Dr. Townsend and Gerald L. K. Smith already had given Lemke their personal endorsements, but fearing a rebuff, they hesitated to seek blanket approval from their group. Recognizing that Lemke's chances of success depended heavily upon complete Townsendite support, the Royal Oak pastor sought and secured a place on the speakers' dais.

Prior to Coughlin's appearance, a bitter debate erupted between Gerald L. K.

Smith and Gomer Smith, no relation, a Townsendite senatorial candidate from Oklahoma. First on the program, the former Share-Our-Wealth lieutenant expatiated upon the atheistic nature of the American labor movement. Swinging his arms wildly as rivulets of sweat poured from his prominent forehead, he warned the assemblage to guard against foreign "isms." Gnashing wooden matches into fine splinters between his teeth and spitting them out to drive home his points, he claimed to see the "bloody hand of Moscow" behind Roosevelt's attempt to establish a dictatorship. In the words of H. L. Mencken, Smith's address comprised "a magnificent amalgam of each and every species of rabble-rousing, with embellishments borrowed from the Algonquin Indians and the Cossacks of the Don. It ran the keyboard from the softest sobs and gurgles to the most ear-splitting whoops and howls."

Mencken might have appreciated these antics, but Gomer Smith, a member of the Democratic Party, as were many Townsendites, resented the Protestant evangelist's attacks on the President. The Oklahoma Democrat's subsequent speech, as "roaring" as his predecessor's, amounted to an eloquent defense of Roosevelt's policies. Far from aiding any internal communist conspiracy, the Chief Executive had in fact rescued the nation from the pernicious doctrine. And as the Oklahoman spoke one sensed a dramatic change in the temper of his elderly audience. With the completion of his remarks, the convention was his—or so it seemed.

Now it was Coughlin's turn. Facing an audience that had wildly cheered Gomer Smith's reference to Roosevelt as a "church-going, Bible-reading, God-fearing man," the priest rose to new oratorical heights as for thirty minutes he extolled Lemke and spoke enthusiastically of the Townsend Plan. Suddenly, the cleric stunned onlookers by ripping off his coat and Roman collar and hurling them to the ground. Roosevelt, he screamed in a Biblical allusion, was both a "liar" and "great betrayer." There were, he continued, paraphrasing Gerald L. K. Smith's earlier remarks, good reasons why the American Communist Party supported the Chief Executive. Finally, reaching an apex of innuendo, the priest announced that Roosevelt's middle initial stood not for "Delano" but for "Doublecrossing."

While the Townsendites applauded boisterously, Father Coughlin embraced Gerald L. K. Smith and Dr. Townsend and proclaimed the solidarity of the Union cause. In the audience, however, Representative Martin M. Smith, a Washington Democrat and the temporary chairman of the convention, watched nervously. Determined that the Townsend Plan not be captured by any party or person, he should have realized that the aged conventioneers would cheer anyone capable of making a sustained emotional appeal. Speaking the previous day, he too had earned accolades when he proclaimed: "We are not going to lose with Lemke; we are going to win with Townsend!" Yet the Washingtonian still believed that the Democrats were in deep trouble, a feeling that was shared by Gomer Smith, who soon initiated a series of broadcasts throughout the Southwest, in which he charged that Coughlin and Gerald L. K. Smith had captured the Townsend movement.

Father Coughlin thus fled the safety and solitude of his radio pulpit for the limelight of the public platform. Consequently, thousands of Americans who earlier admired the divinely inspired work of "a simple Catholic priest" now condemned the atrocious behavior of a demagogue. According to the *Cincinnati Enquirer,* the cleric had "gone to the gutter" displaying "the nature of a beachcomber." Numerous former Coughlinites, including an Oregonian who considered the cleric "a shame and disgrace to each and every Irish-Catholic in the United States," disavowed his extreme tactics. A resident of Detroit wrote Roosevelt to report that local pastors had prohibited the sale of *Social Justice* around their churches. The chairman of Jonathan Coal Mining in Philadelphia called the priest "a charlatan." The leader of New York's National Culture Club assured President Roosevelt that he possessed more religion "than a host of Coughlin's," while W. Anthony George, self-styled "World's Greatest Medium, Spiritualist, and Crystal-Gazer," promised the Chief Executive the 10,000 votes of his followers. The basic implications of this voluminous correspondence were summed up by a Pennsylvanian on July 24, when he said that the President's re-election was "more assured than thirty days ago."

American Catholic leaders soon assured Roosevelt that Coughlin had acted on his own. An Iowa pastor decried the priestly apostate's "cheap barroom methods." Bishop Bernard J. Mahoney of Sioux Falls, South Dakota, condemned "the clerical vulgarian," as did Assistant Rector at Catholic University, the Reverend Maurice Sheehy. Sheehy also advised the Chief Executive that "it would be fatal and beneath the dignity of the presidency to take cognizance of these attacks." Just as Roosevelt had greeted Coughlin's previous tirades with silence, he remained detached from the latest uproar. But he must have chuckled privately, for the priest's epithets, he believed, would definitely strengthen the Democrats and seriously weaken the Union menace.

Amid reports that the Vatican planned to silence him, Father Coughlin apologized publicly to the President on July 23. Claiming that his emotions had gotten the better of him, the cleric admitted that Roosevelt's political intentions were probably even laudable. As the Royal Oak pastor made his confession, meanwhile, Bishop Gallagher concluded an audience with Pope Pius XI in Rome. Contradicting reporters who believed that the pontiff had ordered an end to Coughlin's political activity, Gallagher, upon his return, announced that the subject had not been broached.

William Lemke of course remained the Union Party candidate for President, but Coughlin, his public apologies notwithstanding, acted as if he himself sought that exalted office. At Worcester, Massachusetts, on August 1, he resumed his calamity howling with the warning that a Republican victory in November would precipitate a revolution. A day later, in New Bedford, the priest claimed that just as he had removed Hoover from the White House, so too would he "take a Communist out of the chair once occupied by Washington."

That Father Coughlin remained a hero for thousands of Americans became clear on August 13 when the National Union met in convention in Cleveland. Although the 10,000 delegates attending the conference had come to endorse Lemke and O'Brien, their "father" was undoubtedly the Royal Oak pastor. As Coughlin took his position on the speakers' platform, according to one observer, his followers "went insane," indulging in cries, shrieks, moans, rolling of eyes, and brandishing of arms.

These people were the true believers, the devoted followers who would grant Coughlin anything he sought. Following the keynote address by Senator Rush Holt of West Virginia (Senators Elmer Thomas and Pat McCarran had already refused the honor), the cleric received unanimous approval as president of the National Union Corporation. Nominating and seconding speeches evidenced his charismatic domination. Mrs. Helen E. Martin of New York announced that "for those of us who haven't a material father . . . *he* can be our father and we won't need to feel lonesome." Another delegate proposed: "Resolved that we give thanks to his mother for bearing him." Yet another, a tall, crew-cut Dakotan, epitomized the urgent feeling of Coughlin's congregation of despair: "I am a farmer. I've worked hard. I've raised a big family. Now I've got nothing." Speeches like these went on for hours.

The time had come to endorse Lemke and O'Brien, and the delegates appeared ready to offer a white ballot; yet there was discord, albeit minute. After a "stubborn, white-faced, obviously terror-stricken Pennsylvania Irishman," John H. O'Donnell, dissented, Coughlin haled him to the platform and announced that he was the sole dissenter among 8,153 registered delegates and alternates. For a moment, O'Donnell's life hung in the balance. Shouts of "Judas!" rang out and a middle-aged woman clawed her way forward to scream, "How much did Farley pay you?" "Where'd he go?" demanded another delegate. Realizing the terrible potential of mob psychology, the priest quickly relented, and O'Donnell left the hall under police escort.

The convention came to an end in huge Municipal Stadium on Sunday afternoon. Forty-two thousand Coughlinites cheered the priest as he announced that he would fight on for financial reform. His self-esteem bolstered by three days of frenzied activity, Coughlin concluded his remarks with a fateful promise: "If I don't deliver 9,000,000 votes for William Lemke, I'm through with radio forever." Shortly thereafter, rather anticlimactically, both Lemke and O'Brien addressed the gathering and predicted a Union Party victory in November.

Because Father Coughlin's relationship with Dr. Townsend and Gerald L. K. Smith was marked by increased dissension, the "spirit of Cleveland" was misleading. In fact, the Biblical admonition that "pride goeth before destruction and a haughty spirit before the fall" well described the priest's political crusade, a solitary quest made hopeless by his employment of extreme tactics. That his ill-advised exacerbation of social tensions had become counterproductive was reflected in the renewed criticism now directed at him from within the Church.

On September 3 the Vatican journal *L'Osservatore Romano* denied unequivocally that the Holy See approved Father Coughlin's activities and reiterated the fact that Bishop Gallagher understood "quite well what he was told on the subject." Yet certitude in Rome equalled uncertainty in New York, for when the Detroit prelate returned to the United States a day later aboard the Italian liner *Rex,* he informed newsmen that although the Papacy was not happy with Coughlin there were no plans to restrain him. Giving substance to Gallagher's remark, the radio priest left dockside with the declaration that distinguishing Roosevelt from Landon was like choosing between "carbolic acid and rat poison." *Time* magazine was surreptitiously correct in assessing the situation. Everything, so far as the priest was concerned, was "hunky-dory."

Coughlin's flippancy could not conceal the fact that in many quarters he himself had become a pariah. His moral indignation and oratorical fervor had carried him too far, obliterating the distinction between idealistic cause and demagogic rule. The "un-American" image of the Royal Oak pastor became stronger in the national mind.

"Not a sentence of your newsreel speeches," wrote one Los Angeles resident, "can be heard for the hissing and booing here." An inhabitant of Dearborn, Michigan, equated Coughlin with Al Smith because both men tended "to hear voices and see things under the bed." It was the belief of an Italian immigrant that the cleric had forsaken the Bible and the Ten Commandments. A "poor old man" living in Chicago printed at his own expense a condemnatory "Public Letter to Father Coughlin." A former Coughlinite expressed the feelings of persons disheartened by the priest's activities: "One of the first to enlist in your and our battle for freedom from financial bondage and the money changers, I believed in your sincerity to the fullest extent. Since that time something has come over you . . . you are not what you used to be. I withdraw my membership from the National Union."

And from staid Boston came the following bit of atrocious doggerel, penned by a disgruntled Irish-Catholic:

> *The Reverend Father Sore Ass is*
> *The greatest clown I know,*
> *And, boy, if Barnum was alive he'd*
> *Stage a one man show.*
> *You'd see the Reverend's proper face*
> *(His rear, between the hips),*
> *And noises that can come from there*
> *Can far outdo his lips.*
>
> *Barnum would feed the Rev'rend beans*
> *And get his Doctor Quack,*
> *And satisfaction would be yours*
> *Or else your money back.*
> *The Rev'rend then would back-fire with*
> *His stink bomb. (Sniff) Peeyew!*
> *And when the crap came, who would win*
> *The pot? Laugh. Barnum knew!*

Paying little attention to this growing opposition, Father Coughlin moved on to Chicago where he addressed an estimated 80,000 members of the National Union at Riverview Park. The assemblage roared its approval as its hero denied that the Vatican would silence him. "That's a lie!" he shouted. "If they had cracked down, I wouldn't be here today." New cheers erupted when the cleric derided Landon for hoping to return the country to the gold standard and for remaining silent on such issues as the Works Project Administration, the international bankers, and war debts. Laughter greeted Coughlin's characterization of the Republican nominee as "the world's worst radio speaker." The priest's advice for Landon was candid: "If he wants to go anywhere, he should stay fishing, not go fishing."

Turning his wit on the administration, Coughlin described the President as "the beautiful cover on the New Deal Magazine." Henry Morgenthau earned the sobriquet, "lover of the international bankers"; Rexford Tugwell was "the handshaker with Russia"; Mordecai Ezekiel, a liberal member of the Department of Agriculture, became "the modern Margaret Sanger of the Pigs." The list continued. There was "plow-me-down Wallace" and "Madame" Perkins —"with her three-cornered hat—one corner for communism, one for socialism, and one for Americanism."

"Well," the priest concluded, "we all know for whom we're voting if we vote for Mr. Roosevelt—for the communists, the socialists, the Russian lovers, the Mexican lovers." When Coughlin asked who among the crowd would vote for the President, silence followed. "Against?" A thunderous roar burst forth.

Father Coughlin's two-fisted campaign moved into September and October. On September 13, speaking to an enthusiastic crowd at Ebbets Field in Brooklyn, he denounced the "heathen" industrial system of the United States and charged that David Dubinsky, leader of the International Ladies Garment Workers, had collected $5,000 for the cause of Spanish communism. In New Haven Coughlin predicted that if Roosevelt were re-elected, "the red flag of Communism would be raised in this country by 1940. . . . The Communists are coming out for Mr. Roosevelt and he lacks the courage to denounce them."

On September 20, in Des Moines, Coughlin again sought to link the Roosevelt leadership with the red menace. Before his speech the cleric spoke with Dale Kramer, former secretary of the National Farm Holiday Association, and according to Kramer, told him in "a soft, matter-of-fact tone," that "one thing is sure. Democracy is threatened. It is either fascism or communism. We are at the crossroads." To this statement Kramer replied, "What road do you take Father Coughlin?" The priest answered, "I take the road of fascism."

Although the clergyman's statement simply reflected his belief that fascism was a lesser evil than communism, the remark had broader implications. Prior to Italy's invasion of Ethiopia and Hitler's decision to redress the Versailles Treaty, fascism had in fact impressed many Americans as an alluring social and political experiment. By mid-1936, however, this flirtation had ceased and Continental fascism, increasingly racist, militaristic, and totalitarian, had taken on a demonic image. Accompanying this metamorphosis was the tendency of nervous American liberals, many of whom had earlier supported Mussolini's "social pragmatism," to place Coughlin in the same ideological bailiwick as the European dictators.

Then too, when Father Coughlin discussed fascism he probably envisaged a governmental system based upon advanced Catholic social thought and radical agrarian reform. Both before and during the Union campaign, he never outlined a consistent philosophy but contented himself with vague protests against big business and big labor, accompanied by a heavy emphasis upon nationalism and isolationism, a despair of liberal democratic institutions, and the belief that the press and political parties had been captured by the enemy.

In fact, the only link between Coughlin and the European dictators lay in the staunch support offered the cleric by less-educated, agrarian groups. Conversely, the predilection of lower-middle-class, urban laborers for Coughlin's program, while reflecting the absence of a vigorous American leftist movement to channel working-class discontent, contrasted sharply with the situation in Europe, where laboring groups were usually attracted to communist and socialist parties. In this limited sense, Coughlinism might be interpreted as a "fascism of the left," similar in several respects to the subsequent Argentine *Justicialismo* of Juan D. Perón and to Getulio Vargas's dictatorial labor program in Brazil.

Father Coughlin had based his campaign upon little that was positive and much that was negative in American political life. It was not surprising, therefore, that by late September the crusade lagged noticeably. Most Catholic publications, disgusted by his slanderous remarks and totalitarian propensities, had retracted their support, and after a rally in Cincinnati drew only 12,000 persons, a quarter of the expected turnout, even the priest began to doubt Lemke's chances.

A newspaper reporter covering the Cincinnati meeting marveled at its incongruity: "Poor William Lemke—hindered by the voice and perhaps the mentality of a second-class soap-box orator—is the first presidential candidate who is decidedly a secondary figure at his own rally." After listening to Coughlin hack his way through the hackneyed theme of New Deal communism, the reporter concluded that the priest was indeed a missionary "with all the fervor and fire of the missionaries of old who faced privation and death to carry their message." But, he added, "the problem with Father Coughlin adheres from accepting his premises."

The cleric's premises, which struck some observers as fascistic, had become a great source of embarrassment for American Catholic leaders, and the elephantine machinery of the Church hierarchy finally began to move. Where earlier criticism of the priest had been carefully muted, clerical supporters of the administration now directly confronted their renegade colleague. George Cardinal Mundelein of Chicago castigated the Royal Oak pastor, as did Bishop Mahoney of Sioux Falls, Bishop John F. Noll of Fort Wayne, and Archbishop John McNicholas of Cincinnati. Archbishop McNicholas had attended Coughlin's rally in Cincinnati and was astonished by the priest's announcement that if an "up-start dictator" took over the government, it might be necessary "to resort to bullets instead of ballots."

Reacting to Father Coughlin's insensate attacks on Irish-Catholic politicians such as James Farley, Massachusetts Congressman John McCormack, and Representative O'Connor of New York, a New York City resident wondered "how any Catholic could stomach this . . . knight of the cloth [sic] who knocks over Catholics of Irish descent in order to make us think he is broadminded. . . . " His question appeared to be answered officially on October 8 with the arrival of Vatican envoy Eugenio Cardinal Pacelli. Acting more like a simple ambassador of papal good will than an agent of interdiction, however, Cardinal Pacelli spent three weeks in the United States without mentioning the controversial priest.

As the Vatican hesitated to deal forcefully with Coughlin, Roosevelt and his advisers determined to put him in his place. On October 8 the Democratic National Committee provided Father John A. Ryan, a liberal faculty member at Catholic University, with a national radio network to present its case. Charging that fully nine-tenths of the cleric's monetary program was mere "hocus-pocus," Ryan excoriated Coughlin's "ugly, cowardly, and flagrant calumnies," defended the priest's enemies, and entreated American laborers to vote for a man who truly cared about social justice—Franklin D. Roosevelt.

If Ryan's counterattack accelerated Coughlin's descent from respectability, the broadcast also enraged the priest's ardent supporters. Within two months, in fact, the Catholic University academician received more than one thousand letters, of which only fifty were respectful in tone. This correspondence demonstrated clearly that Coughlin's was now truly a congregation of despair. Rather than mirroring a cross section of ethnic, religious, vocational, and educational backgrounds, the messages were written primarily by poorly educated German- and Irish-Catholics who, when not making grammatical errors, bespoke their total alienation from the President, the New Deal, and ironically, the Catholic Church itself. Roosevelt's government-by-experiment had not solved their urgent problems, and although they considered the Chief Executive essentially honest, they felt he nonetheless had fallen victim to an evil conspiracy. Their only remaining hope was Father Coughlin, who did care whether they lived or died. In terms which evidenced their highly developed sense of class conflict, these Americans praised the battle their Christ-like leader carried on against the rich.

As election day approached, the Royal Oak pastor no longer seemed to care about Lemke and the Union Party. By late October, corroborating an earlier poll in the *Literary Digest,* he remarked that his candidate's vote would be unimpressive but perhaps sufficient to throw the election to Landon.

Ironically, once the chief asset of his party, Father Coughlin had become its greatest liability. The restraint he once possessed was gone; his poise was nonexistent. He had become a rabble-rouser who, having left the sophisticated milieu of the radio studio, now derived satisfaction from driving live audiences into hysterical expressions of evangelistic fidelity. Concomitant with the priest's degeneration, opposition to the lost cause mounted. Father Ryan's acrid denunciation of the cleric was seconded by two well-known Catholic laymen, Joseph P. Kennedy of Boston and John B. Kelly of Philadelphia. Kennedy remarked of his erstwhile friend's attacks that if there were any semblance of communism in the United States, "the words 'liar' and 'betrayer' would have been uttered only once." Kelly, meanwhile, termed the cleric "a disgrace to the cloth of the priesthood."

Other difficulties for Father Coughlin had humorous overtones. In mid-October the lone dissenter at the National Union convention, John O'Donnell, asked a Michigan Circuit Court for an accounting of a sum "in excess of one million dollars," allegedly held by trustees of the National Union. Inasmuch as O'Donnell later dropped the suit, it appears that he had merely seized an opportunity to charge publicly that Father Coughlin had become "an arbitrary and dictatorial tyrant, incapable of governing his emotions, who in the name of the National Union for Social Justice, indulged in orgies of vituperation and irresponsible abuse."

Buffeted by trumped-up legal charges one day, the cleric was showered with feathers the next. As he addressed a rally in Detroit, a crazed heckler leaped to the rostrum and emptied the contents of a pillow onto Coughlin's head. As might be expected, the robust priest pinned the man to the floor, the crowd suggested that he be crucified, and the gathering took on the complexion of a Roman circus.

Few novelties marked the Royal Oak clergyman's last fortnight of campaigning. In a radio sermon on October 24, however, he ventured into the realm of foreign policy by suggesting that the real choice in the upcoming election lay between peace and war. Previewing themes he would stress after 1937, Coughlin claimed that President Roosevelt's leadership of the recent inter-American conference at Buenos Aires indicated anew that the United States planned to join the League of Nations. The League posing a threat to world peace, America would be drawn into war within three years. Worse yet, the Treasury Department, headed by the hated Henry Morgenthau, planned to underwrite the British and French cause in Europe.

The priest's campaign ended as it had begun, with expected attacks upon traditional adversaries. Having labeled Roosevelt "a scab President" a week before, Coughlin appeared humble as he apologized for the remark on October 31. Yet the penitence was short-lived, for in the next moment he began anew with the announcement that "a vote for FDR is a vote for 273,000 Socialists and David Dubinsky and 78,000 Communists who sent funds to Spain to massacre helpless nuns and priests." A day later, Franklin Roosevelt had become "the revivor of the divine right theory" and "the upstart President."

On November 3 the American electorate returned Roosevelt to the White House. Landon carried only Maine and Vermont, giving rise to a humorous variation on an old theme: "As Maine goes, so goes Vermont." While the Republican Party was being reduced to impotence, however, the Unionists encountered disaster. Their total of 892,000 votes, less than two percent of all votes cast and only one-tenth of Coughlin's predicted tally, provided the final denouement to the cleric's "political" career. It had taken time, but the Royal Oak pastor now knew that it is one thing for a mass leader to recruit a following, but quite another to convert that support into a national political force.

Roosevelt's consummate political ability, a mixture of firmness, hope, kindness, and what journalist Raymond Clapper termed "an acute sixth sense," made him unbeatable in 1936. The Chief Executive had proved himself, in Herbert Swope's words, "President of all the people." Roosevelt's first administration had been a classic example of a leader stimulating creative energies among the American people. The years 1932–1936 were for the President and most Americans a period of partnership and shared experiences. His campaign theme, "Four Years Ago and Today," correctly stressed the hustle and bustle of a country returning to life.

While Roosevelt's campaign offered a study in leadership, Father Coughlin's called for an analysis in the psychology of domination. Stifling dissent, the cleric formulated policy and made all important decisions. His desire for omnipotence embittered relations with Townsend, Lemke, and Smith, and his glandular style, a compound of ferocity and fear, alienated potential voters among many of his own followers. Nor did the priest fathom the complexities of American politics. Despite its status as a popular lobby, the National Union for Social Justice never secured sufficient patronage to make the Union Party a significant threat at the polls. In addition, the Unionists were hindered by numerous state electoral laws historically opposed to third parties. In six of the thirty-six states in which the party did appear on the ballot, it was forced to change its name. That the Unionists did not secure recognition in California and Louisiana, finally, testifies to the impotence of Dr. Townsend and Gerald L. K. Smith.

The Union Party also failed to draw support from established political groups. Secretary of Agriculture Henry Wallace, for example, worked diligently to convince American farmers that the administration truly appreciated their plight, while the Non-Partisan Labor League, upon which Coughlin counted for assistance, contributed nearly one million dollars to Democratic coffers. The basic problem here lay in the hesitation of old Progressives and radically oriented liberals to join a party whose chances at best were dubious and which might split the liberal vote and throw the election to

Landon. These were the sentiments of such men as Governor Floyd B. Olson of Minnesota, Robert La Follette, Sidney Hillman, and Mayor Fiorello La Guardia of New York.

For those persons connected with it, the Union campaign of 1936 was a bitter experience. Indeed, Americans who voted the Lemke ticket, predominantly of Irish and German descent, apparently did so because the New Deal had not improved their lives. It was, more than any other factor, their wretchedness and futility that provided the adhesive by which they stuck with the North Dakota Republican.   As for Lemke himself, it is difficult to picture him as a tragic hero and probably the adjective is more fitting than the noun. In one instance he invested $7,000 from personal funds in the campaign and, despite assurances from Father Coughlin, was never reimbursed. Even more degrading were the constant reminders of his insignificance in the campaign. A Union poster epitomizing this fact appeared at one rally: "FATHER COUGHLIN TO SPEAK TONIGHT!" Below this, in small print, were the words: "William Lemke—Union Party Presidential Candidate —will also speak." Granting Lemke's ineptitude as a public speaker, it is still a sad commentary that a presidential candidate rated second-billing at his own rallies.

Having promised to abdicate his radio pulpit if Lemke garnered less than 9 million votes, Coughlin bade a lugubrious farewell to his congregation on Saturday, November 7. The National Union for Social Justice was unceremoniously interred. Franklin Roosevelt could become a dictator if he so chose. Newsmen gloated. The angry pastor of Royal Oak was quiet—for the moment.

5

William Dudley Pelley and the American Silver Shirts

★ ★ ★ In contrast to Father Coughlin's confused and confusing program, William Dudley Pelley and his American Silver Shirts illustrated the nature and problems of an avowedly fascist group that looked toward a reorganization of the United States along racist, corporatist, and military lines. The Silver Legion eschewed a traditional nativist theme, anti-Catholicism, and placed in its stead a curiously diffuse anti-Semitism. The prejudice against Jews that dominated Pelley's publications often verged on autism; yet behind his screaming rhetoric there lurked an important symbolic appeal to small-town Protestant bigots who felt painfully the end of WASP supremacy over the American social order and who sought substitute ways to bolster their prestige. Indeed, status anxieties were as real to Pelley and his followers as were the economic dislocations that drove Catholics to join the Coughlin movement.

William Shakespeare observed that a man can die but once; but this eternal truth seemingly did not apply to Pelley who spent "seven minutes in eternity" in 1928, returned to earth, and subsequently assumed leadership of the proto-fascist Silver Shirts of America. The only son of an itinerant Methodist parson, by his own account Pelley was not merely born in the shoe-production center of Lynn, Massachusetts; rather, he was there "inducted into a new mortal coil at seven minutes to one o'clock in the morning of March 12, 1890."

Spending his boyhood years traversing the rugged northern Massachusetts countryside as he followed his father from call to call, Pelley inhabited a grim world dominated by Protestant orthodoxy. Household conversation, narrowly circumscribed, consisted of such topics as free will, election, higher criticism, and infant damnation. Because of his father's vocation, he formed few friendships while attending schools in Gardner and Springfield, and dropped out after his sophomore year.

As his religious vocation kept his family in penury, George Pelley soon forsook his calling and founded the Pelley Tissue Corporation in Springfield. There his son learned the art of producing toilet paper, but like Henry David Thoreau, who abhorred manufacturing pencils in the family employ, William found little stimulus in the family trade. Though he became company treasurer in 1909, he resented having been denied a full education and therefore began reading promiscuously. He became "one of the worst agnostics that ever had books come to his post-office box in plain wrappers from freak publishing houses."

Describing himself as "a smouldering [sic] young Bolshevik," Pelley found an outlet for his resentments in writing. In 1912 he became publisher of the *Philosopher* magazine. Although he continued to deride institutional religion and other sources of authority, this period of revolt seemed to pass quickly, and in 1913 he began publishing the *Chicopee* (Mass.) *Journal*. Four years later he assumed similar duties with the *Wilmington* (Vt.) *Times* and, concomitantly, wrote features for the *Springfield Homestead* and crime reports for the *Boston Globe*.

Named to a five-man International YMCA Commission in 1917 to analyze the work of Protestant missions in the Far East, Pelley became, after America's entrance into the First World War, a correspondent for the *Saturday Evening Post*. During the winter of 1917–1918, in this capacity he accompanied two employees of the International Harvester Company across the frozen Siberian steppe to Moscow. There, as the Bolshevik Revolution ran its course, he helped rescue nearly one million dollars of company funds and also secured several important diplomatic documents from American Ambassador David R. Francis, later returning these to Washington. It was during this journey that Pelley later claimed to have had his first intimation of a Jewish-communist conspiracy to subvert the Christian nations of the world.

Upon returning to the United States, Pelley embarked upon a career notable for its variety. Under contract with Crowell Publishing, he wrote several novels that drew praise as specimens of dramatic construction. Moving west to Hollywood, he became a writer of scenarios for films starring Lon Chaney, Hoot Gibson, Tom Mix, Colleen Moore, and Cullen Landis. He contributed articles to *Collier's, Good Housekeeping,* and the *American Magazine*. He founded Pelley's Press in New York and the *Hi-Hat* magazine in Hollywood. He became president of Pelley and Eckels Advertising in Los Angeles, established a restaurant chain, the "Brief Meal Corporation," and served as business manager of one of the Dole Pineapple Flights to Hawaii.

These successes were qualified by significant failures. In 1921 Pelley's wife deserted him; his *Hi-Hat* magazine folded after a few issues; the "Brief Meal Corporation" enjoyed only a short existence. His respectable writer's income, moreover, could not offset the fact that fame and fortune had eluded his grasp. Overly generous in self-appraisal, he berated editors and film-makers who rejected his material and adopted a wholly naturalistic view of life. To become successful, he believed, one had first to engage in strife, and the best way to overcome opposition was "to crash through it like an army tank flattening out a breastworks." By early 1925, dominated by "tremendous nervous tension," he seemed headed for a nervous breakdown.

After working on a story for *Collier's* until the early morning hours of May 29, Pelley retired to the bedroom of his modest cottage near Altadena, California. Between three and four A.M., he later remembered, "a ghastly inner shriek tore through my inner conscience." Certain that he was dying, he "plunged down into a mystic depth of cool, blue space." Then friendly arms lifted him onto a beautiful marble-slab pallet, and, after bathing in a crystal-clear Roman pool, he emerged revived and began conversing with passers-by who appeared "sublimated, glorified, and possessed of an Olympian peace." Suddenly, however, amid a whirling, bluish vapor, he was rushed upward. His mind swimming, he awoke "to earthly consciousness" in his bedroom.

The meaning of his extraterrestrial voyage was clear to the suddenly percipient Pelley. "I brought back with me from that Ectstatic [sic] Interlude," he wrote, "something that interpenetrated my physical self and which suddenly began to function in strange powers of perception. I was not the same man that I had been before."

Worried lest he be called a crackpot, Pelley hesitated to make public his experience. In his own mind he had changed a great deal—his "nerves," a product of religious conflict and economic and status frustrations, had disappeared—and he had acquired amazing new powers of stamina and reflection. Upon learning of the incident, the editorial staff of the *American Magazine* had no trouble convincing him that the sensational account would have wide appeal. The contract signed, Pelley related the details of his journey in a sincere, straightforward manner, emphasizing the fact that he was not an occultist but only an ordinary man revealing a deep personal secret. He was, he humbly assured readers, not even certain where he had been. "Call it the Hereafter, call it Heaven, call it Purgatory," he wrote, "call it What you Will. Whatever it is—and where—that humans go after being released, I had gone there that night."

The exotic tale called forth many letters from persons claiming to have had similar experiences and from others who considered him "a spiritualistic nut." Approximately 10 million persons read his story and Pelley, his entrepreneurial instincts stimulated, made a discovery that to him was as important as the radio had been to Father Coughlin: one could write about metaphysical wonders for fun *and* profit. Thus Pelley enlarged his claim to supernatural powers and by 1929 discovered himself to possess a built-in "mental radio" through which he could "tune in on the minds and voices of those in another dimension of being." Using this medium, he undertook a crash course in "hyper-dimensional instruction" in which his "oracular" professors dictated to him "a four-hundred-page book on political economy, so advanced in context and knowledge that it surprised authorities who have perused portions of it."

In 1930 Pelley moved his operations to Asheville, North Carolina, whose location in the Great Smoky Mountains near the highest elevation east of the Rockies indicated that it would be the only eastern American area saved from a prophesied natural cataclysm. The spiritualist could not have chosen a more idyllic site, as residents of the "land of the sky" had long extolled the beauty of their green mountains, fertile valleys, and rushing streams. Firmly established in Buncombe County, Pelley immediately formed "the League for the Liberation," and members from Los Angeles to Boston soon met regularly to discuss the messages sent their leader by disembodied spirits. To keep his followers abreast of new developments he founded Galahad Press in February 1931, financing the transaction by selling more than $13,000 in preferred stock to fifteen persons. Incorporated in New York and moved subsequently to Washington, D.C., Galahad Press, like many of his ventures, verged on bankruptcy until its demise in 1934. Yet in its four years' existence the press served him well, printing *The New Liberator* (*Liberation* after 1932) and numerous spiritual tracts.

Pelley's journal offered "instruction and inspiration from sources above and behind mortality," and its contents, unless designated otherwise, reached him "via the Psychic Radio, from Great Souls who have graduated out of this three-dimensional world into other areas of time and space." Although concentrating upon spectral topics, Pelley also concerned himself with more mundane issues. In an article entitled "The True Significance of Present Russian Atheism," for example, he predicted that the Soviet Union and China would combine forces and that the "petty squabblings of interdependent European nations [would] be swiftly ignored in the mightier menace of a new influx of Goths and Huns battling at the Gates of Europe."

An incurable promoter, Pelley incorporated in Asheville the following year the "Foundation of Christian Economics," an institution whose by-laws provided for the sale of stock, the granting of dividends, and the enrichment of its founder. A "non-profit" organization, the foundation was in fact less devoted to comparative religion than to singular economics. Between 1932 and 1934 Pelley continuously diverted funds from Galahad Press into his personal account and that of the foundation. By early 1934 the "profit-making" press showed a balance of $4,700, while that of the foundation totaled $81,000. To preserve the secrecy necessary to these operations, Pelley ordered Galahad records destroyed in January 1934, but not before North Carolina authorities had begun scrutinizing his activities.

Potential legal troubles mattered less to Pelley than self-aggrandizement, so he also became a college president. Galahad College, located in the old Asheville Women's Club building, endured for one summer session and attracted forty students to classes in public stewardship, spiritual engineering, cosmic mathematics, and social metapsychics. Thereafter the college offered extension courses which the American Civil Liberties Union termed a mixture of "astrology, Hindu mythology, evolution, radiotherapy, endocrinology, and radio broadcasting."

Galahad College was never accredited, but it did fulfill its major task. During a four-month period in 1932, its president received $30,000 simply for mail-order courses in "metapsychics." Not surprisingly, contributors to Pelley's spiritualistic fiefdom were often as bizarre as he. Mrs. Marie Ogden, for instance, directed the "Home of Truth" religious sect and considered herself the reincarnation of the Virgin Mary. After offering $12,000 in bonds to the foundation, however, she deserted the Asheville mystic when it became clear to her that he was "always establishing things and never hanging on to them long enough to entrench them firmly." Subsequently she led a colony to Dry Valley in southern Utah and was arrested when police discovered that she had kept the corpse of a sectarian in her home for over a year while attempting to revive it.

Dr. John R. Brinkley, an eccentric physician who resided in Milford, Kansas, Del Rio, Texas, and Mexico while fleeing from the American Medical Association and the Federal Radio Commission, also contributed a large monetary gift to Pelley's account. Brinkley specialized in rejuvenating elderly Kansans through his "compound operation," in which he transplanted vital portions from the testicles of Toggenberg goats. In addition, he prescribed freely over a powerful radio transmitter and, of course, received a cut on each purchase when his remote-control patients rushed to designated pharmacies to receive their castor oil, aspirin, and other nostrums. In time, although barred from practice in his native Kansas, he became sufficiently wealthy to own a bank, build a park in his home town, and run for governor. In 1932, seeking revenge upon those persons who had interrupted his lucrative career, Brinkley split the Democratic vote and thus facilitated the rise of Republican Alfred M. Landon.

As long as people like Marie Ogden and Dr. Brinkley had money, Pelley reasoned, his was the material they would read. But with the deepening of depression, his sources of income evaporated and he found it increasingly difficult to publish *Liberation* on schedule. In November 1932, after his business manager revealed that he would be unable to finance the foundation payroll, Pelley was forced to travel to New York, where he secured a new literary agent and wrote several short stories. In New York he conferred with Paul Lillienfield-Toal, an official of the North German Lloyd, who predicted that Adolf Hitler would soon seize power in Germany. Pelley returned to Asheville shortly before Christmas and spoke for the first time of organizing a militant group to defend Christian-American Constitutionalism. He remembered that a medium had prophesied the occurrence of a significant event on January 31, 1933, a "pyramid date."

On the evening of January 31 Pelley was working in his office when his secretary brought him a copy of the local newspaper. There it was, an eight-column, banner headline which proclaimed, "ADOLF HITLER BECOMES GERMAN CHANCELLOR!" Something clicked in Pelley's mind as he suddenly recalled a conversation he had carried on with his "Oracle" three years before. "Over in Europe," the medium informed him, "there exists a young Austrian. By trade he is a painter. He is coming to the head of the German people. His work is not yours for his is strictly political. Yours is economic but spiritual as well. He will become the great power in Central Europe. That power of his may extend over Russia, overthrowing the Legions of Darkness. The Day that man ascends to the Chancellorship of the German people, take it as your timetable to launch your organization in America."

Pelley glanced at his secretary. "Tomorrow," he said, "we have the Silver Shirts."

Esoteric issues faded in importance as Pelley determined to create an American countersubversive movement comprising "the cream, the head, and the flower of our Protestant Christian manhood." In his "First Official Despatch [sic]" from Silver Shirt headquarters, he announced that the basic object of the organization would be "to foster, promote, and develop political and patriotic principles for the betterment and welfare of its members." Financial support would be secured through annual dues of twelve dollars, voluntary contributions, endowments, miscellaneous fees, and "by the transaction of any business that the Board of Directors may deem advisable."

The quasi-military framework of the organization was its most notable characteristic. Pelley, as "National Commander," directed operations from Asheville and was aided by a five-man "General Staff." Silver Shirt posts, comprising nine national administrative districts, were to be located in every American community "where Christian people are aware of the problems facing American government." On the community level a Department of Local Posts was organized to secure membership and arrange social events and meetings; a Department of Silver Rangers to supervise military instruction; and a Department of Industrial Relations to handle finances. Other sections included an Office of Junior Affiliates and the Department of Foreign Affiliates.

The by-laws of the Silver Legion restricted membership to persons who were at least eighteen years of age and practicing Christians, and who were either native-born or naturalized citizens. Before attaining active status, furthermore, prospects had to demonstrate "unswerving loyalty to the United States of America as a sovereign people" by taking an oath "to uphold physically, if the need arises, the Constitution of the United States and the constitutional form of representative government."

If the neophyte understood and approved "the premise and tenets of the Christian Commonwealth, whose economic provisions the Silver Shirts would inaugurate upon the debris of the present Judaistic practices," he would pledge "to commit no act against America's despoilers of the present moment that is not countenanced or directed by the Chief of the organization over his signature."

Complete conformity to Pelley's policies was a necessity. Members might be expelled if they failed to uphold "tenets of the Christian faith," or if they committed acts or preached doctrines "inimical to the social success of that faith." They could also lose their shirts if they made "a false representation of race, religious faith, or political principles," if they "promoted or otherwise affiliated with other organizations subversive of the ends of the corporation," or if they "prompted secession movements within the corporation." Finally, Silver Shirts faced exclusion for insubordination, for "relaying information as to the corporation's intimate business or plans to subversive individuals or organizations," for "misusing corporation funds," and for "making unauthorized statements or spreading irresponsible reports."

Because Pelley considered his organization to parallel the Nazi SS, a significant aspect of group ritual was the uniform worn by its members. Silver Shirt garb did not invite anonymity. The men were to wear shirts of silver gray, with a brilliant "L" stitched in red silk on the left breast. Trousers were to be blue corduroy knickers, and were to be worn with puttees, or long socks. On his blue tie each Silver Shirt member would have woven his personalized national number.

Silver Shirt membership burgeoned, but not as quickly as Pelley claimed. Field organizations were dispatched to California, Ohio, Pennsylvania, Maine, Maryland, Utah, and Nebraska. The Asheville nativist also secured aid in proselytizing activities from many respectable citizens, including Protestant clergymen in Los Angeles, Seattle, and Augusta, and several attorneys and physicians. By the end of 1933 the organization had extended operations into twelve states, and from a membership of 700 persons six months earlier, would reach its zenith early in 1934 with approximately 15,000 members.

For the better part of 1933 events moved smoothly for Pelley and his Silver Shirts. Although hostile residents forced him to move his second base of operations from Oklahoma City, he successfully transferred the unit to Los Angeles in January 1934. In fact, it was in southern California that the Silver Legion gained its greatest following. Although Pelley's boast that there were more Silver Shirts in the area than either police or National Guard was inflated, local meetings did draw upwards of 500 persons during the early months of 1934.

Although Pelley attempted to maintain the fiction of a separate existence, there could be no doubt that the Silver Legion rode the flood tide of anti-Semitism sweeping Germany. In his first year as an American *Führer,* he made numerous overtures to German sympathizers in the United States, including Edward Emerson, Fritz Gissibl, Oscar Pfaus, the Reverend Gerald Winrod, and "Count" Anastase Vonsiatsky, leader of the Russian National Fascist Revolutionary Party. As his "foreign adjutant," meanwhile, Pelley chose his friend, Lillienfield-Toal, whose position as a German steamship line officer enabled the Asheville extremist to achieve direct contact with Nazi propaganda agencies such as the *Deutscher Fichte Bund* (German Fighter Society) in Hamburg and *Weltdienst* (World Service) in Erfurt.

Having recognized the potential dangers inherent in operating a Nazi fifth column in the United States, Pelley argued that "the adroit thing to do" would be "to let a spontaneous American movement be born here that has exactly similar principles and precepts to Hitler's; that shall be American in character and personnel; but that shall work shoulder-to-shoulder with German aims and purposes." Yet by July, a mere five months after the birth of the Silver Shirts, these qualifications were ignored by the *Deutsche Zentrale* of the German League of Chicago when this organization awarded the North Carolinian honorary membership, praising him for his work in "purging . . . our nation of its subversive elements maliciously undermining the Federal Constitution."

For good reason increasing numbers of Americans began to perceive in the Silver Legion a threat to their pluralistic society. When dissension among officers in the Los Angeles unit forced Pelley to travel frequently to southern California, members of the California State Legislature voiced resentment over the presence of a totalitarian group. On Capitol Hill Representative Samuel Dickstein of New York, frightened by the implications of anti-Semitism in Hitler's Germany, lobbied for the investigation of American fascism, as did representatives of the Anti-Defamation League of B'nai B'rith, the American Jewish Committee, and the American Jewish Congress.

In fact, in the historic bogey of anti-Semitism, Pelley discovered a symbolic, unifying theme that he modified to fit American necessities. Arguing that a secret cabal of 300 "Judeo-Bolsheviks" located in Hamburg, Paris, London, and New York, controlled most of the world and stood ready to inundate the United States, he derived "proof" of the menace from the depression, numerous bank failures, Prohibition, repeal, gangster activity, the Hoover Moratorium, and the Roosevelt Brain Trust. His revelations in *Liberation,* often of a contradictory nature, emphasized imminent danger. In one issue, the Silver Shirt leader intimated that a Jewish leader had informed a secret Jewish unit operating in the South that "in only a few more months we will be in full control of the United States," and that if those in attendance subscribed generously to a fund, "we will see to it that the American capital is transferred here, although the United States will be a tributary nation to Zion, with headquarters in Jerusalem."

An armchair psychologist could conclude that the "money" was raised because in Pelley's conspiratorial scheme, which amounted to a kind of self-fulfilling prophecy, it had to be. "Gentile Americans should stop talking about good Jews," he warned. "Those who do should provide themselves with darkened bungalows and make sure the windows are raised when Jewish organizations come to town. Don't hoodwink yourself that the rank and file of our Jewish citizenry doesn't know what is going on!"

Other attacks were based on pseudo-sociology. For instance, from a sentence in the Talmud, stating that "all shall be one unit and one people so that no man can say to his neighbor: 'I am better than you,'" Pelley reasoned that "in unhappy Russia, whose government is composed of 376 Jews and just sixteen real Russians, universal vulgarization is made a sort of state religion." Then, in a representative non sequitur, he asked readers to "consider New

York City, so Jewish that on Yom Kippur it is a deserted metropolis despite its Gentile population. *It is the most vulgar city on our planet!* Millions of cultured Gentiles visit Manhattan annually but cannot remain more than a week, so lewd and disgusting is its atmosphere."

To dismiss Pelley as a member of the "lunatic fringe" would seem appropriate; yet such categorization would deny his considerable intellectual depth. He developed fully his concept of the "Christian Commonwealth" in a book entitled *No More Hunger* (1936), although his ideas on the subject appeared in print as early as 1933 when he predicted that "after sixty generations of rumor, Christ will return to the earth to set up a Thousand-year Reign of Righteousness and Peace." His proposed system of government, he assured readers, had "already endured in purity for 300,000 years in Atlantis."

The Christian Commonwealth recalled many of the ideas of Edward Bellamy, the American reformer of the late nineteenth century who wrote *Looking Backward*. Pelley's system of government was posited on a giant corporation entrusted with the task of replacing the profit system with a model based upon the tenets of Christianity. This modern, corporative state would be operated by native-born, white American stockholders who, without having to work, would each receive monthly dividends of $83.33, thus eliminating "the tyranny of hunger over human volition." Those wanting to earn more money could do so as members of a perpetual civil service organization. Excepting its citizens' personal belongings and homes, which could be purchased on credit from the proceeds of their various dividends, the Commonwealth would own everything, thereby destroying the evils of foreclosure, usury, interest, and rent. Because their work was fundamental to national welfare, American farmers would become the Commonwealth's privileged class. Citizens who did not work would be ostracized from the new system, as would aliens who did not subscribe to its tenets. As for the poor white and southern Negro, Pelley proposed to consign them to the status of the American Indian— ward of the state.

Where the Silver Shirts were patterned upon the Nazi model, Pelley's Christian Commonwealth derived in large part from elements in American life. In addition to its utopianism, there was exhibited its theoretician's admiration for hard work, the concept of private property, and esteem for the agrarian life. Less a revolutionary than a counter-revolutionary, and considering himself far from radical, Pelley avowed that his plan was practicable within constitutional limits. Yet inasmuch as no law could become effective without the approval of fifty-one percent of the Commonwealth's residents, it is clear that his constitutional emphasis was important for symbolic reasons. Like other nativist leaders, Pelley realized that mere mention of the Fundamental Laws was sufficient to bring one-tenth of the nation's populace to its knees in prayerful reverence.

But reverence was insufficient to achieve Christian-American utopia, so it fell to the Silver Shirts to propel the country toward this end. "From humble and secret beginnings," Pelley wrote with characteristic understatement in

1933, "this movement will grow to a power to be reckoned with, until it finally assumes all responsibility for governmental, financial, and economic leadership." Here, however, there were problems: in the world of the Silver Shirts, dominated by the fear of conspiracy, public statements and private thoughts soon conflicted; continued obeisance to lawful procedure became difficult; and the line dividing verbal abuse from physical violence grew dim. Thus it was not surprising that Pelley's directive that no force be employed without his approval was honored in its breach. The first violent deed attributed to the group occurred in Salt Lake City in midsummer 1933, when in the presence of police officers local Silver Shirts kidnapped and beat a suspected communist, leaving him for dead. The victim was rescued by a passing motorist, but the parties responsible were never arrested.

Even more militant than the Utah Silver Legion was the San Diego unit, whose activities were particularly geared toward a confrontation with subversives in municipal government. By autumn 1933, this post already had advocated the violent overthrow of the Roosevelt administration and, to rebuff a predicted Bolshevik attack on City Hall on May Day 1934, had purchased large quantities of ammunition and had begun military training in methods of counterattack. The San Diego Silver Legion was no afternoon shooting club. It was an elite, clandestine, military order divided into squads of five men apiece, each of whom knew only his leader and the other three men in his group. Its commander, Willard W. Kemp, had a fetish for firearms and was reputed to pay ten dollars for every rifle a Marine could steal and deliver, twenty dollars for each case of ammunition, and fifty dollars for a machine gun. When he traveled, Kemp always carried a Springfield rifle and four fully loaded ammunition belts. He and his men boasted of having access to more than 12,000 rounds of ammunition with which to destroy communistic Jews (or Jewish communists). On weekends members of the San Diego Legion visited Kemp's ranch in El Cajon to improve their marksmanship.

Actually, in their active preparations to employ force the San Diego Silver Shirts were unlike their parent group and most other countersubversive organizations of the era. They were, rather, in many ways more closely akin to the notorious Black Legion of Detroit, which had been founded in 1933 by unemployed, semiskilled men who in many cases were graduates of the Ku Klux Klan, and who organized themselves into isolated cells and bestowed military titles upon their officers. The Black Legion provided fellowship and community for Americans who lacked character references for the Elks and Odd Fellows. Individuals could not join the group but had to be invited. Neophytes seeking entrance first stood before a loaded revolver aimed at their heart and promised "to be torn from limb to limb and scattered to the carrion" if they betrayed the organization's existence. Then, according to ritual, they were asked if they believed in a Supreme Being and if they could shoot, ride, drink, and lie. If accepted, new members would swear to uphold "Americanism, Protestantism, and womanhood," purchase a dark robe for seven dollars, and commence the good fight against Jews, Negroes, aliens, Catholics, and communists. The Black Legion was trained in terrorism and, as police investigations revealed in 1936, was responsible for the murder of a young Catholic WPA worker, wrongly suspected of beating his pregnant wife.

The success of the Black Legion was predicated upon the group's secrecy; the ultimate failure of the Silver Legion resulted from its leader's penchant for publicity. Pelley did send representatives to confer with army officers in several cities. He also secured the aid of Captain Samuel J. Rubley, U.S. Army Reserve, in training Silver Rangers. But he never understood that his personal idiosyncracies stood between himself and eventual accomplishment. In fact, rather than terrifying his adversaries, Pelley cut a humorous swathe through the depressed and barren fields of American life during the 1930s. On one occasion, in April 1934, he suddenly appeared at the Park Avenue apartment of Miss Dorothy Waring, secretary for Royal Gulden's countersubversive "Order of '76." Completely garbed in silver regalia, he dismissed his bodyguard, removed two revolvers from concealed holsters, and conversed with his hostess for two hours. Thinking her a rich woman, he attempted to arouse Miss Waring's interest in his organization, which, he explained, would shortly march on Washington, D.C. and install him as "white king" of the nation. Then, changing the subject, he took a strand of her blonde hair and subjected it to a "heat analysis" to demonstrate that she was "100% Aryan." Dorothy Waring was a willing listener, for in addition to serving as Gulden's aide, she acted as an undercover agent for the McCormack-Dickstein Committee currently investigating Nazi propaganda in the United States and would subsequently relate the details of the strange meeting to that organization and to its successor, the Dies Committee.

Like Father Coughlin and other countersubversives, Pelley used American history to suit his special purposes, and one of his plagiarisms caused a controversy among American historians. On February 3, 1934, he published an extract he claimed to have taken from the private diary of Charles C. Pinckney of South Carolina, an American diplomat during the Revolutionary War. Although the original document had been destroyed by the army of Union General William Tecumseh Sherman during its Civil War operations, Pelley alleged that he had access to a copy located somewhere in southwest Georgia. Pinckney, so the story went, had taken notes on "chit chat around the table during intermission" at the Constitutional Convention in Philadelphia, and according to one diary entry, Benjamin Franklin had there delivered a long, impassioned tirade against the Jews.

The possibility that Franklin had been anti-Semitic thrilled German propagandists, and Pelley's story consequently appeared in *Weltdienst* in August 1934, in a Swiss Nazi paper, *Volksbund,* and in Julius Streicher's *Der Stürmer.* Subsequently, the account reappeared in the United States, when Robert Edward Edmondson published it in his *Economic Bulletin* on September 25. By October the "Pinckney Prophecy" had become a primary document in the literature of American countersubversion.

The currency given Pelley's fabrication troubled historian Charles A.

Beard, who in his scholarly investigations had never encountered Pinckney's "diary." To counter Pelley's allegation, he and several graduate students undertook further research and concluded that the "Prophecy" was a "barefaced forgery." Presenting his own evidence, Beard argued that the Constitutional Convention was such an important event that Franklin's "anti-Semitism" necessarily would have emerged if it indeed had been a strongly held prejudice. In fact, however, Franklin was an old man who stood above earthly ambition and had no reason to criticize the Jews. On the contrary, he was respected for his liberal views on religion and probably held the Jewish people in high regard. Finally, the distinguished historian argued that the wording of the "Prophecy" was not that of the eighteenth century, and certainly not that of "the learned Dr. Franklin." In fact, certain words in the document, including "Zionism" and "homeland," more closely resembled the language of contemporary Nazi Germany.

Rebuffed by academia, Pelley was also troubled because his "Oracle" never told him how to escape monetary problems. Unlike more successful anti-Semites who prospered by enumerating the horrors of communism to American businessmen, the leader of the Silver Shirts considered extraterrestrial conversations with departed souls (who couldn't take it with them) of paramount importance. Thus during the early months of 1934, he was forced to try to bolster his finances. Organization dues, initially set at twelve dollars per year, were lowered to one dollar in hopes of attracting new members. In an effort to reach the business community, he also initiated a weekly "confidential news-letter," which offered "the inside information on many of the men, the government, and commercial situations now baffling the rank-and-file of our people." But this venture failed after only six issues, as did his subsequent attempt to solicit contributions directly from Berlin.

In mid-April *Liberation* suspended publication, and when a new journal, *Pelley's Weekly,* appeared in August, more than 1,700 former "enthusiastic readers" failed to resubscribe. Even more serious was the bankruptcy of Galahad Press. Pelley's order to destroy press records lest "they give aid and comfort to the enemy" had not prevented investigations from discovering that the insolvency of the institution resulted from Pelley's diversion of over $100,000 of its funds to other accounts—$29,497.42 to his own personal account in the Franklin National Bank in Washington, and over $81,000 to the credit of the "non-profit" Foundation of Christian Economics. On May 1, 1934, in arrears by $200,000, Galahad Press was declared bankrupt in the Superior Court of Buncombe County.

Pursuant to pending legal proceedings, Asheville Superior Court Judge Zebulon Vance Nettles ordered the attachment of all Silver Legion records and indicted Pelley and two assistants, Robert Summerville and Donald D. Kellogg, for fraud and conspiracy. In addition, following a raid on Pelley's headquarters in May, Asheville deputy sheriffs discovered that the Silver Shirts had not been incorporated in North Carolina, but under Delaware laws. Charges against the Silver Legion leader and his associates were thus enlarged to encompass their violation of the North Carolina "Blue Sky" ordinance, which prohibited the operation in the state of any unincorporated organization.

Arrested on May 23 and freed on $2,500 bail, Summerville and Kellogg did not reveal the fact that Pelley was in Los Angeles attempting to heal a rift among leaders in the southern California unit. Nor would they discuss his spiritual idiosyncrasies. As Summerville told a reporter, the source of their leader's supernatural abilities was "likely to be misunderstood by those who have not been trained to understand. They laughed at Joan of Arc, too, when she heard voices."

Pelley's return to Asheville on June 15 was prompted by hearings on un-American activities currently being conducted in the mountain community by the McCormack-Dickstein Committee. Offering no resistance to local authorities, the goateed American *Führer* denied the validity of charges against him. Freed on $2,500 bail, he waited until January 25 when, following the acquittal of Kellogg, he and Summerville were convicted of violating state law. Summerville received a suspended sentence of from one to two years, while Pelley was fined $1,719.50, given a suspended sentence, and placed on five years' probation. Expressing dismay at Silver Shirt anti-Semitism, Judge Nettles also ordered the Legion theoretician not to publish or distribute any periodical literature in North Carolina. Nor could Pelley enter any business entailing the sale of stock.

Attempting to place the affair in perspective, a staff writer for the *Asheville Times* noted that while Silver Shirt machinations "may make good reading for dog days and raise gooseflesh on the timid, they should excite more laughter than fear among the great body of American citizens." The local superpatriots were merely "a ridiculous expression of social unrest and egotism," he continued, and "no rational person can read of their grandiose pronouncements without seeing the joke of it all."

Yet throughout the editorial there coursed the sensitivity of local citizens. "Asheville," the writer concluded, "enjoys the rather dubious distinction of being the headquarters of the Silver Shirts. This honor was not achieved, but thrust upon this city. Asheville enjoys another distinction which should be counted unto us for righteousness. We have seen the Silver Shirt movement for what it is. In laughing at it, we laugh at others who find in it a menace to the Republic."

6

The Myth of Fascism, the Bogey of Anti-Semitism

★ ★ ★ In deprecating the Silver Shirts, the Asheville journalist displayed an urbanity that many persons lacked during the depression. Like most countersubversive groups, the Silver Legion mirrored the tensions wrought by economic chaos and social dislocation. As such, the organization was itself troubled by personal animosities and internal dissensions. Yet rather than recognizing these weaknesses and interpreting the Silver Shirts as a manifestation of domestic woe, many observers chose to stress two alien characteristics of the movement—its apparent connection with European fascism and its leader's espousal of anti-Semitism. This choice was important in that it reflected a pervasive fear among Americans that their democratic system of government had failed. Because groups like Pelley's now offered alternatives to that system, there existed in the nation a tendency to assign specific labels to phenomena that defied facile description. The need to classify the unintelligible, so strong during periods of accelerated social change, became irresistible. Thus, although the threat posed by Pelley and his followers was mythical, it was nonetheless perceived as real by persons whose fear of Nazism led them to identify the Silver Legion with Hitler's SS.

Ironically, until the advent of the *Führer* endowed fascism with a demonic image, many Americans had been deeply impressed with the experimental, pragmatic nature of Benito Mussolini's corporate state. This "flirtation" ceased during the mid-1930s, however, and liberal and conservative writers alike joined the man in the street in search of "fascistic" legions and their allies. The chase was often frenzied and, not surprisingly, individuals who employed the term usually revealed more about their own anxieties than about the menace itself. In fact, to the extent that fascism exerted a kind of mystical influence upon the American people, the term generated more uncertainty and fear than it did dispassionate analysis.

Because of the blatancy of their activities, the shirted organizations were accorded great attention. When he was not questioning the "Fascist methods and Fascist principles" of Roosevelt and his New Dealers, columnist George Sokolsky discovered in groups like Pelley's Silver Shirts, George W. Christians's Crusaders for Economic Liberty, and Harry A. Jung's American Vigilante Federation, evidence of a "Fascist wave" inundating the country. Journalists Harold Loeb and Selden Rodman, meanwhile, extended the definition, explaining that "some varieties are local. Some have branches in many parts of the country; some have sprung from the remnants of the Ku Klux Klan; others have spontaneously arisen to meet a momentary crisis or labor threat."

Several leading American conservatives, including publisher B. C. Forbes and the editors of the *Washington Star* and *Wall Street Review,* found evidence of fascism within the New Deal itself. British statesman Stanley Baldwin believed that American democracy was in eclipse and that England alone remained a bulwark against "the world tide of dictatorship." Some American magazine writers also looked askance at their government. "Must America Go Fascist?" asked a pair of journalists in *Harper's.* They conceded that it well might, as did Hugh Tigner, writing in the liberal *Christian Century.*

Undoubtedly, it was the liberal and radical press that was most responsible for injecting the fascist label into many areas of national life, thereby blurring its meaning and making the term less than useful in describing American extremists during the 1930s. An editorial writer in the *New Republic* epitomized this phenomenon when he argued that a fingerprinting campaign being waged in Berkeley, under the auspices of the local Junior Chamber of Commerce, would allow "people with strong fascist leanings [to] use the device against labor and 'radicals'—a term that, to the Pacific Coast's high blood pressure, includes even the mildest liberals." Even more unsettling were the antilabor policies of employers and growers in the agricultural heartland of southern California, policies that prompted a writer in the *Nation* to charge that "a 100% American Fascism" has produced "prize-winning blooms in California." "From the labor baitings of the 1934 strike to the lynchings of San Jose," he concluded, "the West begins to look like Nazi Germany."

Fascism was also discernible in a company mining town in Fayette County, Pennsylvania, "where only the members of the miner's immediate family, the physician, and the undertaker have a right to enter the home." A writer in the *New Republic,* meanwhile, charged that "America's most openly fascist organization" existed in the guise of the Johnstown, Pennsylvania Citizens' Committee. Not to be outdone by these allegations, the *Nation* retorted that the American Legion, "openly advocating mob violence against militant workers and the leaders of the struggle against the steel trust," had launched a fascistic organization among steel workers in western Pennsylvania. E. M. Hugh-Jones, Professor of Economics at Oxford, likewise discovered the pernicious "ism" in the treatment accorded United Mine Workers in Rosalyn, Washington. "Fascism is here in the West a present fact," he explained. "It operates through intimidation and illegality. It is 'boring from within' by getting control of local situations. This will prepare the way for control of national situations."

Using as her main source the yearly report of the American Civil Liberties Union, Evelyn Seeley reasoned that except for the American Legion, local American Chambers of Commerce represented the most dangerous "agencies of repression and attacks upon minority movements." And, while the Legion seemed in danger of losing its position, the local Chambers—"Our Number One Fascists"—showed no sign of recanting. "They stand firm," Seeley wrote, "in a pattern that varies only with local conditions—strike breaking (open or secret), red-baiting, company-union promotion, fostering of 'runaway' shops with their lowering of wage levels and working conditions, open shop propaganda, keeping education 'safe,' checking 'subversive activities' that cover as broad a field as Mrs. Dilling's Network."

A writer for *Scribner's* was even more specific, warning that fascism was hovering "at the door." His fear that powerful, unnamed capitalists stood ready to destroy the American economic system was echoed by a reporter for the *Nation,* who expressed concern that business leaders who failed to win their battle against democracy by economic methods might resort to the military in order to create a corporate state. In fact, late in 1934 such a rumor swept through Washington after Retired Major Smedley D. Butler informed Congress that a clandestine Wall Street group planned a coup to be led by General Douglas MacArthur or General Hugh Johnson. Although Matthew Josephson dismissed the affair as "a cocktail putsch" in his recent memoirs, a writer for the *New Republic,* close to the scene, considered it far from incredible. "There is," he wrote, "no more incompetent, ignorant, or reckless group of people in the United States, or probably the world, than that surrounding our speculative markets."

If stock brokers and speculators bore watching, so also did leaders in California higher education. Writing in the *New Republic,* Anna Wallace lamented that decision making had become subject to either "a benighted legislature" or "the dictates of the Regents." Unfortunately, she continued, both groups were staffed by men who harbored reactionary political views and denied the legitimacy of dissent. As proof of her allegations, she cited UCLA Provost Ernest Moore's suspension of five students for allegedly plotting to destroy the university. Moore, in a statewide broadcast, had termed his campus "one of the worst hotbeds of Communism in America," and later allowed 150 athletes to form a vigilante committee to rid Westwood of "all students holding extreme political views."

In addition, the liberal journalist discovered fascist tendencies in a student spy system directed at Berkeley by patriotic organizations like the American Legion; in the crucial role of the university in smearing the reputation of gubernatorial candidate Upton Sinclair; in the expulsion of the editor of the

Santa Clara Weekly for refusing to print material deemed advisable by the administration and faculty; in the incarceration of two liberal university students in a San Mateo jail; in the announcement by the president of San Jose State Teachers College that he would welcome the removal of radical students by their patriotic peers; and (of course!) in the administrative admonition to teachers in San Francisco that they would be subject to dismissal if they were seen carrying copies of the *Nation* or *New Republic* on school grounds.

American leftists also commented upon developing fascist tendencies in American law. Carey McWilliams, for example, criticized other "social observers" for dubbing as fascistic all "untoward social phenomena," but he also offered his own warning that fascism need not invariably wear a uniform. "It may," he argued, "parade in the cloak of conservatism and, more frequently, in the guise of reform itself." In the present instance, referring to specific developments in California, McWilliams decried "an unmistakably fascist sentiment" behind the "powerful, concerted, nation-wide drive for a summary criminal procedure."

In short, fascism could be found wherever one looked. If an individual read the *Christian Century,* he discovered that fascism permeated American religion. But fascism also could be found in Hollywood; it flew with the California Esquadrille; it was noticeable in the programs of several urban bosses; it was present in the comic strips; it even peeked out from between the lines of poet Archibald MacLeish:

> She's a tough land under the oak tree mister;
> It may be she can change the word in the book
> As she changes the man's head in his children;
> It may be the earth and the men remain.

Fascism was employed in such diverse contexts, therefore, that the term became useless in explaining depression-era extremism. In the short run the liberal crusade against American fascism helped create in the national mind a domestic threat where none in fact existed, stimulated the egotism of men like Pelley, and slightly augmented membership in groups like the Silver Shirts. In the long run, however, especially in the two years directly preceding Pearl Harbor, the effect of this fascist analogy was more profound. The analogy not only served to link American countersubversives with external, totalitarian forces threatening national security; it also exaggerated the danger posed by the nativist-extremists, blurred their connection with the American past, and, as we shall see in later chapters, complicated the diplomatic debate between noninterventionists and advocates of aid to Great Britain.

Having been identified as an agent of Berlin, Pelley reveled in the concomitant publicity. But he also realized, even before his case went to trial, that because of the attention being given him he might be forced to cease publishing within North Carolina. For this reason he transferred his printing operation to Knoxville, Tennessee, and on August 29, 1934, he released the first edition of *Pelley's Weekly*. At the same time he continued to distribute thousands of leaflets and handbills, while Silver Legion posts sold copies of *Mein Kampf; The Protocols of the Learned Elders of Zion;* John Waters's *Red Justice;* F. Roderich-Stoltheim's *The Riddle of the Jew's Success;* Carveth Wells's *Kapoot* ("laugh and shudder with the author"); and Elizabeth Dilling's *The Red Network: A Who's Who and Handbook of Radicalism for Patriots.*

While anti-Semitism has of course been used in myriad ways in ancient, medieval and modern history, William Dudley Pelley demonstrated the extent to which this melancholy theme fulfilled the requirements of many counter-subversives during the 1930s. In the first place anti-Semitism provided the basic core of the Silver Shirt leader's patriotic vocabulary. Secondly, Pelley's use of anti-Semitic images revealed much about his own personal needs and those of his followers. Finally, as Seymour Martin Lipset has suggested, the Silver Legion itself illustrated an important change that was occurring in the development of American anti-Semitism, a movement from specific to abstract Jewish targets, from ethnic to ideological prejudice.

The conscious employment of anti-Semitism had become by 1934 the central theme in Pelley's propaganda. On September 4 he resurrected Abraham Lincoln to support his own "New Emancipation Proclamation." This document dealt with the "Jewish problem" in America and indicated that once in power the Silver Shirts would establish policy whereby no racial group would be allowed "further occupancy of public or professional life in excess of the ration of its blood members to the remaining sum total of all races [composing] the body politic." In addition, Americans would celebrate a new national holiday, "Alien Registration Day," at which time all persons of Jewish blood or extraction, along with those persons not native-born or naturalized, would be required, "under penalty of confiscation of their goods and a term of imprisonment, to register their nationalities, countries of birth, and dates and manner of entry into this country." Moreover, if a Jew falsified his report or contributed "moral or financial aid to Jewish nationalism," he would be subject to indictment for sedition. In other words, unless he chose to forswear forever his "Jewish allegiance," the American Jew would be classed as a permanent resident alien, divested of all social and civic rights and responsibilities.

His belief that fewer than 5 million American Jews actually threatened national security suggests that the Silver Shirt director suffered from a form of paranoia. In fact, Pelley emerged from the pages of *Liberation* and *Pelley's Weekly* as a modern St. George, entrusted with the heroic task of destroying the Jewish-communist dragon. Yet each time the Silver Legion director figuratively slayed the monster (once a week, in the pages of his newspaper), a more dangerous replica appeared in its stead. Victory, which seemed easily attainable, became impossible in the end, and ironically, the stereotyped Judeo-Bolshevik emerged as an integral facet of Pelley's life.

Although the Silver Shirt commander realized that peddling anti-Semitism could be profitable, his vituperative tirades against the Jews may also be interpreted as projections of latent tendencies he feared to see in himself.   In his deprived youth Pelley had fought the strictures imposed by his evangelistic father; he had had few boyhood friends and later was twice unsuccessful in marriage.   A notable failure in business, he proved unable to achieve the goals he set for himself and consequently could not relate to the society of which he was a part. This necessity denied him, he "died" and "returned to earth"—intending to rid himself of his undesirable qualities and to destroy, at least symbolically, those persons tormenting him. His numerous frustrations and guilt complexes comprised a classic example of what psychologists term the authoritarian personality.

This mythical "Jewish-communist" menace carried with it not only Pelley's accumulated anxieties, and by extension, those of many of his followers, but also the imputed collective guilt of the Jewish people for the crucifixion of Christ. For although the Silver Shirt commander disavowed Methodist orthodoxy during his adolescence, he remained at heart a Christian fundamentalist and never resolved the religious conflict that stemmed from this inconsistency. His doubts concerning the existence of sin, for example, could not be manifested openly lest he risk eternal damnation. But he could still hate the Jews, the "unrepentant parricides," without fear of Divine retribution. In addition to removing any need for Pelley to make qualitative statements about God, the Jew became in essence a surrogate religious and natural father-figure against whom he could actualize his inner torments.

Jean Paul Sartre observed that a successful anti-Semite cannot exist in a vacuum; to thrive he must attract co-believers. And Pelley's subordinates and the rank-and-file often displayed personal idiosyncrasies as eccentric as his own. As second-in-command, "Captain Bob" Summerville, as he was reverently called by close associates, was also a self-avowed spiritualist, who claimed to receive messages from the astral plane. Summerville's father had died when the boy was thirteen, and he was forced to leave the family farm in Indiana and seek livelihood as a Chicago newsboy. Thereafter he became in swift succession a real-estate salesman, an editor of the Montgomery Ward mail-order catalogue, a professional dancer, and at the age of twenty-six, managing editor of *Liberation*. An elitist, he gave himself entirely to the Silver Shirt movement and proclaimed that, if necessary, he was prepared to die for the organization. One of Pelley's secretaries, recalling a date with Summerville, thought him crazed. "Everything he said was just a lot of high-sounding words meaning nothing," she commented. "I figured that anyone who could keep up a conversation for two hours and not say one coherent sentence must have a screw loose somewhere."

Another Silver Shirt leader, Roy F. Zachary, the "National Field Marshal," was a simple-minded, former lumberjack who apparently became moon-struck by the first spiritualist with whom he came in contact. In an interview years later with the Reverend L. M. Birkhead, national director of the Friends of Democracy, Zachary revealed that he had been attracted by the power of his leader's "clairaudient ear," which enabled him "to hear voices that no one else hears." "It's wonderful the way he can get in touch with God," Zachary continued, "it only takes him a few minutes to get in touch with the divine powers."

There were within the movement other exquisite personalities. "Major" L. I. Powell, for example, had been a member of the Ku Klux Klan and a tub-thumper for a local Khaki Shirt unit in Shreveport, Louisiana, before joining Pelley. In Seattle Dr. Howard Merrill directed Silver Shirt operations from the Olympia Hotel until the management ejected him for failing to pay rent. Merrill's reputation was tarnished further by his liaison with a local procuress, whose operation of several brothels in neighboring Bremerton was more widely known than the fact that she was also training her two teenage daughters as prostitutes. She served as Merrill's secretary while he remained at the hotel.

Journalist Eric Sevareid visited a Minneapolis unit and left with the feeling that he had been at a circus freak show. One man informed him that the NRA symbol, the "Blue Eagle," was really the "mark of the beast" mentioned in the Book of Revelations. Inasmuch as the Biblical text indicated that the "beast" would be known only by a number (six hundred, threescore, and six—666), the individual told Sevareid: "Now look at the emblem. Count the teeth in the cog-wheel. It's fifteen. Five and one. Get it? Five and one is six. Count the tail feathers on the bird. Six. That's six and six. Now how many bolts of lightning are there? Six! And that makes 666—the 'mark of the beast.' "

The leader of the Minneapolis Silver Shirts showed Sevareid the goods he had hoarded while awaiting a revolution that the Great Pyramid of Gizah predicted for the Jewish New Year. "If it be God's will that I fall as a martyr to the cause at the hands of these beasts," he announced, "I shall die here in my Christian home, defending my dear wife to the end."

According to Sevareid, another local Silver Legioneer felt certain that the "beastly imprimatur" had been placed on American coins by Henry Morgenthau, while another accused Governor Floyd Olson of fomenting a communist plot and designated his wizened chauffeur, Maurice Rose, a dangerous international banker. Sevareid, suffice it to say, dismissed the Silver Shirts as "quite mad."

Across the continent in California, while he prepared a book on the threat of American fascism, John L. Spivak interviewed "Captain" Eugene Case, a renegade Los Angeles section leader and professional soldier of fortune who fought with the Sixth Cantonese Army in China in 1922 and with General Manzas in Mexico in 1929. Case subsequently founded and operated the El Monte Military Academy until its demise at the outset of the depression. Dissatisfied with the Silver Shirt financial network which allowed Pelley to reap the big harvest, he broke away from the parent group and incorporated his own Silver Shirt unit so that his erstwhile boss "would not get a nickel."

In a revealing comment, Case informed Spivak that Silver Shirt posts were "divided to play for different types. One plays for the riff-raff; you know, what communists call the proletarians. Another post plays for the nuts—the kind that go to fortune tellers and séances. This class is our mainstay. . . . You know, there are more nuts in this part of the world than any place you can name outside of an asylum."

One such deranged person encountered by Spivak was a retired Nebraska farmer who spoke admiringly of Pelley's "God-given" organization, and of the "Christ Government" that existed in Atlantis 300,000 years before. "You never would have suspected that this nice old gent was stark, staring, raving mad," Spivak concluded, "and he's loose—and there are thousands of them throughout the country."

These examples indicate that Silver Shirt anti-Semitism might be best explained by what Sir Ernest Jones has termed the tendency "of the unconscious mind to generalize wildly whenever any strong emotion is felt."   Yet although the historian is tempted to dismiss the Silver Legion as a group of mental cases, to do so would be both pejorative and self-serving. By interpreting the rhetorical bigotry of the Silver Legion as the product of twisted minds, the hypothetical observer must necessarily reject as useless such statements and consign them to the junkheap of historical illegitimacy. This fact suggests that in itself psychological theory is an inadequate tool with which to gauge the significance of Silver Shirt imagery. Not only does psychological theory seem ill-equipped to explain short-term changes in both the level and intensity of prejudice; such an approach also fails to indicate why, from a large number of available targets, a specific ethnic and relgious group should be made the object of opprobrium. Granting the inclination of maladjusted and frightened individuals to seek scapegoats, why did Pelley and his Silver Shirts choose the Jews instead of the Catholics, traditional enemies of American nativists?

Indeed, the historian must go further, recognizing the possibility that within the irrational rhetoric of the Silver Shirt movement there existed an important clue to the nature of actual social conflict occurring during the 1930s. That Pelley made little use of existing tension between Gentile and Jew was not surprising. Direct economic confrontation, usually a distinctly urban phenomenon, tended to engender a specific ethnic discrimination against Jewish-Americans; but ideological anti-Semitism took root in native-American, rural areas inhabited by few Jews. That the Silver Shirts were numerically strongest in small communities in the Midwest and Pacific Coast, the areas found to be most pronouncedly anti-Semitic by *Fortune* magazine, suggests that the anti-Semitism of the Silver Shirts derived less from the values that they appeared to borrow from Nazism than from forces indigenous to American life.

In fact, from the beginnings of their history, Americans have revered work and activity, accomplishment and success. A corresponding set of values, driving the individual to do something even when it might be advisable to do nothing, has proved especially vigorous in agrarian communities whose inhabitants continuously stressed their own superiority over their urban cousins. The resultant mythos of the yeoman farmer entailed a division of society into two groups, productive and symbolic. Farmers, by working the land and producing tangible goods, comprised the bone and sinew of the nation and became its paragons of morality. Conversely, the nonproducers, who engaged in ephemeral pursuits such as bondholding and banking, personified immoral and parasitical man.

This dichotomy underlay the ideology of Jeffersonian Democracy and was the rationale behind Andrew Jackson's destruction of the Second National Bank of the United States, but it was not until the 1890s that the fevered imaginations of Populist crusaders imbued traditional agrarian biases with anti-Semitic implications. Frustrated in their attempts to secure desired reforms and unwilling to concede their own shortcomings, men like William Jennings Bryan and Ignatius Donnelly exhibited religious fervor in their attacks on urban civilization. Bryan lamented "the cross of gold"; Donnelly blamed conniving, hidden conspirators for the farmer's plight; William "Coin" Harvey sought to sever the grasping tentacles of international financiers. In alluding to Jewish conspiracies, these and other Populist leaders bespoke their complete alienation from society, their fear of anarchy and the coming collapse of civilization, and their despair over the power of money.

Linked closely with invidious influences allegedly emanating from the exotic Eastern metropolis, the symbol of the international Jew corroborated for rural Americans their own view of Jewish "mystery" and thus became a hobgoblin of rustic imaginations. Scattered among nations, welcome nowhere, and victimized by all types of hardship, the Jew clung tenaciously to his ancient heritage and, despite his alien status, retained his identity. And because of the Jew's uniqueness, inexplicable characteristics (Rabbinical divination, for example, or a murder solved by a Jewish detective with "second sight") were attributed to him by agrarian Americans.

Directly following the First World War, a wave of chauvinism swept America as numerous superpatriots, disgusted with the ways of Europe, wholeheartedly endorsed President Warren G. Harding's statement that "you just didn't want a surrender of the United States of America. You wanted America to go under American ideals." Returning prosperity after 1923 quieted many such individuals, but evidence of "100% Americanism" remained, illustrated by Chamber of Commerce literature, immigration quotas, and the statements of big businessmen. On a less respectable level, the revived Ku Klux Klan discovered the term "alien" to have many meanings—Catholic in Protestant areas; Oriental on the West Coast; Negro in the South; and Jew in New York.

However, the patriotic celebrity of the 1920s was not the white-hooded night rider but instead, automobile mogul Henry Ford, who by popularizing and modernizing anti-Semitic themes emerged as the indispensable link between the mild ethnic prejudice of a more simple agrarian past and the more virulent anti-Semitism of the 1930s. Ford was gifted in technological matters but was otherwise "an incredibly naive, simple, and ignorant man" who possessed the knowledge of "a grammar-school boy having trouble making the fourth grade." On May 22, 1920, shortly after the apex of the Red Scare, his weekly newspaper, the *Dearborn Independent,* carried the headline: "THE INTERNATIONAL JEW: THE WORLD'S PROBLEM." The accompanying story proved one thing: that Ford had accepted as truth the greatest anti-Semitic forgery of history—the *Protocols of the Learned Elders of Zion.*

A series of twenty-four documents allegedly stolen from a Jewish cabal planning world domination, the *Protocols* were actually fabricated around 1905 by Sergei Nilus, a Russian secret police agent, and were subsequently employed by Tsar Nicholas II to explain domestic ills, stave off reforms, and justify his pogroms. Though discredited by scholars and journalists, the *Protocols* were widely circulated and, in the process, acquired a vitality of their own. By the 1920s, in fact, they provided believers with a theory of historical causation and a complete interpretation of the modern world as well.

Aided by two assistants, William Cameron and Ernest Liebold, Ford soon became the most notorious American proponent of the conspiracy theory. A child of rural America who reached maturity during an era of increased anti-Jewish prejudice, he was fascinated by the *Protocols* and found in the agrarian Midwest—the home of erstwhile, frustrated reformers and a citizenry disoriented by the complexities of modern civilization—a willing audience for his message. Understandably, in Ford's revised interpretation, the *Protocols* were remarkable for their sentiment of outraged, rustic morality. With a circulation of 300,000, the *Independent* carried twenty articles indicating in tantalizing detail the designs of international Jewry. After the serialization was concluded in October, Ford condensed the articles into a book, *The International Jew,* and his dealers either sold or gave away a half million copies in the ensuing five years.

In addition to stressing historic anti-Semitic themes, such as the Jew's alleged "racial" characteristics, financial chicanery, and political intrigue, Ford and his associates drove the credibility of their readers to its outer limits. Nothing was too sensational. The relaxation of American morals after the war, for instance, stemmed from the desire of "Jewish" financial interests "to render them loose in the first place and keep them loose." "Jewish landlords," moreover, set exorbitant rents; "Jewish clothing concerns" were responsible for the decadent flapper skirt; and, finally, Jews produced cheap Hollywood films, promoted gambling, played "skunk-cabbage" jazz, wrote purple prose, and performed under the hot lights of the cabaret.

Ignoring the fact that as a cultural group the Jews possessed the lowest crime rate in the United States, Ford and his assistants manufactured evidence to prove that the Jews were "the conscious enemies of all that Anglo-Saxons mean by civilization." In this spirit the *Dearborn Independent* warned Christian-Americans to avoid the works of Ovid lest they play into the hands of the Learned Elders of Zion. One issue of the journal, citing "scientific sources," reported a planned conspiracy to use drink and immoral women to weaken the physiques of Gentiles. If this ploy failed, Jewish plotters would invade Christian homes during the night and inoculate their inhabitants with various kinds of disease, especially the dreaded syphilis.

According to the *Independent,* the Jews had extended their power to all corners of the globe. Indeed, a "Jewish interpreter" had accompanied Columbus on his epochal voyage, and Queen Isabella had been in fact a "Jewish front"—the money for her charge's explorations being raised by "secret Jews." And so it went. Benedict Arnold had turned traitor during the Revolutionary War at the behest of "Semitic warmongers." Jews dodged the draft during the First World War to allow more Gentiles to kill one another. And, finally, the repertoire would not be complete without mention of "Shoeless" Joe Jackson, the semiliterate, star outfielder for the Chicago "Black Sox," who threw games during the 1919 World Series at the request of, naturally, "the international Jew."

Henry Ford subsequently retracted and apologized for his allegations, which sprang more from naiveté than malice. Nonetheless he had become the link connecting the genteel, anti-Jewish prejudice of late-nineteenth-century America and the more sinister anti-Semitism espoused by Pelley and other contemporary extremists. It was not surprising, furthermore, that *The International Jew* became a standard reference work for the Silver Shirt leader, as it did for Nazi theorists Joseph Goebbels and Alfred Rosenberg. The point is that without Ford's spadework, the extremists of the 1930s would have had to work much more diligently to garner source material. The father of mass production gave American anti-Semites, in most instances very unoriginal people, ready-made arguments.

Inasmuch as anti-Semitism is an extremely complex phenomenon, any generalization concerning its nature runs the risk of oversimplification. Yet from the evidence available, it appears that the hatred which the Silver Shirts directed at Jewish-Americans derived its character from the agrarian and nationalist milieu that influenced Henry Ford during the previous decade. By no means the yeoman farmer of national mythology, the typical Silver Legioneer nonetheless perceived himself as a defender of this ethos and harbored what may be termed "surrogate agrarian" prejudices—not against Jews themselves, but against the Jewish stereotype. An avowed paragon of individualism, patriotism, nationalism, and morality, the Silver Shirt opposed what he interpreted as a collectivist-urban-liberal-international-subversive enemy. Furthermore, given the exigencies of depression and the irrationality that characterized many members of the organization, it seems that the very absence of large Jewish groups in the vicinity of Silver Shirt posts enabled Pelley to employ anti-Semitism as an all-encompassing, world-historical doctrine. Silver Shirt members might have several Jewish friends, but this fact did not block their acceptance of the negative Jewish stereotype. The Jew was their mortal enemy. He had to be destroyed.

7

Status Politics and Foreign Relations

★ ★ ★ According to Pelley and his followers, the major problem that beset the nation during the mid-1930s was an exceedingly difficult one. There were mortal enemies abroad, to be sure, but unlike earlier days these enemies were not merely Catholics or Jews. No, the menace was more serious than that. It was more subjective, more abstract, and more political. No longer were the levelers immigrants from European shores; now they were trades-unionists, radicals, and intellectual New Dealers and their fellow travelers. Suddenly, or so it seemed, these groups had gained primacy in the nation. Their emergence was not so abrupt as Pelley's rhetoric would have it, yet the imagery that appeared in *Liberation* and *Pelley's Weekly* did reflect the extreme side of a pervasive fear that also influenced many "respectable Americans." In his study of the relationship between Progressivism and the New Deal, historian Otis L. Graham touched on this problem when he observed of the conservative critique of Roosevelt's program that "the only possible use to which their talk of dictatorship, the end of the Republic, class revolution, etc., may be put is as a clue to the depth and nature of the deprivation being worked against certain men and classes in America."

Although the Democratic administration moved slowly in behalf of ethnic minorities, small businessmen, and the laborer, its extension of political power to these historically dispossessed groups mortified Americans long accustomed to a superior station in society. Their attempts at reform, marked by a spirit of noblesse oblige, memories of food baskets delivered to indigent families at Christmas, and membership in a deferential society, had been generally patronizing. Now, however, the egalitarianism of the New Deal seemed to be transforming American life. Centripetal tendencies inherent in state planning replaced the centrifugal forces of rugged individualism; the "freedom from" privation supplanted the "freedom to do" what one pleased. As a symbol of this change, Franklin D. Roosevelt was most easily identifiable and, not illogically, considered to be singularly responsible.

It was the President's decision to seek a redistribution of national wealth, coupled with his attacks upon "fat-cat" newspaper publishers and "economic royalists," that provoked the ire of wealthy American Protestants. Their enmity may have been stimulated by the sardonic smile with which the Chief Executive issued his remarks, or the insecurity they themselves felt at the prospect of governmental innovation. What mattered most, however, was that everything they valued appeared to be threatened, and that the man at the head of the movement had turned traitor to his and their tradition of urbane gentility. For a rich man to equivocate on the subject of "That Man" was to invite epithets like "nigger-lover" and "Jew-lover." But as historians E. Digby Baltzell and George Wolfskill have pointed out, these oaths were mild when compared with the maledictions applied to the President. If Roosevelt was not "a Renegade Democrat," he was "an extravagant, destructive, vacillating, unprincipled charlatan." Referring to his crippled legs, detractors termed him "an invalid, lacking in physical strength." He was, moreover, a moral weakling, "a psychological captive, intellectually shallow, unbelievably gullible," in short, "a dupe" surrounded by "radicals, crackpots, quarterbacks, and foreign-thinking brain-trusters, some of whom are better known in Russia than in the United States." In bank offices, country-club locker rooms, and lawyers' chambers, apocrypha-become-truth was the order of the day. The President was "an inveterate liar, immoral (hadn't you heard about his affair with Frances Perkins?), a syphilitic, a tool of Negroes and Jews, a madman given to unbroken gales of immoderate laughter, an alcoholic, a megalomaniac dreaming his dreams of dictatorship."

Roosevelt was not the sole target of abuse by status-threatened Americans. His associates were also subject to vituperation. Secretary of Labor Perkins, for example, drew scorn as "Mildred Wutzki—Russian-born Jewess." Miss Perkins attempted to allay the rumor by announcing that her real name had always been Frances Perkins until her married name made her Mrs. Paul Wilson. Decrying race prejudice, she declared that "such unworthy innuendo must be repugnant to honorable men and women. If I were a Jew, I would make no secret of it. I would be proud to acknowledge it."

Nonetheless, many American Protestants allowed status resentments to influence their opinions of administration leaders. When Eleanor Roosevelt visited Howard University and was photographed with two ROTC cadets, the subsequent "nigger pictures" enjoyed wide circulation among extremists and Republican reactionaries. Their antipathy toward the New Deal was summed up in the following verse purporting to be a conversation between Mr. and Mrs. Roosevelt:

You kiss the negroes
I'll kiss the Jews
We'll stay in the White House
As long as we choose.

The prospect of social and racial equality was sufficiently frightening to cause many wealthy citizens to generalize wildly. Their cries of outrage, which ironically were directed against their own perceptions of the Jew as a symbol of evil, were less a manifestation of traditional class, or interest politics, than an extension of the more expressive "status-prestige" element in American life. For these individuals, Jews and Negroes became "negative reference groups" through which a semblance of social superiority might be retained.

Though by no means so wealthy as Park Avenue *rentiers*, Pelley and his Silver Shirts nonetheless identified with this latter group. Out of work or the victims of economic reverses, Silver Legioneers clung to whatever status they could salvage and, concomitantly, any prestige that might offset their lowly position on the social and economic scale. Their quest, difficult, even poignant in light of the fact that many of them were elderly, had little education, and in many cases enjoyed no community respect, inexorably led them to seek a patriotic solution. Their outlook on life, which in contrast to the "purer" gentility of well-appointed WASPs might be termed "shabby genteel," corresponded to Pelley's cultural fundamentalism. In arguing that Johnny-come-lately minorities and urban laborers had ruined the good society for which their forefathers fought, the Silver Shirt theorist created for his subordinates a kind of symbolic community based upon mutually held xenophobic assumptions and ethnic stereotypes. At the same time he provided followers strong reassurance concerning their nationality—a system, in anthropological terms, of "workabilities"—something the New Deal failed to accomplish.

Because Roosevelt and his advisers met problems as they were and not as they were preconceived by men like William Dudley Pelley, and because the Democrats promised neither to restore a halcyon past nor to create a future utopia, sincere Americans of varied political persuasions construed New Deal politics as aimless experimentation. In fact, what the countersubversives especially failed to comprehend was the fact that the Democratic program was less a "scheme" than a dramatically innovative approach to problem-solving that differed vastly from their own peculiar type of political solitaire.

Reflecting this phenomenon, Pelley could not fathom national and international affairs except in terms of the easily understood, manipulable, and protean metaphor—the Jewish world conspiracy. Had not the McCormack-Dickstein Committee and the North Carolina courts, as agents of this plot, attempted to silence the Silver Shirt leader because he admired Adolf Hitler? At least this was the conclusion Pelley reached in mid-1935, upon completing his magnum opus on the subject of American foreign relations.

Six years in preparation, *Nations-In-Law* was a remarkable volume insofar as it indicated Pelley's intellectual complexity and suggested a connection between his concern with social status and his conception of foreign policy. In fact, the book revealed an author beset with numerous contradictions. A staunch Christian, he doubted the existence of sin; an internationalist, he condemned the League of Nations; a would-be politician, he eschewed politics as it was practiced in America; an Aryan racist, he decried intolerance; an unethical promoter, he hoped to create a system of ethical relations between the nations of the world.

Looming large in Pelley's analysis was the theme of American destiny. Because each people of the earth had a particular mission, he termed the United States "a bright and shining light" that would "cast a pattern visible to all races as the thing which all mankind can attain in a political structure over diverse nationals and racial groupings." American history being "a forecast and prototype of universal world history in the thousand, brilliant years ahead," the United States would become "the immortal instrument of that splendid dispensation." Before this utopian end might be achieved, however, there remained three prerequisites—exclusion of the "megalomaniacal Jew," elimination of the anarchy and mediocrity of American politics, and the adoption of the principles of "internationality," rather than "internationalism." Only then could the United States graduate from adolescence to adulthood among nations, and prepare herself for membership in Pelley's proposed "Aryan Federation."

Not surprisingly, it was the Jew who blocked America's destiny. Plagiarizing liberally from Henry Ford's *The International Jew*, Pelley linked the Semitic menace with communism, "a satanic reversal and misrepresentation of what it purports to be." Misrepresenting itself as communality, communism in fact resulted in "factional and racial despotism" which made "no real attempt to dictate for the good of the whole, but for the gradual liquidation of those who oppose its freakish tyranny." A year of Hitler or Mussolini, he believed, would be preferable to "an hour of true Stalinism, for at least the Fascism of the former dictators is premised on a tacit inspirational ideal that is fecund in spiritual values, whereas sovietism is inspirationally spiritual in hypothesis only."

"Let the Hebrews wail as they will," he continued, "and point to the numbers of Gentiles in important executive positions under sovietism, but the facts have it that Bolshevism from the start has been financed by Hebrews in places of real power."

Enlarging upon this theme, Pelley noted the presence in the United States of a "species of retrograde high priestism, an effeminate, oriental caliphate premised on racial megalomania." Having engineered American entrance into the Great War, this "predatory faction" subsequently assumed clandestine power over American finances and communications. In the guise of Roosevelt's Brain Trust, it had secured sufficient power to "secretly determine who is going to be elevated to positions of political power and what they are going to do." "Really," Pelley argued, "we have descended in these catastrophic years to a government of the people for the promotion of a super-Jewish world state." The New Deal had "whittled all men down to a common man, made puppets out of evolving freemen, and returned us to an exploded political barbarism that has only introduced ruin and stagnation wherever it has been attempted."

Adopting an elitist's approach to national problems, the Silver Shirt director argued that strong, efficient leadership provided the sole means by which the nation might escape its desperate situation. Whether or not they realized the fact, true leaders had "lived long before coming into the mortal coil of earthly life," and were thus members of a cosmic order. Creatures of the "Divine Intellect," these men were the world's natural aristocrats. In fact, Pelley revered the abstract concept of aristocracy and hoped to transform it into reality. But he did not employ the term in its common usage. His aristocrat earned the title because of his "force of intellect." Because men were not born equal, such elitist types by necessity would lead America's social and spiritual evolution. Government of the people, or democracy, stifled initiative and was unworkable. And even if he were not held captive by Jewish influence, the average man would be unable to manage his own affairs.

Pelley's analysis followed closely that of Alexis de Tocqueville. But where the Frenchman only suggested the dangers inherent in a "tyranny of the majority," the Asheville extremist asserted that such tyranny had already resulted in bedlam because of man's "perniciously encouraged tendency to crucify its aristocrats of the intellect by mistakenly ignoring them, forcing them into academic cloisters while childishly raising up Mr. Average Man as the standard and epitome of social and political acumen."

Asserting, as did historian Charles Beard, that American history was "one long Armageddon of sectionalism," Pelley viewed American progress in terms of the actions of great men. Here were the aristocrats of whom he wrote. American independence, for example, came only through the genius of George Washington, who brought "order and military victory, only to retire to Mt. Vernon with more odium than was currently heaped on Benedict Arnold." If Washington brought "thirteen struggling and apathetic colonies into the semblance of a nation," Supreme Court Justice John Marshall subsequently held the country together "more than a dozen times" during his tenure of thirty-four years.

In modern American history, Presidents Theodore Roosevelt and, surprisingly, Calvin Coolidge appeared to have proved themselves "aristocrats of the intellect." The spirited Roosevelt was "the archangel of the public sovereignty inspired and guided instead of compressed and flogged into regimentation." With his call, "Let's all go together and have a bully time in the going," Roosevelt "did for the nation what was natural and proper in the line of its destiny." He led his countrymen "by assimilating the future in terms of the present."

Like Theodore Roosevelt, Coolidge possessed the requisites of leadership. He had, Pelley asserted, "a gift for guiding men along the lines they chose to

go so long as it was upward, and letting them seem to direct their affairs."
Even more significant was Coolidge's distaste for what he termed "the political mind." In fact, Pelley probably lifted the concept directly from the quiet
President's *Autobiography*, wherein Coolidge described the political mind as
a "strange mixture of vanity and timidity, of an obsequious attitude at one
time, and a delusion of grandeur at another. . . . The political mind is the
product of men in public life who have been twice spoiled. They have been
spoiled with praise and they have been spoiled with abuse. With them nothing is natural; everything is artificial."

To Pelley the political mind denoted a man who sought power because of
the meanness of his birth or his station in life. The concept also suggested exaggerated conceit; the use of one's office rather than his individual character
to secure power; an animal love of money; a tendency towards personal display; the selfish desire for enhanced prestige; the love of cheap glory; and, finally, contempt for his followers. A man who possessed these characteristics
was not a true leader, but a demagogue who would either lead his backers or
not serve them at all. Having gained power, furthermore, this kind of politician would advise his supporters to "take what they got" and "like it." Politics was thus a field of chicanery, and most politicians, expressing their "emotional sterility," sought office simply because they had "axes to grind."
Indeed thousands of so-called "statesmen" were in actuality "nothing more
than performing primates," and Pelley attributed their success to the fact that
"the crowd loves the show, with its basic human attractions, and it will follow
the showman down any grade and off into any bag, for its eyes are apt to be
on the showman's antics and not on the pathway he is pursuing."

Franklin D. Roosevelt epitomized this phenomenon by "rocketing to a theatrical popularity like any Hollywood blonde making lachrymose appeals to
his people over the radio to do this or that." The President's "grand gesture
at leadership" notwithstanding, Roosevelt had surrendered his "sacred prerogative to a little knot of schemers who capitalize on their control of his office to enhance themselves and their alien compatriots at government expense." Here Pelley referred to the Brain Trust, which he termed "neither a
Brains-trust nor Mr. Roosevelt's," but "a so-called Intelligenzia [sic], largely
made up of ambitious young Jews and Jewesses who have purloined Christian
names and strut in their camoflauge [sic] before the public which in turn is
unaware that they are encouraged and often financed by the theoretical Wise
Men of Zion . . . in actualising [sic] the secret Jewish-World State."

Pelley's basic recommendation was a proposed "Aryan Federation" which
would include the United States, Germany, and Great Britain, "all blood
cousins by consanguinity and with well-nigh identical cultures and ethics." To
a man as ethnocentric as Pelley, this point was of utmost importance. "From
time immemorial," he wrote, echoing earlier racist writers such as Lothrop
Stoddard and Madison Grant, "the Aryan, particularly the Anglo-Saxon, has
carried in his blood the consciousness of his importance in and to the social
structure." The new federation, Pelley believed, would allow "the most wor-

thy race to enjoy its enoblement [sic] without danger or threat from the ignorant, malicious, envious, and debased, with all the intermediary degrees of progress and self-expression down the rungs of the ladder of world society."

The time had come for Americans to recognize that their nation lacked a foreign policy. Isolationism, "a screen for timidity," reflected a "bigoted and provincial attitude of condescencion [sic]" towards one's neighbors. Believing, as did the German philosopher Hegel, that nations and races represented rungs along the ladder of world progress, Pelley excused this attitude because the American people were, in reality, "an adolescent unit both in time and experience." Echoing Charles Dickens's critique of "Brother Jonathan" during the 1840s, Pelley called America "a land of bombast and huckstering, of knife and fork diplomacy and cuspidor culture," a country whose diplomats reveled in "going about in suspenders and imprinting boot heel marks on the polished floors of more sophisticated nations." Because they represented "the blatant flapper among nations," American envoys were labeled as "Super-Babbitts not knowing how to cope with professionals." United States representatives abroad lacked social and cultural graces, and other nations scorned them as agents of "a garish creditor from whom more favors could be gained by playing up to her vanity."

If Pelley did not embrace isolationism, neither did he accept "internationalism," as that term was commonly understood. Synonymous with the policy of world Jewry, internationalism would never allow the United States to assume the status of an adult nation. Even if the Jew did not exist, the concept of internationalism was dangerous because most statesmen were global extensions of domestic demagogues, "hard-headed sophists who had to have their hands on two dollars before letting their own two dollars go." Nor did internationalism fit Pelley's Divine Scheme; it failed to express accurately "the true essence of what it should to the world at large." "Making one race or one nation of all races or nations," Pelley suggested, "would work against all laws of spiritual evolution. It would work against nature, and would be disruptive and subversive to the edicts of God Himself."

What was required, both to prevent war and to further the progress of the Aryan race, was a "renasence [sic] of fellowship" to be accomplished by adopting the principle of "internationality," which sought not to "destroy culture," as did internationalism, "but to augment ethics" through government to a point when, in Alfred Lord Tennyson's words:

> . . . the war drum throbbed no longer, and the
> Battle-flags were furled
> In the Parliament of Man, the Federation
> of the world.

But Pelley's "Parliament" would have nothing to do with "the Kosher-manipulated" World Court or League of Nations. Aryans in Germany, the United States, and Britain would work together to preserve "the very thing men looked upon as a great danger—national, or racial solidarity."

The principle of internationality, or "live and let live for all races," excepting the Jew, would become America's permanent foreign policy. Wars, which were inevitable in light of Pelley's Divine Law of Compensation and the baseness of human nature, would cease. Selfish nationalism, a product of international demagoguery, would become a memory. Patriotism would itself assume a new definition, as citizens no longer ignored the defects of their country, but possessed "an active knowledge of the sum and substance of living," emitted "moral individuality and mass integrity," cooperated with all peoples "to effect the greatest good for the greatest number," and displayed the desire "to be a power for constructive altruism expressed not in terms of high moral suasion, but in concrete acts of sensible brotherhood."

Pelley believed a second global war to be imminent and compared the troubled world scene with the status of the United States under the Articles of Confederation. Like the original thirteen states, the nations of the 1930s were marked by different cultures, ambitions, and forms of worship. As the Silver Shirt theorist considered these divergencies to be the result of invariable climates and terrain, there existed no hope of reconciling national differences within the framework of traditional diplomacy. Balances of power were obsolete, as were the concepts of international law and the freedom of the seas. The only hope for world peace, rather, lay "in alignments of similar political cultures acting to minimize friction with their great reserves of racial strength."

Where peace-keeping machinery had failed in the past, the Aryan Federation would succeed, because it would be a true parliament of man, not just "a chamber of deputies for the delegates of national senates." This had been the flaw of the League of Nations, an alliance that contained the seeds of its own destruction. Pelley's new organization would escape this hazard. Although he did not completely outline the functions of the federation, the new, deliberative body was similar in form to the federal system of the United States. Its actions would be guided by the consent of member nations, whose citizens would retain their previous national identity. Issues would be decided by a senate in which each nation would have equal representation, and in a house of representatives where representation would be based on population. The peace force backed by the federation would be a kind of external national guard, while the capital of the new order would be located in some neutral spot, "like the Azores."

Pelley hoped that the federation might be created before the next war, but by 1935 the time had not yet arrived. Citizens first had to await a mysterious "Great Causation." Then their president, having known of "this spiritual machinery for years," would "have orders to lead the American people into a real parliament of man." This passage, combined with the tone of the entire volume, suggests that the Silver Shirt leader had begun to think about the presidency and the election of 1936. Indeed, Pelley expected "to have a great deal to do with giving America a permanent foreign policy." Perhaps his ascendance to the White House would fulfill the prophesied event.

Adopting the slogan, "For Christ and Constitution!" Pelley announced his candidacy on September 10, 1935. "At the sign of the cross!" he cried. "I propose to serve my country as its next President! The announcement you have been waiting for!" Although he did not specify whether his decision was the promised "Great Causation," the self-styled messiah appropriated the rhetoric of Abolitionist leader William Lloyd Garrison to prove his sincerity. Pelley would lead his National Christian Party "without a shade of equivocation, without retreating a single inch from my four-year position as the unalterable foe of Communistic Jewry, without the slightest compromise with venal politics or trafficking with professional politicians—offering the bilked and hysterical American people a roster of all-Christian executives!"

Pelley named Willard Kemp of California as his running mate, but Kemp remained an unimportant figure. All that mattered to Pelley was Pelley. "I promise to follow FDR in the Chief Executive's chair of this debauched and prostrate nation," he announced, "and undo the unchallenged mischief of four years of soviet bureaucracy." Soon afterwards he promised that the contest of 1936 would be based "on 'The Cross and Constitution' against 'the Six-Pointed Star of oriental Sovietism.' " No longer could the American people remain indifferent to their fate. The choice was, in Pelley's words, between "Christ or chaos!"

The Judeo-Bolshevik conspiracy had blocked all efforts to achieve change through legitimate political channels, so Pelley spent the ensuing months attempting to generate support for his candidacy. Father Coughlin and Dr. Townsend might have been sincere men, he reasoned, but neither offered "any real obstruction to the plans of the Russocrats." Nor did the Republican Party harbour a savior. "Deep behind the scenes," Pelley intimated, "the Republicans also have to conform to the secret dictates of the same group of money-drunk internationalists who brought ruin on the Democrats." Indeed, the only choice left was "the man who suddenly and dauntlessly made the Christian Party a power in the United States—a pioneer in the strictly American movement to smash the megalo-maniacal clutch of apostate Jewry on our Christian institutions—William Dudley Pelley!"

In light of Pelley's claim to preternatural abilities, it was surprising that he had no idea how obscure his dark-horse "party" would really be. In fact, forty-seven states refused him admission to the November ballot. Only in the state of Washington did he campaign actively, presenting seven speeches in the five weeks preceding election day. The addresses contained his presentation of "the final solution" to the "Jewish problem" in the United States:

I propose to disfranchise the Jews by Constitutional amendment to make it impossible for a Jew to own property in the United States excepting under the same licensing system employed against Occidentals in Japan; to limit Jews in the professions, trades, and sciences by licensing according to their quota of representation in the population.

Voters in Washington responded by giving Pelley 1,598 of a total of approximately 700,000 votes cast in the state, a development that the Silver Shirt leader dismissed as a result of sabotage of voting machines by Jewish conspirators. Returning to Asheville as if the debacle had never occurred, he was again in business a week later as his newspaper carried the following headline: "HOG-WILD RED RULE BY JEWS!" Because of the Democratic landslide, he reasoned that "hoodwinked Americans" faced four more years of "pro-Soviet Rooseveltism" which would destroy "America's economic structure, push the Republican Party into political desuetude, and enthrone a dynasty of communist Jews to alter constitutional government for the Elders of Zion."

An indefatigable entrepreneur who enjoyed little earthly success before his momentary "death" in 1928, Pelley subsequently parlayed a strange combination of patriotism, perverted Protestantism, mysticism, and anti-Semitism into a small but raucous following. Called into existence by the coincidence of domestic depression and Adolf Hitler's accession to power, the American Silver Shirts occupied the fringes of political life and attracted men and women who, in addition to being deeply suspicious of the changing values of their society, often were themselves suffering from various types of mental aberration.

As did other contemporary extremist groups, the Silver Legion prided itself as a custodian of American tradition. Yet their countersubversive rhetoric did not hide the fact that in one important respect the Silver Shirts were a subversive force. In upholding the values they treasured, Pelley and his supporters paradoxically sought their destruction. In the related concepts of the "Christian Commonwealth" and the "Aryan Federation," furthermore, Pelley had created a metaphor for a very American institution—the exclusive country club—whose membership was usually restricted to white, Anglo-Saxon Protestants who disliked Jews. In the Asheville patriot's vision of the good society, as illustrated in his various writings, there was clearly demonstrated a consuming concern for status. But Pelley and his supporters never achieved the prestige and respect they so revered.

In their misguided effort to secure national esteem, the Silver Shirts soon emerged as American "fascists." This process was facilitated less by their own efforts than by the reaction of nervous citizens to the activities of Adolf Hitler and Benito Mussolini. To many critics the anti-Semitism of the Silver Legion, together with the group's military hierarchy, secret ritual, and anti-democratic world view, appeared to be patterned on the German model. What many Americans did not understand was that Pelley was as American as Henry Ford and that his organization was more closely related to the Odd Fellows Lodge than to the Nazi SS. But if the Silver Shirt "threat" to democracy seemed serious in 1936, as it did to many observers, the perceived menace would assume even more sinister connotations after 1937, as the United States moved inexorably toward diplomatic and military confrontation with European totalitarianism and Japanese militarism.

8

The German-American Bund: Enter Fritz Kuhn

■■■■
★ ★ ★
■■■■ Although Father Coughlin's National Union for Social Justice and, to a lesser extent, Pelley's Silver Shirts were more the products of a domestic than alien milieu, American nativist-extremism during the 1930s was widely interpreted as being foreign oriented and for this reason suffered from an inner contradiction. Historically, xenophobic groups like the Know-Nothings, American Protective Association, and Ku Klux Klan sought to protect American ideals and traditions against those of foreign nations: in the decade before Pearl Harbor, the extremists reversed the pattern. Considering the government already in the hands of an insidious alien conspiracy, they borrowed the vocabulary of Italian and German propagandists and appeared to seek the wholesale transfer of fascist ideology and institutions to American soil.

In actuality, it was the nativists' attempt to cloak these alien symbols and icons in a mantle of Americanism that attested most clearly to their sudden and painful awareness of the disjunction between their own values and reality. For them and their supporters, the unprecedented social and economic conditions of the era, combined with the rise of totalitarianism in Europe, had transformed the national faith in equality into a cruel joke and signaled the end of opportunity. Their political style, which ranged from the wild distortions of the Coughlinites to the autism of the Silver Legion, stemmed from personal and collective bewilderment and represented an antithesis to national consensus, a denial of shared loyalties, a demurrer to unifying commitment.

Because they considered the American experiment a failure, the extremists were forced to look elsewhere for visions of salvation. Father Coughlin appropriated the ancient text of Christianity as the domain of the poverty-stricken. His populistic imagery, recalling the literature and rhetoric of the anti-Masonic, Jacksonian, and agrarian rebellions of the nineteenth century, marked a direct moral confrontation with the established order and at the same time provided him the means to secure power for himself and succor for his downtrodden followers.

Pelley turned toward certain images in Protestant fundamentalism. By placing heavy emphasis upon millennialism, ethnic purity, and the importance of personal identity and individual achievement, he provided the Silver Shirts with a symbolic bulwark against the forces of social and political modernization, and his followers in turn responded with a fanatical zeal that indicated their belief that only a return to the original faith could restore order, freedom, and morality.

If the Coughlinites and Silver Legioneers illustrated many of the tensions which troubled America during the depression, it remained the task of another group of patriots to demonstrate clearly that countersubversive movements could have more far-reaching effects. In "the Friends of the New Germany" and its better-known successor, the "German-American Bund," there existed curious anomalies—two truly subversive organizations posing as saviors against subversion. In attempting to ride the "wave of the future" and at the same time develop an "American" image, the domestic Nazis embarked on an impossible task; yet in their persistent and humorous attempt to have it both ways, they clearly accelerated the deterioration of German-American diplomatic relations.

The origins of American Nazism actually antedated by a decade Hitler's accession to power. During the early 1920s with the Weimar Republic threatened by inflation and civil war, many Germans migrated to the United States. One immigrant, Kurt G. W. Luedecke, who had participated in the abortive Munich beer-hall *putsch,* disguised himself as a traveling salesman in order to disseminate propaganda in New York and Washington and generate financial support for his European comrades. However, he proved an inept fund-raiser and settled in Brookline, Massachusetts, where he established the Swastika Press. Another newcomer, Fritz Gissibl, worked as a typesetter for the *Chicago Daily News* before founding "Teutonia," an organization designed to attract German immigrants who earlier battled communism in the Motherland. Unlike Luedecke, Gissibl received orders directly from Germany; but his mission to raise funds also ended in failure.

Nevertheless, by 1933 numerous local units of the unrelated National Socialist German Labor Party had appeared in the United States, though these groups also lacked overall coordination and direction. Three years earlier, while serving as Washington correspondent for the Nazi journal, *Der Volkischer Beobachter,* Luedecke had attempted to interest several congressmen in the prospect of unifying German propaganda efforts in America. But he discovered that the legislators were too concerned with issues posed by the depression to give his proposal serious heed.

Once established as chancellor, Adolf Hitler swiftly embarked on a program designed to redress what he considered the staggering inequities of the Versailles Treaty. Because this goal was to be accomplished at the expense of Britain and France through diplomatic and other means, the *Führer* realized that cordial relations with the United States would comprise a *sine qua non* of German policy. Yet he also knew that serious obstacles blocked the path toward rapprochement. For one thing, as Luedecke and Gissibl discovered, the American people had not forgotten the war and still considered Germany an enemy. The principles of Nazism, furthermore, were anathema to their democratic values, a point that America's Jewish population would emphasize. Finally, there remained the serious question whether German-Americans themselves would lend spiritual support to the new regime.

Such considerations led the German leader to conclude that too heavy a dependence on overt political propaganda would be counterproductive in the attempt to win American friendship. To be sure, the Foreign Ministry hoped to strengthen American isolationism by stressing Woodrow Wilson's failure to honor his moral pledge to Germany in 1918, the inability of the Allies to pay their war debts, and the economic advantages to be derived from trade with Berlin. But in the main the Nazi hierarchy decided upon a policy of restraining American interest in foreign politics by relying on tourist and cultural propaganda.

American antipathy toward Nazi Party locals led the Foreign Ministry to order their dissolution in April 1933, yet this directive did not signify Hitler's abandonment of the idea of organizing sympathetic German-Americans. Shortly thereafter, a former leader of the Detroit branch of Teutonia, Heinz Spanknoebel, was summoned to Berlin to confer with Nazi functionaries Rudolf Hess and Robert Ley. Disguised as a clergyman, Spanknoebel returned to the United States and founded *Der Bund der Freunde des Neuen Deutschlands,* or "the Friends of the New Germany."

Although German officials hoped that the Friends would prove less obnoxious than had the Nazi Party units, Spanknoebel's employment of coercive rather than persuasive tactics succeeded only in making enemies for the New Germany. Subsidized by the North German Lloyd and the Hamburg-American Steamship Line, the former employee of Henry Ford settled in metropolitan Yorkville, immediately seized control of the *Staats-Zeitung,* a German-language paper, and attempted to capture the *Stahlhelm,* a group of German-American war veterans, and the United German Societies of New York. Throughout the summer and fall of 1933, his position threatened by internecine strife, Spanknoebel toured the Middle Atlantic states, boasting that his was the sole National Socialist organization in North America. Seeking to preserve an American identity, he distributed stickers bearing the swastika alongside the insignia of the Ku Klux Klan. Uniformed stormtroopers often accompanied him on his rounds, and on one occasion, during a particularly virulent anti-Semitic speech in Newark, their presence provoked a nasty brawl.

In September Spanknoebel missed a chance to secure dominion over the United German Societies of New York when that organization's Jewish members, aghast at his blatant anti-Semitism, bolted the group. Taking note of the fear the Friends were spreading in New York's Jewish community, Representative Samuel Dickstein of the House Committee on Immigration and Naturalization announced his intention to investigate aliens who had entered the United States under false pretenses. In addition, after Samuel Untermyer, president of the Non-Sectarian Anti-Nazi League, charged that the cost of German propaganda in the United States had reached an annual total of 3 million dollars, a federal grand jury in New York initiated hearings on local Nazi activities.

The grand jury report of November 10 detailed Spanknoebel's connection with the Reich and noted his failure to register as a foreign agent. A subpoena issued for his arrest went unserved, however, as two weeks before, realizing that he would soon be a fugitive from justice, Spanknoebel apparently booked passage aboard the German liner *Deutschland* as it left New York. Attempting to disassociate itself from its boisterous American offspring, the German government, speaking through Propaganda Minister Goebbels, immediately denied any knowledge of Spanknoebel's activities, while Ernst Bohle, the director of Germans Abroad, announced that in the future, direction of the Friends would be turned over to American citizens.

These official attempts to minimize American objections to the existence of the Friends did not count for much, however, as the indefatigable and slightly hysterical Dickstein joined with Representative John McCormack of Massachusetts to launch a congressional investigation of fascist and communist activities within the United States. The widely publicized report of their special House Committee revealed that many nativist groups had adopted Hitler's cause and that two business firms, Ivy Lee-T. J. Ross and Carl Byoir and Associates, had in fact distributed Nazi literature. In May 1934, alarmed at this and other reports of extremist affairs, President Roosevelt conferred with top advisers, including J. Edgar Hoover and Attorney General Homer Cummings.

The unexceptional members of the Friends of the New Germany should have evoked more ridicule than fear. That they did not may be explained in large part by the tendency of Americans to define their activities in the context of domestic developments in Nazi Germany. In the popular mind the Friends thus ceased to be unemployed, lower-middle-class immigrants (or immigrants' sons) seeking some excitement to buoy their spirits through the dog days of depression; rather, they were endowed with demonic characteristics more properly descriptive of their German progenitors and were seen as sinister functionaries in Hitler's American branch office.

Reports of Nazi fifth columnists goose-stepping their way across the fields of a summer camp near New York City consequently took on increased significance after Hitler initiated a calculated program of anti-Semitism that culminated in the "Blood Purge" of July 1934. This event, which included several mass executions perpetrated ostensibly to eliminate "extremists" of the left and right, shocked humanitarian Americans and led Ambassador William Dodd to remark of the *Führer,* "I have a sense of horror when I look at the man."

By blackening the American image of the German leader, Dodd's comment paradoxically influenced Hitler's decision to install as Ambassador to the United States, Hans Luther, an economist and former chancellor of the Weimar Republic. In the words of the *Führer,* Luther's main qualification was that he would show "nothing startling or wild in German foreign policy." In a further attempt to downplay fears of Nazi ferocity, Hitler informed Dodd that he would not allow Reich propaganda to reach the United States and added that any disobedient subordinate would "be thrown into the North Sea." To judge from the subsequent propaganda releases of the Friends, Bund, Silver Shirts, and ultimately, Father Coughlin, those waters should have been filled with bodies; yet German records listed no drownings.

Controversy surrounding the American Nazis increased dramatically during the first months of 1934, seemingly in direct proportion to the number of column inches that New York newspapers accorded Hitler's atrocities against the Jews. The Friends themselves contributed to this clamor when, for example, they established the *Deutsch Amerikanische Wirtschafts Ausschuss* (DAWA) to counter the economic boycott of German goods sponsored by the Anti-Nazi League. But for the most part it was a pervasive American distaste for the theoretical aspects of Nazism, especially racism, that served to fasten attention upon the group. Exemplifying this trend, representatives of the American Jewish Congress, organized labor, and the American Legion staged a mock trial at Madison Square Garden on March 7, with Mayor Fiorello La Guardia, Senator Millard Tydings of Maryland, Al Smith, and Raymond Moley appearing to "bear witness" to German crimes against humanity.

In maintaining their role as demagogues, Father Coughlin and William Dudley Pelley were required, willy-nilly, to make a good deal of noise. The Friends of the New Germany, "un-American" by dint of their choice of appellation, should have realized that to mitigate this tactical error while also generating support for Hitler, sophistication and stealth would prove of more strategic significance than *Sturm und Drang.* But because the domestic Nazis themselves were unable to agree on tactics, commotion and internal bickering were the rule rather than the exception.

This problem was illustrated late in 1934 when Anton Hagele led a revolt of young Turks from the New York *Turnhalle* after deriding President Herbert Schnuch as "worse than a Jew" for his inefficient leadership. Hagele's forces subsequently seized control of the Friends' journal and emerged two weeks later as the "American National Socialist League." According to Schnuch, this development merely purged the organization of "Jewish dupes," but Kurt Luedecke, loyal to Hagele, pointed out that the schism occurred because the Friends could no longer satisfy "that part of its membership which wanted to see action and nothing but action." "If we are only coming near

our goal," Luedecke explained, "there will be no Jew left in these United
States. Here is our toast—TO THE LAST JEW!"

A bit melodramatic, to be sure, but such intramural squabbling convinced
many German-American residents of Yorkville that the organization was
simply a "racket" carried on by a few selfish men seeking to enrich themselves. Nevertheless, despite warnings from the German Embassy and the
conservative Steuben Society that the Friends were intensifying American
distrust of Berlin, the director of the *Auslandsorganisation*, Ernst Bohle,
clung to his belief that his department ought not to disavow the group. Ambassador Luther concurred, remarking that the Friends comprised "the only
association championing New Germany," and thus there was no possibility of
breaking off completely.

Early in 1935 the Friends became involved in an issue which, according to
journalist John Lardner, "drove lawyers, writers, state executives, and wit-
nesses into a mad spin of histrionics and hysteria." Bruno Hauptmann, a
Bronx carpenter of German birth, stood trial for the kidnap-murder, three
years before, of the infant son of Mr. and Mrs. Charles A. Lindbergh. As expected, most Americans called for Hauptmann's swift conviction and execution. But seeing a chance for publicity, the Friends quickly undertook a spirited defense of the accused.

Indicating that Hauptmann was a scapegoat, a publicist for the
organization argued that because Lindbergh was "the Nordic hero of the
United States," his child represented "Gentile perfection," and for this reason
"Jewish money stepped in and silenced revelations that would have shaken
the Christian world out of its torpor." Another document, placing the trial in
the context of German-American relations, noted that "the voluptuousness
with which the Jew press of New York tried to shift public sentiment against
Hauptmann and his home country has been demonstrated in such terms as
'Nazi-killer,' 'Nazi kidnapper,' and 'German machinegunner.' "

The Friends did not prevent Hauptmann's execution, but their activities in
his behalf, combined with their continued support of the Third Reich, attracted increased scrutiny. In fact, scarcely a week passed without some notice of their pursuits appearing in the *New York Times*. In January the group
celebrated the Saar Plebiscite, by which the rich Central European area came
under Berlin's control. Two months later, when the Friends organized new
units in White Plains, Yonkers, and New Rochelle, Jewish War Veterans in
the latter community threatened to take legal action to curtail the American
Nazis. In April the Friends sponsored a dance to celebrate Hitler's birthday,
and two weeks later, at a mass meeting in New York, adopted resolutions defending German rearmament and denouncing international communism.
After a summer festival at Yaphank, Long Island, there remained no doubt
that Dr. Ignatz Griebl, now leading the Friends, considered it his paramount
duty to unify German-Americans in support of Nazism.

In the interim, German propaganda sent the Yorkville yahoos decreased
in volume, but augmented Nazi military prowess, combined with the Anglo-

German Naval Agreement of 1935 and anti-Semitic disorders in Berlin, further antagonized American opinion. A growing spirit of Germanophobia was manifest in the denunciation of the Nazi *Kurfürstendamn* by Representative Emanuel Celler of New York and Senator William H. King of Utah, and in Mayor La Guardia's refusal to issue a masseur's license to a German resident of Manhattan. Concomitant with these events, a mob boarded the German resident liner *Bremen* in New York Harbor and tore the Nazi flag from its staff, while the editorial board of *Commonweal* joined the Anti-Nazi League in calling for American abstention from the forthcoming Olympic Games in Berlin.

Thus by mid-1935, the Friends of the New Germany had become a definite liability in the German book of accounts. His earlier support for the organization replaced by dismay, Ambassador Luther entreated the Foreign Ministry to return to its original policy of de-emphasizing politics in attempting to unify the German-American community. Responding to this plea, Foreign Minister Konstantin von Neurath subsequently directed German consuls in the United States to inform German citizens in their areas that they must resign from all German-American groups. The directive was not obeyed, however, as the Friends refused to believe that Nazi leaders would treat them so cavalierly. When the *New York Times* printed the order, the editor of the *Beobachter,* Walter Kappe, denounced it as "a Jewish lie by a Jewish paper." Soon afterwards, an incredulous Fritz Gissibl traveled to Berlin to check personally the veracity of the directive. When he returned to the United States in November, he notified the Foreign Ministry that Germans within the organization still refused to believe that Berlin wanted them to resign. For this reason, Rudolf Hess reiterated the point with the admonition that this time there could be no misunderstanding.

Although many American congressmen appeared to sympathize with Germany's reoccupation of the Rhineland on March 7, 1936, it was clear that in the American mind there would be no resurrection of Hitler's reputation. Indeed, protest was widespread, as the United Mine Workers passed a resolution denouncing the Reich; the American Federation of Protestants, Catholics, and Jews went on record condemning German anti-Semitism; famed conductor Arturo Toscanini accepted an invitation to lead the Palestine Symphony Orchestra; and the American Jewish Congress announced that it had raised $20,000 to further the cause of anti-Nazi propaganda in the United States. In view of such resentment, Berlin's ardor toward the Friends cooled considerably. German authorities preferred to remain on good terms with conservative German-American groups such as the Steuben Society and the United German Societies of New York, both of which had earlier repudiated the domestic Nazis. Accordingly, on April 1, Ernst Bohle ordered the dissolution of the Friends of the New Germany, whose continuation, he argued, would entirely wreck German-American relations.

Yet the departure of the Friends from the fringes of American political life did not mark the end of German-American extremism, for on the very day the group succumbed, the German-American Bund (*Amerika Deutscher Volksbund*) appeared in its stead. According to its leader, Fritz Kuhn, who had assumed control of the Friends the preceding December, the Bund had no connections with Berlin and was open only to American citizens. Attempting to cleanse his group of the stigma of Nazism, Kuhn pointed out that his was "a militant group of patriotic Americans" who embraced "the Constitution, Flag, and Institutions of the United States." In the primal drama of patriotic conduct, the Bundists, as self-appointed countersubversives, would rescue the heritage bequeathed Americans by the Founding Fathers and stand fast against "all Atheistic teachings and all abuse of the pulpits designed to undermine the Morals, Ethics, or Patriotism of Americans; all Racial Intermixture between Asiatics, Africans, or non-Aryans; all Subversive Internationalism; the liberal-pacifist forces undermining the morale of youth; Alien-controlled, international so-called Labor Movements; and the Rackets of International finance."

There was little to distinguish the rhetoric of the Bundists from that which characterized the Silver Shirt crusade. Like Pelley, Kuhn believed that a symbolic coalition between George Washington and Adolf Hitler would result in "all Americans defending Aryan culture and the Code of Ethics on which this national was founded, helping to build a great American movement of Liberation . . . in order that the dictatorship of a . . . Jewish international minority . . . may be broken."

Far from being *gemütlich,* group ritual was calculated to appeal to the emotions of persons who already had embraced the tenets of the Third Reich. But there was more to it than this, for in a curious way membership in the organization allowed German-Americans who, like Father Coughlin's Irish-Catholics, had themselves earlier been enemies of American nativists, to reverse the relationship. Now, the aliens themselves had become nativists in good standing, self-avowed custodians of national security. This fact was apparent at a gathering in the Brooklyn *Schwabenhalle* only a day after the Bund's inception. There, amid swastika and American flags, patrols of *Ordnungsdienst,* or "security guards," clicked their heels smartly as Kuhn and his associates described sinister Jewish conspirators who had invaded the government of the United States. At the beginning of the meeting the group pledged allegiance to the Stars and Stripes and, at the end, joined in a rendition of the *"Horst Wessel Lied,"* the Nazi anthem containing the line, "Death to the Jew."

By far the most obnoxious feature of the Bund, aside from its racism, was its leader. Described by *Time* magazine as "pompous and garrulous," Fritz Kuhn strove to keep his name and that of his organization in the headlines. To the consternation of Ambassador Luther and his successor, Dr. Hans Dieckhoff, the *Bundesführer* behaved "like an embryo Göring" while assaying the role of storm trooper between 1936 and 1939.

Born in Munich in 1895, Kuhn served with the German army during the war in France, Rumania, Italy, and the Balkans and was wounded in action.

Subsequently he studied chemistry at the University of Munich and drank deeply of nascent Nazism, becoming a member of the terroristic *Epp Freikorps* (1919) and *Oberland Freikorps* (1921). He joined the Nazi Party in 1921 and in the same year was convicted and sentenced to four months' imprisonment for raiding the coat pockets of fellow students. Fleeing to Mexico in 1923 with 2,000 marks stolen from a sympathetic warehouseman who had befriended him, Kuhn found work as an industrial chemist until 1927, when he came to the United States. In 1933, after laboring for six years in Henry Ford's Dearborn plant, he became a naturalized American citizen and celebrated the event by joining the Friends of the New Germany. Thereafter he served as a leader of the Detroit local, head of the organization's Middle-West Division, and finally in December 1935, as national president.

Kuhn named as his chief lieutenant James Wheeler-Hill, the illegitimate son of a Russian father and English mother, who served primarily as a liaison between the Bund and other American extremist groups. Another officer, Severn Winterscheidt, had formed a close friendship with the notorious German anti-Semite, Julius Streicher, before coming to the United States in 1931. Upon joining the Bund, he edited the *Deutscher Weckruf und Beobachter* until 1938, when he was convicted of molesting a young girl in a New York movie theatre.

Such was the human material comprising the hierarchy of the organization; and like Pelley and Father Coughlin, Fritz Kuhn accorded his associates no responsibilities. Inasmuch as the Bund amounted to a species of property to which he held absolute title, his announcement that the group would function according to the *Führerprinzip* that guided Nazi Germany marked a cynical attempt to convince supporters that any diminution in his own power would menace the entire social order.

Seeking to avoid the tactical errors that had plagued the Friends, Kuhn constructed a constitution that preserved anonymity of membership and secrecy in the operation of individual cells. Yet aside from this departure, he resurrected in its entirety the organizational framework established by the earlier group. In fact, the ostensible "Americanization" of the Bund belied the fact that for all practical purposes the organization remained a spiritual offshoot of German Nazism. Although it was not, as many critics charged, a disciplined army of spies and saboteurs, the organization continued to receive propaganda directly from Berlin, and despite the Foreign Ministry's directive prohibiting its nationals from membership, the Bund roster retained a majority of German citizens.

However, the group was unable to develop effective techniques for enlisting new recruits. Employing pressure tactics to gain control of German-American societies and families, the Bund generally encountered apathy among residents of Yorkville, who admired Baron von Steuben, a hero during the American Revolution, as much as they detested Hitler. For them the statement by the *Deutscher Weckruf und Beobachter* that Americans of German descent could be good citizens "only if they are and remain good Germans" was absurd. Nevertheless, although they earned the reputation of being "thick heads," the Bundists did alarm some residents of Yorkville who failed to protest for fear that relatives in Germany would be harmed.

Even more unsettling to many Americans was the establishment of Bund summer camps in areas with large German populations. At sites such as Camp Siegfried at Yaphank, Long Island, Hindenberg at Grafton, Wisconsin, and Nordlund, near Andover, New Jersey, campers studied German language and culture, listened to discussions of the Jewish menace, and worked hard to keep physically fit. By midsummer 1937, supported by campers' fees, annual dues, and "special assessments" levied upon friendly German-American businessmen, more than thirty such camps were operating within the United States. This alone kept the Bund in constant legal difficulty, and also enraged American opponents of Hitler.

Because of Fritz Kuhn's unclear connection with Berlin, the Bund became a cause célèbre in 1937. He had visited the German capital the previous year, ostensibly to attend the Olympic Games, and there he presented Hitler a copy of the organization's *Golden Book* and $3,000 for the German Winter Relief Fund. Upon his return to the United States he claimed that the *Führer* had told him to "go back and carry on your fight." Kuhn also carried with him a photograph depicting him and three associates engaged in conversation with Hitler. In addition, Kuhn made the remarkable statement that the German chancellor had given him total power over the Embassy and the entire consular network in America.

The swift denial of Kuhn's allegations by the German Foreign Ministry did not prevent the self-impressed *Bundesführer* from acting as if he possessed official sanction. In the midst of the 1936 presidential campaign, he offered his support to Alfred M. Landon and announced that Hitler approved of the Kansas Republican because he would "produce a more friendly position of the United States toward our Fatherland." Acutely embarrassed, the German Embassy quickly repudiated the endorsement, and Berlin followed suit two days later. Yet with rumors circulating that the Bund had infiltrated German-language departments in several American high schools, the denials did not convince many citizens that Fritz Kuhn was not in league with the most famous of Austrian corporals.

In light of his hatred of Nazism, it was not surprising that Samuel Dickstein exaggerated the Bund's relationship with Germany. But by stressing this theme, the New York Democrat augmented the publicity being accorded the group and thereby made of it something it was not—a danger to the internal security of the United States. Prone to hyperbole, he made headlines when he charged that Kuhn commanded no less than 200,000 persons, a tenth of whom were preparing for actual military combat. In addition, Dickstein claimed to possess the names of thousands of German agents and sympathizers who had secreted themselves throughout the nation. These allegations bordered on the absurd and were ridiculed by many of Dickstein's colleagues.

Nevertheless, the wide currency given the New York congressman's allegations generated within the American mind a fear of alien subversion.

Because the Bundists equated publicity with success, they welcomed discussion of the "Jewish question," an issue with which national leaders, apart from expressing their moral outrage, were powerless to deal. Yet even here, the critical remarks made by American politicians had the effect not only of exacerbating German-American diplomatic tension, but also of providing Kuhn a forum from which to press the attack upon "Jewish" communism. During the course of a speech to the Women's Division of the American Jewish Congress on March 3, for example, Mayor La Guardia applauded a listener's suggestion to erect a building dedicated to freedom of thought at the forthcoming World's Fair. The impulsive "Little Flower" then added a novel suggestion of his own, proposing to build a chamber of horrors, crowned by a figure of "that brown-shirted fanatic now menacing the peace of the world." The edifice, La Guardia believed, would provide a fitting home for the German exhibit.

Because the mayor's proposal violated an unwritten diplomatic rule restraining public officials from criticizing nations at peace with the United States, Ambassador Luther sought and was granted a swift apology by Secretary of State Cordell Hull. A Tennessean whose national service dated from the administration of Woodrow Wilson, Hull no doubt privately approved La Guardia's suggestion, but because of his position he remained unable to express his feelings publicly.

Unconstrained by this diplomatic protocol, La Guardia sought to discomfit the Bundists, whom he despised, by stating his regret that his mother had only a slight infusion of Jewish blood, unfortunately "not enough to boast of." This verbal stiletto punctured Fritz Kuhn's inflated ego, and the Bund leader warned the mayor to refrain from making the World's Fair "a battleground of religion." La Guardia, he added, had his facts wrong: Germany was not preparing for war. The Reich was a peaceful government that threatened no one. Two months later, Kuhn indicated that the time had come for the city father to leave the United States. He had not, explained the *Bundesführer*, "come over on the *Mayflower*." That La Guardia was in fact a native-born American citizen, while Kuhn himself had been naturalized only four years before, was immaterial. The point was that like Franklin "Rosenfeld," the CIO, and the New York court system, the mayor was a cog in the Jewish-communist world conspiracy and would help destroy the country if given the chance. "We will fight like our forefathers for this country!" Kuhn screamed at 600 followers in the *Turnhalle*.

What La Guardia and Kuhn actually said during their exchange was less significant than what many Americans chose to hear. In itself the war of words was inconsequential; yet because reaction to the affair tended to polarize opinion in symbolic terms, the interchange foreshadowed the metaphorical context in which the Great Debate on American foreign policy would develop after 1937. Indeed, to judge by the rhetoric and imagery employed by persons who wrote to the mayor and Roosevelt, a conflict over the meaning of patriotism was already underway on the domestic front. Most correspondents, including a resident of Providence, Rhode Island, who compared La Guardia's ideals with those of Roger Williams, strongly supported the city father. Some New Yorkers went so far as to send him checks and money orders to help erect his "chamber of horrors," while the Plainfield, New Jersey, branch of the American League against War and Fascism proposed that he make a similar denunciation of Mussolini.   Samuel L. Untermyer of the Anti-Nazi League and several Jewish- and German-American groups also condemned Kuhn. Untermyer, recovering from illness in Palm Springs, wired the League's annual convention in New York and explained that Hull himself owed La Guardia an apology for what amounted to a gratuitous insult. "All hail to Mayor La Guardia!" read Untermyer's emotional telegram.

From the other side came equally emotional attempts to impugn the loyalty of the controversial mayor. A German-American resident of Kansas City wrote La Guardia that he could find his "own calibre right here among the gangland Dagoes in KC." A New Yorker, probably a Bundist, ordered the city father to cease aiding "the real menace—the Russian-Subversive-Communists—most of whom are Jewish." An indignant physician wrote Roosevelt from Waterbury, Connecticut, asking "Does free speech under our Constitution imply that a Semitic-infused La Guardia can hide behind the curtain of an American Chief Magistrate? Cannot something be done to stop Huey Longism, as exemplified by La Guardia?"

To be sure, there were some Americans who considered La Guardia's insult unwise for more realistic reasons. Many of these were of course Jewish-Americans who feared a deterioration in relations between Washington and Berlin. A former resident of Düsseldorf, for example, remarked that although the mayor's words could not hurt him, he had left behind his seventy-seven-year-old mother and 450,000 other Jews. More direct in his approach, a New Yorker expressed dismay for similar reasons. "We Jews certainly need help in these trying times," he wrote to La Guardia, "but not by making stupid remarks about foreign governments. Keep your hands off foreign affairs! Do your job right here in this city!"

But American foreign relations, complicated in an intangible yet significant way by the "Jewish Question," were becoming important. On February 12, a Bund meeting at the Hippodrome in New York attracted an audience of 4,000 persons, who listened attentively as German, Russian, Italian, and English speakers attacked communism, the Loyalist government in Spain, and the Anti-Nazi League. Flags of fascist Italy, Nazi Germany, the former Spanish monarchy, and Imperial Russia stood next to the Stars and Stripes. For Fritz Kuhn and his goose-stepping cohorts, the cause of Nazism had assumed new importance: Hitler had cast his lot with Franco's Spanish rebels. Now there was something about which the Bundists could really cheer.

The nativist-extremism of the mid-1930s was thus an important manifestation of the kind of social strain that generally accompanies periods of great change. Just as the employment of countersubversive metaphors during the depression was not peculiar to a single class or ideological persuasion, no single cause brought men and women to rally around ultrapatriotic banners. Yet despite their many differences, the Coughlinites, Silver Shirts and Bundists were unified by the style of their conspiratorial rhetoric, which, as a language unto itself, generated its own vitality and suggested, through self-fulfilling prophecy (usually to the point of dreary redundancy), universal validity.

Indeed, Father Coughlin's so-called "radical" critique of Wall Street bankers and international financiers was similar in nature to the "reactionary" Silver Shirt and Bundist denunciations of the Judeo-Bolshevik world conspiracy. In the first place, although the priest had not yet publicly espoused anti-Semitism, within his image of the international banker there lurked a Jewish stereotype, the use of which was probably understood and approved by most of his followers. Secondly, these "radical" and "reactionary" versions of conspiracy theory established within countersubversive ranks the importance of what might be termed an apocalyptic imagination, that is, a way of looking at the world characterized in some instances by a deep sense of foreboding and in others by premonitions of imminent disaster or by actual visions of doom. This sort of eschatological *Weltanschauung* reflected the feeling of many Americans that it was more reassuring to ascribe the direction of events to enemy forces than to admit that all was chaos. Thus the cement which bound together the nativists of the 1930s was a compound of individual and collective disillusionment, itself the product of the contemporary disjunction between personal aspirations and actual conditions. It was not surprising, therefore, that such an ethos of economic and social dislocation stimulated within the nativist imagination a nexus between seemingly disparate enemies.

Because of the nature of their feelings about life in general and the Roosevelt administration in particular, Coughlin, Pelley and Kuhn had become, together with their respective supporters, spiritual aliens posing as patriotic nationalists. While channeling the diffuse hostility of their followers, the extremists alleged that a Soviet-style totalitarianism had been transplanted to Washington, an assertion that was apparently corroborated by the accession of the political intellectuals, some of whom incidentally were Jewish, and the encroachment, for the first time on a large scale, of the Federal Government upon the daily lives of the American people. These developments became even more unsettling in view of the skillful manner in which the yahoos manipulated fragmentary and highly circumstantial evidence to document their allegations. That their warnings carried a modicum of truth and an intimation of actual conflict sufficed to stimulate the imaginations of their subordinates, many of whom did not comprehend the implications of the bigotry being espoused by their leaders. Indeed, had all the evidence been available, these crusades of countersubversion probably would not have existed.

Yet by early 1937 the nativists' allegation that Judeo-Bolshevik conspirators had infiltrated the office of the Chief Executive had brought into the open an issue heavily imbued with emotive and moral connotations as a result of events in Germany. Coughlin, Pelley and Kuhn had fired the opening guns in a domestic war concerning the symbolic meaning of Americanism. Here, however, the extremists were at a disadvantage, for as they warned their countrymen against communists who had captured key government positions, most Americans who looked towards Europe saw only a threatened renewal of the bloody wars of self-destruction that had plagued the Continent from time immemorial and consequently did not distinguish between communism and fascism. This popular view that both versions of totalitarianism were evil and best avoided shaped the nature of the antiextremist counterattack launched by concerned leaders like La Guardia and Dickstein, men who also employed a countersubversive rhetoric and imagery to portray the nativists in their true light—as enemies of the Republic.

Because isolationist sentiment was at its peak in 1937, the problem of loyalty in a democratic, pluralist society had not become crucial. Should the United States be drawn closer to the impending crisis in Europe, however, the peacetime distaste for foreign "isms" might easily give way to a wartime terror of alien spies and saboteurs.

9

Spain, China, and American Neutrality

★ ★ ★ In late summer 1936, as British historian D. W. Brogan waited to purchase a ticket at the Union Pacific railroad station in Kansas City, a clerk inquired if he was European. When Brogan replied affirmatively, the agent remarked tersely, "Well don't go back—it's going to hell."

Despite nearly two decades of disillusionment with the Great War and the Versailles Treaty, the United States found it impossible to ignore global strife. From 1937 to late in 1941 the American people and their leaders faced complex diplomatic problems whose apparent solutions led inexorably to participation in European and Far Eastern affairs. These crises profoundly affected the careers of the extremists, who, although sharing the common desire to keep apart from foreign imbroglios, did so because they approved the policies being pursued by the European dictators and Japanese militarists. This was clearly a tactical mistake, for while the national consensus had been menaced by internal forces during the nadir of depression, Americans now slowly began to perceive the growing external threat to the Republic; and consequently the yahoos' inverted nativism—in essence a sort of antinationalism poorly disguised as superpatriotism—stood in all-too-bold relief.

This augmented notoriety resulted in the complete disappearance of the extremists' thin veneer of respectability and accompanied the emergence, for the first time in American history, of the Federal Government as protector of civil liberties and minority rights. Compared to the vicious repression of these same rights and liberties in Spain, Portugal, Germany, Italy, and the Soviet Union, the United States again became a beacon of light in a world of darkness. For the extremists and their supporters, however, who rejected the pluralistic spirit of the New Deal, America offered no hope. And if they could not embrace the projected Rooseveltian good society, then they would wreak figurative vengeance on it by taking their cues from its antithesis.

To understand the nature of the bitter reaction accorded the extremists after 1937, one must remember that despite their foreign orientation, Father Coughlin, William Pelley, and even Fritz Kuhn developed their rhetorical style and peculiar images of countersubversion within the domestic context of the depression. The extremists were, to be sure, a band of guerrilla fighters whose unifying force remained from the outset the hatred wrought by continuing economic and social deprivation. In 1936 their contest against the established order was dismissed by many Americans, who were accustomed to and relatively tolerant of the perorations of home-grown demagogues as a side show of no lasting import. After 1937, owing more to world troubles and the anxieties of American liberals than to their own efforts, the domestic extremists underwent a metamorphosis in the popular mind and emerged as traitorous, well-organized, Nazi fifth columnists.

The menace of American fascism, endowed with a new and sinister significance as a result of global developments, again became a national issue. As it did, the extremists began to influence America's foreign policy in an indirect and subtle way. On one level, their propaganda contributed to the deterioration of German-American relations by reinforcing Hitler's belief that the United States lay in the clutches of apostate world Jewry. This irony was offset by another, the extremists' unwitting provision of some very good arguments favoring American intervention in behalf of Great Britain. In a symbolic sense, the extremists' emotional style and their injection into the great diplomatic debate of the bogey of anti-Semitism proved even more significant. By late summer 1941, following Charles A. Lindbergh's address at Des Moines, Iowa, interventionists capitalized on this theme to destroy the cause of respectable American isolationism. Rather than spending precious time fighting the Roosevelt administration's interventionist diplomacy, isolationists were forced to spend the "last minutes of peace" explaining that they were not Nazis.

The process by which the extremists unwittingly sabotaged the isolationist effort was a complicated one, beginning with the civil war that erupted in Spain in July 1936. The conflict, rooted in the vicissitudes of internal Spanish politics after 1931, threatened to become a general European war after Germany, Italy, and Portugal offered aid to rebel leader Francisco Franco, and the Soviet Union gave support to the de jure republican government. This situation placed the issue of American neutrality in clearer perspective than had the Italo-Ethiopian war of the previous year, for when Italian forces invaded Ethiopia, Roosevelt and Secretary of State Cordell Hull had assumed that the impartial arms embargo of the 1935 Neutrality Law would hinder Mussolini's warriors. But because Ethiopia was a poor nation lacking the money, transportation facilities, and arms that Italy possessed, the legislation did not gauge the disparate strength of the two countries. Nor did the Law of 1935 guarantee abstention from any large-scale conflict. Being remote, the

Italo-Ethiopian war failed to make a significant mark upon the American mind. Yet as the President pointed out, no doubt referring to the possibility of larger conflict, the embargo "might have exactly the opposite effect from that which was intended. The inflexible provisions might drag us into war instead of keeping us out."

Toward the Spanish Civil War, therefore, the Chief Executive attempted to follow a policy of strict neutrality. After he urged extension of the amended Neutrality Law of 1936 to cover civil wars, Congress resolved jointly on January 8, 1937, to forbid the export of munitions "for the use of either of the opposing forces in Spain." The proposed legislation, amended on January 22 by Senator Key Pittman of Nevada to allow belligerent nations to buy nonmilitary goods in the United States and to transport them in their own ships, provided the substance of debate occupying the nation's legislators in the early part of the year. In effect, the American people were being asked if they were willing to forfeit the profits of neutral trade in order to avoid involvement in war. They could have either peace or prosperity, but as they desired both, cash-and-carry provided the compromise solution.

Although sharing Roosevelt's worry that the Iberian conflagration might become a general holocaust, most Americans viewed the issue with apathy. Some individuals, however, felt strongly committed to one of the warring sides. In university lecture halls, Protestant church pulpits, and the liberal press, the cause of Spanish republicanism found staunch adherents. In addition, ships sailed from American shores, filled with idealists who interpreted the contest as an apocalyptic battle between the forces of democracy and European fascism.

On the other hand, most members of the American Catholic hierarchy felt about Franco the same way they did about transubstantiation and the Virgin Mary. For them, as for many lay Catholics, the rebel leader appeared to be a holy soldier waging war against modern infidels. Compared on occasion with Christ Himself, Franco would save traditional, Christian Spain from onrushing hordes of international communists. So strong was this approbation, in fact, that Catholics who criticized Franco, including French philosopher Jacques Maritain, and Americans like Kathleen Norris, George Schuster, and Dorothy Day, often were condemned as traitors by their co-religionists.

The partiality with which American Catholics regarded Franco's rebels allowed Father Coughlin opportunity to attempt to recapture some of the respectability he had lost during the Union campaign, a performance termed by a resident of central California, "bigoted, fanatical, and beyond excusability." In this sense the Spanish strife was a godsend to a man who lived for the adulation of the crowd and, consequently, critics who had scoffed at his earlier "retirement" from radio laughed in derision when he cut short his self-imposed exile to deliver a special New Year's greeting. Although the cleric announced that he would return to regular broadcasting only if *Social Justice* circulation increased markedly, his actual reappearance was prompted by the sudden death on January 20 of Bishop Michael Gallagher. The Detroit prelate had blazed the path toward social justice, Coughlin pointed out, and this was no time to allow the weeds of inaction to cover that glory road.

Immediately there was renewed controversy, as from his tower promontory in Royal Oak the priest denounced John L. Lewis, leader of the infant CIO, for his major role in directing a sit-down strike that paralyzed General Motors in Flint. After Michigan Governor Frank Murphy refused to employ state militia to rout the strikers, Coughlin angrily concluded that although Lewis was not a communist, the future of American communism depended upon the leonine labor leader's success. At the same time the cleric called for a rebirth of the National Union in order to fight President Roosevelt's plan to liberalize the Supreme Court by "packing" it with justices sympathetic to social reform. Believing that Court and Constitution were not to be disturbed, Coughlin advised his audience to wire Washington legislators to thwart the measure. Whether his epistle was crucial in the eventual defeat of the scheme remains a moot point, however, as the Royal Oak pastor's was only one voice among millions that condemned the President's ill-advised measure.

Even before Bishop Gallagher's death, the priest offered an explanation of the battle currently raging in Spain. In a column in *Social Justice* he noted that Germany faced "an extremely difficult diplomatic task" in combating Spanish communism, and that Hitler became involved only because of his admirable opposition to the Soviet Union and his desire to bring peace to the Iberian Peninsula. It was the Soviet presence in Spain that mattered, and as Coughlin tempered his Anglophobia to enumerate various "acts of Communist sabotage in the British battle fleet," he readied himself to oppose actively Senator Pittman's cash-and-carry proposal.

Employing recognizable countersubversive rhetoric, the cleric warned that American munitions makers planned to sacrifice neutrality for immense profits. Another world war was imminent and, he indicated, the American people remained oblivious to "undercover and secret" diplomacy in Washington. In a masterpiece of invention he indicated that an internationalist conspiracy had already forced the abdication of King Edward VIII of England. The monarch's professed love for Mrs. Wallis Simpson, a sophisticated American divorcée, actually represented the ultimate success of international bankers who had worked for years to drive "the strong-willed Windsor" from the throne. Because these conspirators now threatened America, citizens could protect themselves only by maintaining "an America self-sustained and self-contained, free from foreign entanglements and foreign influence."

Questioning what he considered an inordinate amount of national discussion concerning the peril posed by "the helpless dictator powers," Coughlin argued that Germany could never be "the remote or proximate cause of the next war." Current European tensions stemmed from basic conflicts between "have" and "have-not" nations. While Germany belonged to the latter group, Britain and France enjoyed "the tremendous natural advantage in availing themselves of the vast resources of the United States." In case of Continental war, the passage of cash-and-carry neutrality would force the United States to become "an unwilling ally of the 'haves.' "

To prevent this from occurring and to buttress the isolationist cause, the Royal Oak pastor offered a symbolic interpretation of George Washington's Farewell Address of 1796. For all the extremists and for many other Americans as well, the document served as a figurative rock of ages. On February 21, therefore, the cleric celebrated Washington's Birthday by genuflecting before this isolationist monument. The radio sermon revealed him at his best, and those listening might well have believed that they were instead attending a séance. After praising Washington's "Great Rule," the priest asked his audience "reverently to roll down the curtain of time to take one last look." What Coughlin's hearers "saw" was a vision, permeated by "the mists of time," of Washington warning his men to hold fast against entangling alliances, then sitting back as his comrades filed by, bidding their eternal farewells. Suddenly he spoke: "I shall be obliged to you if each will come and take me by the hand. . . ."

But before the Father of his Country could continue, the radio priest, his voice quavering with emotion, interrupted: "Fellow citizens, close your eyes, lift up your heads! Clasp the hand of your beloved leader! His hand holds your hand. It is a sacred pact between the living and the dead. It is your pledge to hold fast to tradition. . . ."

His understanding and use of American history dominated by his concern for drama, Father Coughlin neither considered the pragmatic nature of the Address nor the facts that the document had not been presented orally but in a newspaper, and that much of it had been written by the great Anglophile, Alexander Hamilton. But these were minor matters; most Americans were not historians and, in any event, the oral presentation constituted a much more evocative medium.

Conspiratorial hypotheses also marked William Dudley Pelley's analysis of foreign affairs; yet, although the Silver Shirt leader believed that the "triumphant Jewish oligarchy" in Washington controlled the conduct of American diplomacy, he demonstrated little initial interest in the proposed neutrality legislation. Attempting to repolish the tarnished image of his Silver Legion for the promised counterattack against the forces of Judeo-Bolshevism, he conferred with another well-known American anti-Semite, aging, white-haired James True, who gained notoriety in 1936 when he told the editor of the radical *New Masses:* "We're not going to drive the Jews out of this country! We're going to bury 'em right here!"

In the course of their discussion, Pelley nominated Representative Samuel Dickstein of New York as public enemy number one and explained that "letting Jews like Dickstein conduct investigations of Gentiles in the name of Gentile patriotism, or permitting wild-haired little kikes to hold important federal positions . . . are phases of the Jewish psychosis" besetting America. The two men decided to "blow Dickstein out of Washington," a threat that would be accomplished with True's great new invention, a stubby, hardwood truncheon designated a "Kike-Killer." Having patented his shillelagh as an "amusement device," True boasted that it would make a policeman's nightstick look like a twig. Of course there existed no possibility that either man would succeed in using the weapon on Dickstein, but the story of the "Kike-Killer" amused many people.

Pelley did not campaign actively against cash-and-carry, but he opposed the measure in spirit by revealing in *Liberation* "Secret Facts About Europe for Vigilante Silver Shirts." Espousing a kind of "domino theory," he explained that "the set-up in Washington" suggested that the United States was "already being governed from some central source in Europe." Just as the various nations of the world were parts of a larger whole, events occurring in different countries comprised segments of a larger pattern. "Moves on the European chess-board," he intimated, "are already a phase of the same game where the American moves are Supreme Court alterations, the sit-down strikes, the strange behavior of Madam Perkins, and even the psychology of the President himself." Moreover, if the American people failed to restrict the "red horror" of Spanish Loyalism to Europe, they had better begin thinking of that "terror" as an advanced blueprint of what eventually would befall the United States.

Charging that the nation's "captured press" had failed to report the truth concerning the Spanish "blood-drench," the Silver Shirt leader echoed Father Coughlin by asserting that Benito Mussolini had extended aid to Franco only to prevent "a successful Communist Government in Spain from moving closer to Gibraltar." In fact, control of the gateway to the Mediterranean was the strategic issue in the Spanish war; the nation that held Gibraltar would have the British Empire at its mercy. Hitler and Mussolini thus provided the last hope for European freedom and the safety of world Christianity.

The passage on May 1 of a new, "permanent" neutrality law marked a reorientation of American foreign policy in favor of maritime powers. Although reiterating existing provisions against the shipment of arms and munitions and the extension of loans to belligerents, the law also embodied Senator Pittman's cash-and-carry proviso which stated that during the ensuing two years maritime trade would be lawful when belligerent nations purchased nonmilitary goods and removed them in their own vessels. In addition, the new law granted Roosevelt the power of designating goods to be classified as nonmilitary in nature.

Congressional isolationists opposed cash-and-carry in principle, primarily because it surrendered America's freedom of the seas to Britain and France. Isolationists on Capitol Hill did not hold Germany and Italy in high regard and in fact often spoke of the two countries with more bitterness than did administration spokesmen. Yet inasmuch as their sincere desire to avoid war theoretically limited the steps the United States might take unilaterally to preclude such an eventuality, respectable opponents of aid to the democracies found themselves in a position that with the passage of time became increasingly untenable. If, in other words, their demand for the continued freedom to make decisions assumed as a constant premise the existence of an unlimited range of options, they failed to see that Italian and German actions could quickly circumscribe their ability to make unencumbered choices. In addition, because Britain and France were the only nations with which the United States would side in any event, the isolationists also found themselves in the morally troubling position of consistently opposing proposals that might aid the democracies.

No such dilemma existed for the extremists, whose hatred of Britain and acceptance of variations on the Judeo-Bolshevik theme left them the singular task of preventing American involvement in European quarrels, no matter what the consequences. Far from having American interests at heart, the yahoos hoped that under Adolf Hitler the Continent would become an armed Nazi camp devoted to stamping out the communist menace. In this sense, the extremists were not isolationists at all, but in a manner similar to Alexander Hamilton, who supported Britain in the wars of the French Revolution, they stood foursquare behind the *Führer* and Mussolini. For the perverted patriots, then, passage of cash-and-carry only confirmed existence of a conspiratorial cabal in Washington. Their arguments, ironically enough, had assumed the measure would pass (after all, the government *was* in the hands of the enemy), and in the nature of all self-fulfilling prophecies, it did.

The irrational arguments employed by the extremists of course exerted little direct influence upon the neutrality debate. Father Coughlin's vociferous opposition to Spain's Loyalist government may have contributed to Roosevelt's decision to maintain an embargo on goods headed for Spanish shores, but it is difficult to separate the priest's influence from the isolationist sentiment that permeated the United States. In addition, extremist hysteria concerning the measure tended to cloud the fact that it was never truly effective and, indeed, probably figured in Franco's eventual victory. In the early months of 1937, finally, international questions remained less important than domestic issues, as reflected in Roosevelt's own failure to recognize clearly the threat posed by the dictators, and in the fact that his Court plan engendered much more controversy than did his advocacy of cash-and-carry.

Nevertheless, the stage was slowly being set for the eventual identification of the extremists with the respectable isolationist mainstream. Ironically, the catalyst for this was Representative Dickstein of New York, a Jewish liberal representing a predominantly Jewish constituency, who had become acutely concerned over alleged Nazi inroads in the United States. Four days after Pittman introduced his cash-and-carry proposal, Dickstein called for a new investigation of Nazi and fascist propaganda. Arguing that since the congressional investigation of 1935 there had been "black-hooded wings and white-hooded wings and brown shirts and blue shirts and black shirts and dirty shirts spreading throughout the United States," the excitable congressman demanded that such "110% Americans" be "sent back where they belong."

Dickstein's proposal, a domestic manifestation of augmented global ten-

sion, received support from congressmen who had received anti-Semitic propaganda, but other legislators, including Conservative Hamilton Fish of New
York who termed the suggestion a "regular alien and sedition law," scoffed at
the New York Democrat's allegations. Most perceptive, perhaps, was Texas
Democrat Maury Maverick who warned that the hate literature he had received was "only a beginning to what will come if we pass this resolution."
By investigating American anti-Semitic organizations, he argued, the House
would start "a wave of anti-Semitic propaganda all over the country," and the
inquiry would become "a boomerang of intolerance."

By July congressional support for Dickstein's proposed fascist hunt had
grown markedly, but events during that summer and fall produced a more
conservative national temper and thereby influenced the direction of the
forthcoming inquiry. First, the spectre of domestic radicalism, given meaning
by strikes called by Sidney Hillman's textile workers and the United Auto
Workers, plainly frightened property-oriented, middle-class Americans. Even
more unsettling was President Roosevelt's refusal to use force against the strikers, a failure many citizens interpreted as an executive assault upon property rights concomitant with his attack upon the Court. A third shock occurred in August, with the beginning of a "recession" that quickly erased
economic gains made during the preceding two years.

Domestic gloom darkened with the advent of a serious crisis in the Far
East. On July 7 Japanese troops attacked Chinese forces at the Marco Polo
Bridge near Peiping. Three weeks later, Japanese planes bombed Shanghai,
and hostilities that had smoldered since 1932 burst into full flame. Japan's in-
discriminate attack upon Shanghai's civilian population appalled humanitarian
Americans, but the President refused to invoke the Neutrality Law of May 1.
Technically justified in his unwillingness because Japan had not formally declared war, he, like most Americans, also favored the Chinese in their fight
against the Empire of the Rising Sun. The weaknesses of Spanish Loyalist
forces vivid in his mind, Roosevelt reasoned that an application of the legislation would result in similar hardship being visited upon the armies of
Chiang Kai-shek. At the same time, the Chief Executive and Secretary Hull
also believed that given the "set" of American public opinion, conflict with
Japan should be avoided at all costs. Because American impatience might reduce chances for a negotiated Far Eastern settlement, Hull's moral castigation
of Japanese militarism issued on July 16 stood as the basic American policy
concerning the conflict.

By September the foreign policy debate was heating up. Most Americans
hoped that Roosevelt would invoke the neutrality legislation, while others
worried lest cash-and-carry give the Executive too much leeway. Of the latter
group Senator Gerald P. Nye of North Dakota was most outspoken, calling
for "a hard-and-fast policy of neutrality" that could be changed "only by the
vote of Congress."

"Why," he asked, reiterating the conclusions of his investigating committee, "should we sell armaments and implements of war for the sake of profits,

greed, and blood money, which may also be used against our own soldiers? Why should we prepare the nations of the world for war and become the symbol of arms and armaments and the dollar sign for wholesale slaughter?" Given the mood of the country, Nye's were convincing arguments.

Yet other prominent citizens considered American neutrality an impossible goal in a world threatened by war. According to financier Bernard Baruch, who had been instrumental in popularizing the idea of cash-and-carry, the United States could maintain the freedom of the seas only by fighting for it. Closer to the seat of power, Eleanor Roosevelt believed that if America remained aloof, the country would pay "in a lower standard of living and decreased trade relations." The world was too closely knit "for one part to go broke and the other not to feel it."

But with Britain and France occupied by difficulties in Spain, and Chiang Kai-shek unable to mobilize his forces to rebuff the onrushing Japanese, strong American support for the principle of collective security remained a remote possibility. News reporters, therefore, were unsurprised on September 14 when FDR announced that American merchantmen would no longer be permitted to "transport to China or Japan any of the arms, ammunition, or implements of war" listed in the Law of May 1.

Confronted with serious domestic and international problems, the Democratic administration suffered another blow in late September with the revelation that newly-appointed Supreme Court Justice Hugo Black had been at one time a member of the Ku Klux Klan. Black's nomination, and the Senate's celerity in confirming him, led to a torrent of criticism from men of such varied political views as Senator Burton K. Wheeler of Montana and columnist Westbrook Pegler. A writer for the *Chicago Tribune* gloated: "There is a Klan and there are Kleagles, Kladds, Kludds, Klonvocations, etc. To these Mr. Roosevelt had added a Klonstitution and a Supreme Klort!"

In the wake of these difficulties, the President undertook a goodwill tour aimed at mending Western political fences. Returning to Washington, he made the last speech of his journey in Chicago on October 5. It was one of the most memorable addresses of his entire career. Believing that he could lead a socially conscious nation only if he had the support of public opinion, he set out to educate the American people on the subject of the breakdown of international order. In fact, he appeared suddenly to be a staunch advocate of collective security: "When an epidemic of physical disease starts to spread, the community approves and joins in a quarantine . . . War is a contagion whether it be declared or undeclared . . . There must be positive endeavors to preserve peace. Therefore, America actively engages in the search for peace."

Although it will probably never be know if the quarantine proposal constituted a "candid and clear statement in behalf of collective action against aggressors," the immediate reaction to the speech by isolationists in and out of Congress indicated that it did. The proposal received warm support from proadministration papers, including the *Washington Post* and *New York*

Times, but many observers, probably the majority, charged that the President had resorted to rattling the sabre so as to divert attention from his domestic failures.

Whatever his aim, Roosevelt retreated quickly enough from the high ground of Chicago, for as he spoke to reporters the following day he evaded questions concerning the specific peace efforts he had in mind and contended that his statements in no way conflicted with current neutrality legislation. In a radio chat five days later, he also eschewed the term "quarantine" and announced that he only wanted the American people "to be wise enough to realize that aloofness from war is not promoted by unawareness of war. In a world of mutual suspicions, peace must be affirmatively reached for. It cannot be wished for."

But when such a chance occurred in Brussels in November, the Chief Executive hesitated to place the weight of the United States on the scale of peace. Japan, contending that the China "incident" was a domestic matter, had not sent a delegation despite requests from Washington and from European leaders. As the Continental delegates discussed the possibility of employing sanctions against Tokyo, the State Department, which was still determined not to provoke the Japanese, cabled its representative that coercive measures did not fall within the scope of the meeting. On November 24, after its members (Italy excepted) passed a weak resolution condemning Japan for violating the Nine-Power Treaty of 1922, the conference adjourned. In addition to proving abortive in its immediate objective of halting Nippon's sweep through China, the Brussels Conference also marked the failure, for the moment, of Roosevelt's attempt to reorient American policy toward a more positive global role.

As during the debate on cash-and-carry, the extremists did not directly impinge on administration policy in the period between Roosevelt's Quarantine Speech and the Brussels Conference. In fact, their current status indicated that if domestic factors have often influenced the conduct and execution of American diplomacy, this was a case where the reverse was true. Foreign crises were clearly having an internal effect, as intensified conflict in Spain and the Far East seemed to exacerbate the yahoos' respective problem. In the last part of 1937 and the early months of the new year, Father Coughlin encountered hostility from his new superior, Archbishop Edward Mooney; Pelley's hysterical anti-Semitism increased demands for a House inquiry into American fascism; and Kuhn and his boisterous Bundists brought "goose pimples to haters of dictatorships, lovers of democracy, and communists."

Speculation concerning Archbishop Mooney's attitude toward Coughlin appeared to be settled in June when Mooney announced that "Father Coughlin does not want to be an issue." Upon his return to Royal Oak, however, the radio priest demonstrated that he remained the slashing phrasemaker of old. A week before the President would make his Quarantine Speech, the cleric discussed Hugo Black's nomination to the Supreme Court. "It is my hope," Coughlin announced during a press conference, "that Justice Black will live to be 200 years old. May he be a monument to . . . Mr. Roosevelt's personal stupidity."

Where Bishop Gallagher had offered his ambitious underling a blanket imprimatur, his successor quickly separated himself from Coughlin's accusations. Castigating the priest for his attack on the President, the Detroit prelate also belittled the cleric's observation that the CIO was a communist organization. When Mooney failed to approve Coughlin's subsequent statement answering the criticism, the former prince of the airwaves abruptly canceled a contract for a series of future broadcasts. This decision thrilled journalist Howard Brubaker, who wrote that because of the archbishop's "splendid work," Father Coughlin "is to be silent for twenty-six weeks over a nationwide network."

But while Brubaker and other critics gloated, the priest hired Walter Baertschi, national coordinator of what remained of the Social Justice movement, to lobby for his return to the air. He also sold *Social Justice* to Baertschi and announced that the Toledo resident would serve as president of the Social Justice Publishing Company until he returned to broadcasting. Baertschi did his job well, organizing a "Committee of Five Million," and spearheading a letter-writing campaign to convince the Vatican of the validity of Coughlin's cause.

When Vatican officials echoed Archbishop Mooney's belief that the former radio shepherd had become a black sheep, Coughlin relented and called upon his followers to cease agitating in his behalf. Soon afterwards, he confounded observers by announcing that he would return to the air, and indeed, on January 9, 1938, he delivered his first radio sermon since publicly disagreeing with Mooney. According to a story in *Social Justice,* Coughlin had cast the dove of peace to his superior. Perhaps the archbishop would "learn to love the pastor of the Shrine of the Little Flower."

Before being sidelined by these difficulties, the cleric analyzed developments in the Far East. His initial reaction to the crisis demonstrated the ease with which he modified his Catholicism to support the aims of non-Christian Japan. Coughlin interpreted the undeclared war as a diplomatic device that allowed Japan "to gain the objectives of war without incurring the historical responsibility for having waged war." Whatever sins they had committed, these Oriental cousins of Franco's Spanish Nationalists were fighting "the battle of Christianity and orderly government . . . against the infection of communism."

Throughout August and September the pages of *Social Justice* were filled with warnings to the American people, innuendoes against the President, and defenses of Japanese policy. On August 30, emphasizing the precarious diplomatic position of the United States, Coughlin warned that if Roosevelt either branded Japan a belligerent or proclaimed an embargo on scrap-iron shipments to the Nipponese, war between the two nations would occur shortly thereafter. Although anticommunism now stood as the big gun in the priest's arsenal, his retention of the attitudes of Midwestern radicalism that had characterized his earlier career was manifest in his belief that the real cause of hostilities lay in the tensions generated by rival international investors. His combination of communists and international financiers as the nation's paramount enemies might have seemed illogical, but this was beside the point. The wider the conspiracy, Coughlin reasoned, the more people who would believe, and in this sense he was simply touching all possible bases to convince his followers of the seriousness of their danger. As defense counsel for the American people, a role he had grown to love, he wondered whether the losses sustained during the First World War would be offset "by the private gains to be had by putting our army and navy behind the right to sail dangerous waters in pursuit of foreign dollars."

Superficially, Father Coughlin's desire to avoid war seemed to be as sincere as the feelings of most Americans. His commentary during the early autumn displayed a relative clarity and restraint, qualities that would be lacking after 1938. "It would appear," the priest wrote in one illustrative editorial in September, "that any policy of this country, as a neutral, which could result in giving a military or a strategic advantage to one side or another in a quarrel that does not directly concern us, not only is not a neutral policy, but one which may well get us into plenty of trouble we could otherwise avoid."

Yet if Father Coughlin's rhetoric often sounded very similar to that employed by William Jennings Bryan during the latter's short stint as Secretary of State under Woodrow Wilson, the fact remained that in no way could the priest be classified as an isolationist. Like Pelley and Kuhn, he was a partisan who desired war—as long as it involved the right parties and did not include the United States. Coughlin identified Japan's quest as synonymous with American national self-interest, and consequently it was the Japanese position in the Far East that drew continuous praise in *Social Justice*. A victory over the forces of Chiang Kai-shek, in sum, would place Japan "in a much better position to prepare and fight an ultimate war with Communist Russia, probably with the aid of Germany and Italy."

Compared with Father Coughlin's relatively tranquil response to the Far Eastern crisis, William Pelley's reaction was characteristically hysterical. Hoping to avoid another organizational defeat such as that which followed the McCormack-Dickstein hearings of 1935, the Asheville *Führer* had reorganized the Silver Shirts into secret Councils of Safety during the summer. But because of his unrestrained anti-Semitism, he only succeeded in gaining the renewed attention of Dickstein, presidential secretaries Marvin McIntyre and Stephen Early, and FBI Director J. Edgar Hoover.

In the way of substantive analysis there was little new in Pelley's outbursts. Already having informed his readers of the "true facts" in Spain, he, like Coughlin, merely transformed Franco's rebels into Japanese warriors and Spanish Loyalists into the armies of Chiang Kai-shek. Under the headline, "DON'T BE FOOLED BY THIS JAPANESE-CHINESE BRAWL!" he argued that "Japan has truly begun our American battle against Red Judaism in the Far East. Every thrust at Nippon means giving aid and comfort to

America's most vicious enemy—the Jewish Red!" In case of war between the Soviet Union and Japan, he warned, a clandestine agreement between Roosevelt and Soviet Foreign Minister Maxim Litvinov ("alias Finkelstein") *"would practically place our Pacific Fleet at Stalin's disposal,"* and the United States would become "an ally of the Jewish *murderbund* in Europe."

A month later, in a front-page story dealing with "Inside Facts on the War in China," Pelley justified Japan's failure to issue a formal declaration of war because there was no way for Tokyo to declare war on "a Chinese government that does not exist. Japan is warring against a successfully organized and utilized Red Chaos in China."

Pelley's condemnation of the Quarantine Address surpassed in viciousness his earlier criticism of the Chief Executive. In an article entitled "Japan Merits Friends, Not Vicious Critics," the Silver Shirt leader charged that "the sick man of hide [sic] park" planned "to fanaggle [sic] the United States into this war on the side of Red Russia." The "Red Jews," he continued, "lost out in Italy, they lost out in Germany, they lost out in Spain—they bid fair to lose out in China." But now, unfortunately, as a last resort, "those great Washington Jews propose to identify the United States as a Leftist nation and put her into the second world war to defend Sovietism and make the world safe for Communistic Jews!"

Pelley accused the President of working up war hysteria in order to restore his waning popularity. "Roosevelt sounds off," he wrote, "he runs true to form. This time it is Japan, not Germany, who is the mad dog abroad—who must be quarantined lest it lethally bite some good little Red-Jewish government in the leg." In effect Roosevelt had severed

the Gordian Knot of complications by explaining suddenly: "Oh! My goodness! Look at what Japan is doing over there in China!"

The whole thing is, of course, a wholesale defense of Jewish communism facing disaster in a world that has finally had its convincing demonstration of exactly what Jewish communism is.

SHALL THE UNITED STATES GO TO WAR AT THE FANAGGLING [SIC] OF A KOSHER PRESIDENT TO MAKE THE WORLD SAFE FOR CONTINUED JEWISH BLOODGUT?

Obviously, the answer to this rhetorical flourish was "no." If America did fight, Pelley reasoned, the entire male population of the country would become slaves of Jewish interests. But it was clear to him that this was exactly what the President planned.

With Father Coughlin and Pelley thus limited to rhetorical attacks upon administration sympathy for China, it remained the task of Fritz Kuhn and the German-American Bund to act out their discontent. During 1937 and 1938, the conduct of the organization thrust it into the limelight as the paradigm of American fascism, a position it would hold until Charles A. Lindbergh's apostasy in Des Moines, three years later. To reach this unenviable apex was relatively easy. Success was synonymous with publicity, and the

Nazi pretenders consequently strove heroically to maintain an American image. That their futile quest was taken seriously by many Americans who should have known better indicated, if nothing else, that developments in Nazi Germany were fast becoming a national issue. Ironically, no group recognized this fact more clearly than the vast majority of Yorkville's German-Americans, who, in addition to being one more generation removed from the Fatherland than in 1917, also remembered with anxiety the intense chauvinism that swept over them following America's plunge into war. For these Americans, lessons had been learned: avoid controversy; steer clear of the Bund. Yet the Bund could not keep apart from difficulties of its own creation. In addition to making many citizens aware of the repellent characteristics of Nazism, the group complicated New York City politics and also accelerated the deterioration of German-American relations.

In July, after the opening of Camp Nordlund near Andover, New Jersey, and the subsequent appearance at the site of Dr. Salvatore Caridi and a regiment of Italian-American fascisti, several American leaders began to act as if the Axis Pact, concluded earlier by Hitler and Mussolini, had been re-enacted in the United States. Undocumented charges flew furiously, as Samuel Untermyer of the Anti-Nazi League announced that Nordlund was directly controlled by Berlin; Representatives Martin Dies of Texas and William Citron of New Jersey demanded an FBI investigation; and Congressmen Fred Hartley of New York and J. Parnell Thomas of New Jersey joined the determined Dickstein to call for open congressional hearings. After Dickstein entered the names of forty-six alleged "Nazi spies and agitators" in the *Congressional Record,* Fritz Kuhn also entered the fray, announcing that he welcomed any and all investigations to prove the "American-ness" of his organization. On August 18 this desire was consummated when the Justice Department initiated an inquiry concerning the summer *Bundhavens,* and the *Chicago Times* dispatched undercover reporter John Metcalfe to join the Yorkville Nazis and write a series of articles detailing their activities.

Kuhn approved of maximum exposure for his organization, no matter what the context, but J. C. Fitting, an officer in the New Jersey branch, was much more sensitive. In September he wrote the *Literary Digest* to decry an earlier article referring to "the Nazis and their Camp Nordlund" and a picture depicting the American flag "trailing in the dust" beneath the swastika. Seeking to protect the American image of his organization, Fitting termed the picture "part of the unscrupulous campaign of slander" directed against American patriots. "We have pledged that this corruption shall never bring down our Stars and Stripes," he continued, "and fix in place of them the Hammer and Sickle. As a sign of a world fight against this pest, we honor the Swastika, never forgetting to honor more our own Stars and Stripes."

Some Nordlund campers said nothing at all about the Stars and Stripes; one such group constructed a rudimentary stovepipe cannon and "pointed" it at Representative Dickstein. A sign on the rusty weapon read: "Attention Mr. Dickstein and Other Snoopers—Nazi Munitions Camp—A. Krupp—

Made in Germany." It should also be noted that the ammunition to be shot from the cannon consisted of empty beer bottles—made, of course, in Germany.

While the harassment of the Bund continued, Kuhn turned his attention to United States foreign policy. Taking his copy directly from German sources, the *Bundesführer* explained at the outset that he would attempt merely to be "a good propagandist for Hitler" by explaining "the true facts that made him go National Socialist rather than Soviet Bolshevist." Because the President had rejected the Japanese warning against the real epidemic, communism, Kuhn termed Roosevelt's quarantine proposal the work of a madman. Placing himself squarely on the side of the Empire of the Rising Sun, the Bundist leader hoped that "in the interests of world peace" Japan would foil the "Judeo-Bolshevik powers without too serious sacrifice." In the meantime the United States should ignore "Bolshevized China."

Explaining in detail the probable motives that led the President to make his fateful announcement, Kuhn took as a basic premise the fact that Great Britain was the only country currently preparing for war, and that a secret alliance "probably" existed between the British and the United States. His second hypothesis, more clever than the first, was also more believable in light of growing anti-Japanese sentiment in the United States. When Japan invaded world markets with cheap goods—"clever imitations of standard brands of manufactured products"—she trespassed upon what theretofore had been a sacred preserve of English manufacturers. For this reason Japan had been singled out as a sacrificial lamb by certain economic interests in the United States and Britain. Roosevelt's speech in Chicago thus proved that Japan would "be crushed to save the English trader from going bankrupt."

Kuhn admitted that he was no intellectual giant but, like Pelley, always asserted that those persons who opposed him were "morons." Of this group, because of his geographical propinquity and unabashed hatred for Hitler, Mayor Fiorello La Guardia was the most despicable. In early September, therefore, with an eye on the upcoming New York mayoral elections, the Yorkville Nazi wrote in the *Free American* that "La Guardia must be defeated; he is the candidate of Browder's Communists, Louis Untermyer, and Rabbi Wise. . . . La Guardia allows Jew mobs to picket importers of German products and to burn German goods in the street."

Kuhn might have had kinder words for the city father, for two days before La Guardia's re-election the mayor decided to allow the Bund to stage a parade through Yorkville to the New York Hippodrome, where the organization would take part in "The Political Awakening of German Stock." Since the march would occur two days after the observance of "Anti-Nazi Week" in Manhattan, many observers believed that with passions at fever pitch the procession would end with Bund blood bubbling in the gutter.

His undisguised animosity toward Nazism notwithstanding, La Guardia acted from a characteristic sense of fair play in deciding that no legal reason existed to deny the Bundists their march. America remained a free country, he pointed out, in contrast to contemporary Germany, and to allow the parade to occur on schedule would provide an excellent way to illustrate this very point. La Guardia's adoption of a tactically impeccable position seemed to be vindicated when predictions of a "Lexington Avenue Massacre" did not materialize. If anything, the parade was an anticlimax. Giving the lie to the tabloid *Journal-American,* which in the best tradition of yellow journalism asserted that the march "ended in a riot," only 800 of the expected 2,000 Bundists appeared, and only half of these wore uniforms. In addition, the Nazi pretenders were outnumbered nearly two-to-one by police and detectives who watched the event, thus holding scuffles between "heilers" and "hissers" to a minimum.

Believing the best approach to the problem of domestic Nazism would be to let the Bundists "walk through a wall of silence," La Guardia had asked his supporters not to attend the parade, "even out of curiosity." This plan was at once sensible and impossible, as Americans not only love parades, they also relish side show freaks. It was not surprising, therefore, that the mayor's political opponents in Tammany Hall immediately branded him "a Nazi-lover" and released a flier charging that "Today La Guardia sold out to the Nazis." Speaking for the city's Jewish community, Judge Jonah J. Goldstein accused the city father of issuing the parade permit to get votes and called for his defeat: "La Guardia is a demagogue who with one hand plays on the heart strings of the Jews, and with the other issues a permit to Storm Troopers to goose-step from Yorkville to the Hippodrome."

La Guardia dismissed these allegations as part of a "whispering campaign hatched by fanatics and picked up by Tammany Hall," but as far as many American liberals were concerned, the Bund amounted to nothing less than a malignancy in the body politic. According to Samuel Untermyer, the organization constituted a definite Nazi conspiracy "now virtually admitted in speeches by members of the German cabinet." In an address to the Asbury Park branch of the Jewish War Veterans of the United States, he called for drastic legislation against this "band of alien Ku-Kluxers, meeting in secrecy, drilling and marching to the goose-step, bedecked in the military garb of the country they have abandoned." In a humorous footnote to the affair, the Reverend L. M. Birkhead announced plans to organize in Germany branches of his own group, the "Friends of Democracy," if he could secure permission from German Ambassador Hans Dieckhoff.

But for the moment the Bundists remained their own worst enemies. After the organization purchased 178 acres of land in the Kettletown section of Southbury, Connecticut, residents of the hamlet held a mass rally on November 23 and, avoiding "perfervid Americanism or patriotic enactments," decided simply to resist the Bund as a nuisance destructive of local property value. Employing terms such as "natural beauty," "pleasing aspects," and "historic character" to describe their community, city fathers created a zoning commission to prevent the Bundists from spoiling their rural placidity.

If the residents of Southbury met the Bund with "a solemn humor worthy of the state which once fashioned the wooden nutmeg," most Americans were not able to exhibit similar equanimity. Their vision affected by sombre shadows cast across the Atlantic by German Nazis, they were left with a view that made the Yorkville Nazis larger than life. That American policy makers also were growing increasingly fearful of the German resurgence was manifest on August 4, 1937, during the course of an important address in Norfolk by Ambassador William Dodd. Although he did not refer to Germany directly when he announced that the objective of some European powers was to frighten and even destroy democracy everywhere, his reference was clear. Soon afterwards, Secretary Hull attempted to assure Ambassador Dieckhoff that Dodd's hobbies were Jeffersonian Democracy and world peace and that on both subjects he was "somewhat insane." But when the downcast American diplomat resigned and returned to the United States in January 1938, he remained convinced that the world was on a collision course with catastrophe.

Dodd's despair was not the only factor complicating diplomatic relations between Washington and Berlin, for when Prentiss Gilbert, the American charge in the German capital, accepted an invitation to attend the Nazi Party Congress in Nuremberg, many Americans were outraged. Apparently approved by Hull as a measure that might improve relations, Gilbert's visit had the opposite effect. The American representative was somewhat more successful in October 1937, however, when he complained at length to Berlin about the activities of Germans in the United States. Although Washington did not blame Ernest Bohle's *Auslandsorganisation* for what was occurring in Yorkville, Gilbert reported that "the mere fact that it was believed in America that the German colonies there took orders from Germany made [Americans] nervous."

On October 11 the Foreign Ministry replied to Gilbert by again ordering "all German authorities [to] sever their connections with the Bund, and all German citizens [to] end their memberships." The Freytag Memorandum signified a reorientation of Reich policy concerning the Bund. The author of the document, together with Dieckhoff, recognized that although the withdrawal of German citizens would deal the group a mortal blow, Kuhn's worthies had become a definite liability on Berlin's book of accounts. To downplay the significance of the American Nazis, therefore, the Foreign Office announced a policy of re-emphasizing German cultural propaganda in the United States. The *Auslandsorganisation* and the *Volksdeutscher Mittelstelle* were notified to exclude the Bund in future dispatches, and Kuhn himself was directed to burn all previous correspondence from the *VM*. Because continued dealings with the group might stimulate a violent reaction—perhaps, in Dieckhoff's words, "even destroying the German element in the United States," Nazi leaders were instructed not to exert any kind of political influence upon their American imitators. Finally, in March 1938, concomitant with a public edict prohibiting German citizens from membership in the Bund, the Foreign Ministry informed Washington not only that the rule would be enforced strictly, but also that the Bundists would be prohibited from using the swastika in their ritual.

This news staggered *Bundesführer* Kuhn, who had traveled to Berlin the preceding February and had returned convinced, to the point of boasting, that Propaganda Minister Joseph Goebbels and Hermann Göring were among his closest supporters. Quickly he repeated his hegira to the Nazi capital and, upon arriving, remonstrated bitterly but to no avail with Hitler's close aide, Captain Fritz Wiedemann. Thus there was nothing to do but to return again to New York. Kuhn continued to boast that he remained an intimate of Adolf Hitler, but the words had an ashy taste to them. The Yorkville extremist was now on his own.

Interestingly enough, it was Kuhn's view of America and not that of the German diplomats that was nearly synonymous with Hitler's. In October 1937, after reading the document with "great interest," the Nazi chancellor transmitted to the Foreign Ministry a detailed memorandum entitled *"Roosevelt —Amerika—Eine Gefahr"* ("Roosevelt—America—A Danger"). The author of the memorandum, Hans von Rechenberg, was no stranger to the Ministry, having been fired from his post as its Hamburg director thirteen years before. Condemned as an originator of harebrained schemes, von Rechenberg subsequently migrated to Green Cove Springs, Florida, where he found work as a dairy farmer.

Written sometime in 1937, the Rechenberg Memorandum hypothesized that the New Deal marked "the fulfillment of the Communist Manifesto and the paving of the way for Communism in the United States," and that the Roosevelt era thus signified "the beginning of the final catastrophe for America." Extremists everywhere could applaud this thesis, but officials in the Foreign Ministry scorned it. Not only did the document fail to "add to the under- standing of America and Franklin D. Roosevelt," it amounted to "one-sided and unreliable propaganda." Contradicting Rechenberg's evidence, which purported to demonstrate exclusive Jewish control of American banking, Freytag, director of the American desk, indicated that this was patent nonsense and added that Roosevelt could not be held responsible for speeches made by public officials such as La Guardia. Ambassador Dieckhoff exhibited similar disdain for the document, warning that Germany had underestimated American strength in 1917 and that to do so again would be courting disaster.

The professionals in the Foreign Office indicated that the Rechenberg Memorandum ought to be ignored, but because they did not make German foreign policy their rational proposals went unheeded. Conversely and ironically—inasmuch as the American countersubversives had been making similar charges to the point of dreary redundancy—the document confirmed Hitler's belief that Judeo-Bolshevik cabalists indeed had seized control of the government in Washington.

While Fritz Kuhn continued to play the role of Hitler's American cousin, Representative Dickstein found it increasingly easy to generate support for his proposed investigation of domestic extremism. Himself the victim of fear that bordered on hysteria, the New York lawmaker spoke loudly and often of the threat posed by the Bund and other Nazi sympathizers. These emotional pleas again led Representative Maury Maverick to caution House colleagues against their tendency to fish for herring in times of crisis. Yet despite the Texas Democrat's warning that such an investigation might itself cause racial feeling by "wasting time on small minorities which are misguided and have no influence," the House approved the creation of an investigative committee in May 1938. Maverick became a prophet almost immediately as the new House Committee on Un-American Activities, chaired by Democrat Martin Dies of Texas, considered the internal communist conspiracy to be America's *bête noire* and consequently expanded fully three-quarters of its time inquiring into the activities of alleged agents of Moscow.

Much like the nationalistic jingoes of the troubled 1890s and the official vigilantes during the Red Scare of 1919–1920, the Dies Committee bore witness to an historical American tendency to attempt to discredit enemies of the Republic by categorizing them as un-American. In the present instance, however, the continuing American dialogue with and distrust of Marxian socialism, the liberal orientation (and, by implication, socialist appearance) of the New Deal, and the dearth of a national experience with anything that could be equated with contemporary Nazism, combined to determine the Committee's decision that domestic communism was by far the greatest menace.

Thus, a cruel joke had been played on Dickstein. Before the Committee had moved very far in its work, it attracted support from Father Coughlin, Pelley, and other Americans located in the Nazi rooting section. In addition, although critics termed the Committee "a three-ringed circus" and an "hysterical witch hunt," most Americans approved its purpose. This fact was not ignored by the extremists, who realized that praise of the organization might be translated into apparent respectability, a quality they clearly lacked. By September 1938, for example, Coughlin, who had cared little about the Committee at its inception, offered thanks to the group for revealing "what was going on" and, in fact, named Dies as *Social Justice*'s "Man of the Week," worthy of the applause of every "honest, America-loving, Red-hating U.S. citizen."

If the support the extremists lent the Committee's search for communist conspirators represented their attempt to secure public approbation, the tactical success of their effort was offset by its negative implications. The point was that in the five years preceding Pearl Harbor, most Americans considered Nazism and communism as two sides of the same totalitarian coin. In their conscious rejection of all Continental "isms," Americans deliberately articulated distorted similarities between the two ideologies, either ignoring outright their differences or obscuring them within a matrix of loosely drawn analogies. In the popular mind both Russia and Germany had succumbed to the "moral collapse" that threatened to engulf all Europe, a premise that prefigured isolationist Senator William A. Borah's metaphorical description of both "isms" as "jackals baying at the moon of constitutional government."

For many of the nation's leaders, as for the man in the street, the basic distinction between Nazism and communism lay in the different moustaches adorning Hitler and Joe Stalin. A choice between the two dictators was in reality an option between Satan and Lucifer. Itself a manifestation of augmented ideological conflict between Americanism and totalitarian ideology, the popularity of this strange but compelling sort of illogical logic suggested that the negative symbols and images which the Dies Committee derived from its investigation of communist infiltrators might also describe the domestic fascists. For this reason, in the long run, Coughlin, Pelley and Kuhn stood to suffer as a result of the Committee's work. Much as they would abhor the fact, had they indeed been capable of realizing it, the American supporters of Continental fascism would discover that the American people had placed them in the same ideological bullpen as their archenemies, the hated Bolsheviks.

By the end of 1937 public opinion was clear on two points: first, even after Japanese bombers sank the U.S.S. *Panay* on December .12, most Americans remained determined to avoid war; and second, their opposition to Nazism was equally staunch. These conflicting attitudes not only indicated the inner contradiction that later became the bane of respectable isolationism; they comprised the essential framework of the subsequent Great Debate on American foreign policy and thus substantiated Louis Hartz's observation that in a conflict of ideas, Americanism tends to become absolute, and that the process automatically "hampers creative action abroad by identifying the alien with the unintelligible, and inspires hysteria at home by generating the anxiety that unintelligible things produce."

The countersubversives represented one side of this anxiety, the majority of Americans the other. What had been a family quarrel before 1937 had now become an international conflict, and this fundamental change, in addition to transforming the inverted nativists into alien conspirators, endowed them with the very images and symbols they had employed to warn the nation against the Jewish-communist conspiracy in Washington. Contrary to their avowed roles as patriotic nationalists, the extremists suddenly discovered themselves on the other side of the fence, in the camp of the enemy.

This free, connotative association of demonic characteristics in the national mind provided an important reason why the extremists received more attention than they warranted. Their ostensible weakness, in fact, was clear to anyone who could discuss them without losing his temper or perspective. Numerically insignificant, supporters of Coughlin, Pelley, Kuhn, and myriad lesser "fascists" lacked the cohesion necessary to pose a threat to the Republic. In addition, there existed little chance that their leaders could submerge individual differences to join forces. Coughlin's Catholicism, for example, was anathema to the WASPs who supported Pelley, while the Bund's unabashed fealty to Germany proved unsettling to those alumni of the Ku Klux

Klan who had, after all, become "good American" Silver Shirts. In sum, from the outset of this crucial juncture in American diplomatic history, varied nativist themes operated at cross-purposes.

But just as they blurred distinctions between communism and Nazism, well-intentioned American opponents of Hitler and Stalin tended to minimize these weaknesses, and the sensational publicity accorded the extremists produced in the United States a popular image of a unified, Nazi fifth column. Thus, if the countersubversives exerted little, if any, direct pressure upon the course of the 1937 neutrality debates, their very presence on the fringes contributed to a deepening metaphorical crisis in German-American relations. In addition, in case of an external crisis that affected American national security more acutely than the "undeclared" Sino-Japanese War, the extremists could be counted on to play an important symbolic role in the foreign policy debate. The once-unified ranks of American isolationism showed signs of cracking, as several prominent liberals had identified American self-interest with the fate of European democracy. At the same time, a few conservative legislators in the isolationist ranks had taken to using rhetorical images quite similar to the language of the extremists. Of course, these solons abhorred the principles of Nazism in private conversation, but the time was fast approaching when they would have to make their feelings publicly explicit, lest internationalists equate their views with those promulgated by men like Pelley and Kuhn. There was no little irony here, for if the conspiratorial view of history that motivated the countersubversives seemed superficially consistent with the nation's isolationist tradition, their partisan support of European fascism and Japanese expansion placed them outside the mainstream of American separatism. Though they would have denied the fact, the extremists were from the beginning as "internationalist" in their thinking as the most ardent supporters of Western democracy.

On the eve of the new year a major task facing responsible isolationist spokesmen lay in the maintenance of sufficient distance between themselves and the extremists. Their success in this assignment would determine to a large extent their eventual ability to persuade the American people that their well-being indeed depended upon the continued ability to remain aloof from global troubles.

10

Father Coughlin's Patriotic Dilemma

★ ★ ★ As Americans pondered the implications of developments in Europe and the Far East, the extremists continued to insist that the danger to the United States came not from Germany or Japan, but from an insidious, internal conspiracy with headquarters in Washington, D.C. For Father Coughlin this belief held critical consequences during the two years preceding the outbreak of war on the Continent. The Royal Oak clergyman's creation of a "Christian Front" to combat the conspiracy and his emergence as an unabashed anti-Semite marked the final stage in his transition from an advocate of social reform into an outspoken opponent of global democracy. The priest's behavior during this period demonstrated that if he initiated his public career honestly professing a patriotic creed, by the end of 1939 he had become its prisoner.

This critical juncture in Coughlin's life mirrored a deeper crisis in American Catholicism. Because they were always located outside the historical mainstream of national political and social life, American Catholics had always exhibited extreme sensitivity to being termed anything but wholly devoted to the Republic. Since the 1880s, in fact, most Church leaders had attempted to erase this stigma by integrating their hyphenated congregations within the larger matrix of society. The hierarchy strove to convince Protestants that their fears of papal conspiracies were groundless and that Catholic immigrants and their descendants were loyal citizens. This program of Americanization helped unify ethnically diverse peoples and thus countered the institution's minority status and lessened the threat of bigotry. In addition, the desire to cast off the "ghetto mentality" of the outsider and to become assimilated within the national consensus produced numerous Catholic professions of devotion to enduring national traditions and values; undercut the forces of hyphenate nationalism during the First World War; and influenced the hierarchy's identification of Roman Catholicism with Americanism during the chauvinistic 1920s.

The Catholic quest for an American identity was interrupted by the Great Depression, which shattered secular optimism and left in the place of consensus a vacuum of doubt. As a result, a perceptive historian has written, "Catholic social thought during the 1930s was characterized by unanimous and enthusiastic approval of official Church teachings, and wide, often bitter, disagreement over their meaning and application." Not surprisingly, these years witnessed the emergence of parish priests like Father Coughlin, committed to endowing their religion with social meaning, and a laity that was deeply involved in domestic political questions. But the collapse of national consensus also confronted believers with a dilemma concerning the acceptable means that might be employed to rebuild the nation: would the faithful appropriate American or international sources for inspiration and support? The problem was articulated in 1931, when Pope Pius XI issued his encyclical, *Quadragesimo Anno*, which called for a fundamental confrontation between individual Catholics and their society. This, of course, was no problem for intellectuals such as Father John A. Ryan, Father James Gillis, and members of the editorial staffs of the *Catholic World, Catholic Worker,* and *America,* who accepted the premise of the document and generated within the Church a new spirit of inquiry that supplanted earlier, untested assumptions and reflex professions of faith in the Republic.

For many American Catholics, however, probably the majority, the explicit challenge of the encyclical was too fearsome because it augured the revival of anti-Catholic prejudice and the basic issue of national loyalty. Thus they sought refuge in the Royal Oak pastor's exaggerated nationalism and anticommunist rhetoric, while Church leaders and intellectuals debated the nature of the coming good society. In fact, Coughlin's militant anticommunism, which possessed clear and authoritative sanction both within the Church and the United States, amounted to nothing short of a psychological masterstroke that enabled him to minimize the tension between the two conflicting sources of Catholic authority—Vatican edicts on the one hand and the historical, national ethos on the other.

The priest's conspiratorial imagery, which allowed his followers to reconcile their external loyalty to the Pope with their loyalty to American nationalism, effectively guided many of the faithful through the uncertainties of the depression. But with the advent of serious diplomatic crises in Europe and the Far East, what had been his greatest asset became Father Coughlin's chief liability. With the signing of the Nazi-Soviet nonaggression pact in August 1939 and the outbreak of war shortly thereafter, the cleric suddenly found himself trapped on the wrong side of the gulf he had theretofore bridged so successfully.

In the main a victim of his own primitive rhetoric, Father Coughlin encountered his greatest difficulty at a time when the Church itself was adopting a pronouncedly militant, anticommunist position. Although a majority of the faithful, having benefited from New Deal reforms, retained Democratic loyalties and saw no reason to label Roosevelt a communist, let alone a "Jewish dupe," a large minority was severely critical of his attempts to liberalize the Supreme Court, reorganize the executive branch of government, and purge his party of renegade senators. Catholic critics of the administration feared that an excessive centralization of power in the executive would weaken their Constitutional protection against religious persecution.

The antipathy of the Church toward anything that smacked of un-Americanism also manifested the institution's insecurity amid augmented global strife, and it was this uncertainty, combined with the overriding national fear of being drawn into another world war, that suggested to the priest that he might again achieve marked success. Ironically, however, Father Coughlin became a casualty of the bitter propaganda war that he had helped initiate, a conflict that currently raged between American adversaries of Nazism and Catholic anticommunists.

This symbolic battle, in which the major weapons were allegations of unpatriotic feelings issued by both sides, illustrated a major tension in Catholic nationalism during the late 1930s, and it was this problem that eventually became one of the sources of Coughlin's downfall. In 1937 Father Wilfrid Parsons, a former editor of *Commonweal,* wrote that Continental analyses of European politics had become polarized in terms of fascism *vs.* communism, and warned that if a similar tendency developed in the United States, too vociferous an opposition to communism might land American Catholics within fascist ranks. Father Parsons' warning bore bitter fruit in 1938 and early 1939, as non-Catholic hostility toward the Church burgeoned. While Catholics generally remained in step with the national desire to maintain neutrality, many Church spokesmen offered reasons why fascism was preferable to atheistic, Soviet communism. By contradicting the prevailing American view that both versions of Continental totalitarianism were indistinguishable and similarly despicable, this Catholic view, though understandable, was problematic because it left the Church open to the charge, especially by liberal Protestants and academicians, of acting as an apologist for Nazism.

Had it not been for the signing of the Nazi-Soviet nonaggression pact ten days earlier, the eruption of general warfare in Europe would have made even more critical the Catholic inclination to distinguish between communism and fascism. As it was, by strengthening in the American mind the symbolic stereotype of "red fascism," the Molotov–von Ribbentrop Treaty terminated for the Church the troublesome need to differentiate between the two "isms" and also removed a foundation of Catholic isolationism—the fear that somehow the United States might become allied with the Soviet Union in a war against Nazi Germany.

In linking Berlin's fortunes with those of the Kremlin, the accord also placed Father Coughlin in an untenable position. Probably the most glandular anticommunist within the Church, the cleric had done more than his share to popularize the issue that now, paradoxically, threatened to destroy his patriotic pretensions. By implicitly linking an anticommunist position with antifascism, the Nazi-Soviet pact had the effect of turning his countersubversive rhetoric against him. Because even an apparent statement in favor of fascism now could be construed as approval of totalitarianism generally, patriotic American isolationism demanded explicit antipathy toward all totalitarian systems. But by the end of 1939 the evidence available to the American people indicated that the priest had adopted a diplomatic stance closely allied with Berlin's. In publishing excerpts from the discredited *Protocols of Zion,* and by proposing a militaristic solution, à la Franco, to national problems, Coughlin provoked a reaction which indicated that while Americans during the 1930s exhibited a new tolerance for cultural and religious diversity, they retained their distaste for persons suspected of harboring divided national loyalties.

It was, however, with renewed hope that the radio priest had renewed his broadcasts in January 1938. The New Deal seemed in danger of coming apart after President Roosevelt had been checkmated in his attempt to "pack" the Supreme Court and to bring peace to the battleground of labor-management relations. Now, seeking to reorganize the executive branch of government, the President drew the wrath of an increasingly truculent Congress. Conversely, although many critics argued that Coughlin had embraced fascism, by April sixty-three stations carried his radio perorations; *Social Justice* circulation figures approached 350,000; and, according to the *Detroit Times,* the response of more than 80,000 listeners to the cleric's plea to defeat the administration's Reorganization Bill constituted one of the greatest of his career.

After debating the idea for some time, Father Coughlin announced in April the formation of local groups of twenty-five persons who would dedicate themselves to studying the principles of social justice. In June he indicated that he awaited the moment when these "platoons" would become "a great thinking army that can swing our nation back to sanity and right-thinking." Taking his cue from Spain's rebel leader, Francisco Franco, the priest called for the creation of an organization to combat the Popular Front, a heterogeneous group of loosely allied American communists and liberal fellow travelers. "If there must be fronts," he wrote, "let us have the Christian Front."

For the moment the Christian Front lacked a clearly formulated program. In Father Coughlin's mind the group probably represented little more than a symbolic American bulwark against subversion. But there could be no doubt that it was the position of the United States vis-à-vis Europe that led the priest to make his suggestion, for the year 1938 was as much a watershed in Continental and Far Eastern affairs as it was in his own career. As he worked tirelessly to demonstrate that American involvement would be a monumental error, Coughlin dismissed Japanese aggression in China by comparing it with Great Britain's historic drive for empire. Americans, he believed, ought to pay more attention to Japan's slogan, "Asia for the Asiatics!" Later, attempting to excuse Nazi expansion, the cleric announced that he approved in spirit the Austrian Anschluss and the Munich Conference because they preserved world peace. Analyzing the latter agreement, he tempered his Anglophobia long enough to praise British Prime Minister Neville Chamberlain as "one of the most outstanding statesmen in the history of the British Empire."

Father Coughlin's diplomatic pronouncements again illustrated his tendency to apply selectively abstract religious and moral absolutes to complex and changing social and political conditions. Superficial at best, this method of argument was also dangerous as it tended to ignore the basic differences between ideal and real categories. The priest's failure to appreciate this dichotomy, in fact, led him in November to a new level of extremism. After his radio sermon of November 20 he was no longer merely an outspoken adversary of the administration; he seemed now to conform to the popular American stereotype of a Nazi anti-Semite.

Since July *Social Justice* had carried in serial form the *Protocols of the Learned Elders of Zion*. Although the priest expressed doubt as to whether the documents had in fact been written by the mythical Zionists, he considered the veracity of the *Protocols* to be an academic question. What was important, he assured readers in a twist of logic, was the corroboration by the *Protocols* of "very definite happenings which are occurring in our midst."

But on November 20 the cleric echoed Pelley and Kuhn—and Goebbels and Hitler—when he stated flatly that international communism stemmed from Jewish direction of the Russian Revolution of 1917, and that Nazism arose as a "defense mechanism" to prevent a similar episode in Germany. The American people, therefore, had to move swiftly not only to halt an international Jewish conspiracy to spread Bolshevism, but also to rescue "deluded" American Jews from their unscrupulous leaders. In another broadcast a week later Coughlin extracted excerpts from this sermon as he attempted to demonstrate that he was not an anti-Semite. His exegesis proved abortive, however, when a moment later he cited Irish priest Denis Fahey's "The Mystical Body of Christ in the Modern World," an article from a 1920 issue of the *American Hebrew,* and the *Protocols* to support his belief that "the Russian-Jewish Revolution, largely the outcome of Jewish thinking and of Jewish discontent, [would] figure in history as the overshadowing result of the world war."

These intemperate remarks, buttressed by the incredible allegation that the American banking firm of Kuhn, Loeb & Company had underwritten the Bolshevik victory, made Father Coughlin a subject of adoration for extremists at home and Nazis abroad. Ostensibly, the priest had become an Aryan supremacist, and according to the Berlin correspondent of the *New York Times,* his radio sermon had made him "the German hero in America." William Dudley Pelley, meanwhile, termed the broadcast "the prize Silver Shirt speech of the year," and the Bund's *Free American* paid tribute to the "heroic courage" displayed by the cleric, one of "the few outstanding Americans who has the courage of his convictions, and whom the Jews have not yet been able to intimidate."

By no means a racist in the same sense as were Nazi theorist Alfred Rosenberg, Propaganda Minister Goebbels, or, for that matter, William Pelley, Father Coughlin apparently adopted the theme of anti-Semitism as a pragmatic means to connect in the minds of his followers the twin evils of Bolshevism and high finance. Logically located at opposite ends of the philosophical spectrum, bankers and communists were now linked symbolically by the indisputable "fact" of their being Jewish. This allegation remained generally consistent with the basic negative thrust of the priest's earlier attempts to maintain America's sense of mission and innocence in a world quickly going to hell. His previous usage of the term "international banker" certainly had "Jewish" connotations, and it took but a short step to make explicit what he and many listeners had believed for some time. Because the virus of anti-Semitism was itself spreading throughout the country, the confused and power-hungry clergyman apparently anticipated, albeit erroneously, a backlash of unified opinion that would go to any extreme to avoid American participation in war. For Father Coughlin the espousal of anti-Semitism was not, as it would be for the Nazi leaders, or for Pelley or Kuhn (in their moments of grandiose delusion), an end in itself. Rather, the cleric's attack upon Jewish cabalists represented yet another of his groping attempts to augment his radio congregation.

Whether or not Father Coughlin occupied the same philosophical ground as Rosenberg and Goebbels, though, was a question that few Americans cared to ask. Less than a month earlier the Nazis had undertaken their most vicious campaign to date against German Jewry, a wanton crusade that culminated in a desecration of synagogues and other religious symbols. This event, known as "Crystal Night," pricked the American conscience and fanned the fires of indignation that greeted Coughlin's fateful sermon. With Archbishop Mooney remaining silent, no doubt fearing renewed controversy, the management of Station WMCA in New York, which originated the speech, washed its hands of the cleric and invited Professor Johann Smertenko of the Anti-Nazi League to refute his accusations. Alexander Kerensky, who led the Russian Provisional Government before the November Revolution, informed the *New York Times* that Coughlin's sermon was full of distortions and misinformation, especially the charge that twenty-four of twenty-five alleged fomentors of the uprising were Jewish. Another ill-fated participant, Leon Trotsky, concurred with Kerensky's statement, as did the editorial staff of the *American Hebrew* and the management of Kuhn, Loeb & Company.

In addition to generating a wave of fear in American Jewish circles, Coughlin's anti-Semitic outburst flabbergasted Catholic leaders who had recognized the need for good will and hope in a world scarred by hatred and were currently engaged in a quiet campaign to heal divisions within the Church. Immediately George Cardinal Mundelein of Chicago, President Roosevelt's closest friend among Catholic prelates, denied that the radio priest had the authority to speak for the Church. In further efforts to offset the cleric's remarks, the Reverend Maurice Sheehy of Catholic University called attention to the historic pro-Jewish policy of the Papacy, and Father John A. Ryan, writing in the liberal journal *Commonweal,* urged good Catholics not to join an avowed anti-Semitic campaign. A conservative Catholic, columnist Westbrook Pegler, termed the priest's bigotry particularly inappropriate because "Irish immigrants to this country were hated and persecuted for their religion and blood." The Reverend William C. Kernan, rector of Trinity Episcopal Church in Bayonne, New Jersey, called the sermon "the most dangerous threat to Christianity that we Christians have ever faced." Editorial writers in *Commonweal* and the *New Republic* pointed out that in his zeal the priest had become a fanatic.

The nearly unanimous, negative reaction of the Catholic hierarchy to Father Coughlin's calumny did not restrain the cleric's partisans. In fact, a subsequent decision by the management of WMCA to discontinue his sermons galvanized loyal Coughlinites into mounting a loud defense of their hero's right of free speech. This campaign reached its zenith at a dinner on December 15, arranged by Father Edward Lodge Curran, president of the International Catholic Truth Society and a sponsor of the anticommunist and mildly anti-Semitic *Brooklyn Tablet.* Staged under the auspices of the "Committee for the Defense of the American Constitution," the banquet featured Judge Herbert O'Brien, who praised Coughlin's earlier efforts in saving the nation from the World Court, the Court-packing scheme, and the Reorganization Bill. Following the speeches, the assemblage passed a unanimous resolution calling upon the Federal Communications Commission to revoke the license of Station WMCA. Three days later professional anti-Semite Allen Zoll led two thousand pickets to the steps of the WMCA building, and for the next nine months, noisy Coughlinites picketed the station, hoping, in Zoll's words, "to put WMCA out of business."

His adoption of anti-Semitism may have made Father Coughlin more controversial, but it did not immediately diminish his appeal. In January 1939 pollster George Gallup reported that during December the priest had maintained a listening audience of 13 million Americans over a forty-station network. Three and a half million persons listened regularly to his Sunday jeremiads, and two-thirds of this number approved what it heard. Most of Coughlin's followers, Gallup concluded, were city-dwelling members of the Democratic Party who were engaged in occupations placing them in lower-income brackets. These statistics, by convincing the priest that his powers of electronic persuasion remained strong, contributed to his decision to test his strength against the President's once again, this time concerning a crucial diplomatic issue.

Throughout 1938 Roosevelt had exhibited his dissatisfaction with the embargo clause that prohibited the shipment of all arms to warring nations, and in January 1939, he sought its repeal. "We have learned that when we deliberately try to legislate neutrality," he warned in his annual message, "our neutrality laws may operate unevenly and unfairly. We ought not to let that happen any more." Referring to an inflexibility that had already given succor to Italy, Nationalist Spain, and Japan, the President desired a new provision that would enable American policy makers to distinguish between aggressor nations and their adversaries.

The possibility of being drawn closer to the troubles besetting Europe and Asia dismayed American isolationists, so much so that liberal writers in the *New Republic* and *Nation* found themselves in substantial agreement with the reactionary publisher of the *Chicago Tribune,* Colonel Robert R. McCormick. One of the angriest voices in the antiadministration phalanx, however, emanated from Royal Oak. On January 15 Coughlin warned that the recent decision by the Senate Foreign Relations Committee to consider neutrality revision was but a last-ditch effort to aid communist forces in Spain, and, as the priest had done earlier, he implored his listeners to wire their senators not to tamper with neutrality. "The only way for America to keep out of war," he cried, "is to keep on keeping out of war, and this means not engaging in the sale of arms, munitions, and implements of war!" A day later, approximately one hundred thousand wires arrived on Capitol Hill, and Chairman Key Pittman's powerful committee bowed before the microphone messiah's apparent power shortly thereafter.

Pittman's discretion reflected the administration's caution in the face of overwhelming opposition to overseas commitments, yet Roosevelt still searched for a way to revise the neutrality law. While maintaining a public position that belied his ultimate goal, he spoke often of the terrible potential for global war, and his message was given added urgency in March when Germany absorbed Czechoslovakia.

As the "professor" in the White House proceeded with his patient yet persistent lecture on the subject of national security, Father Coughlin fought to prevent repeal of the embargo. But the priest's arguments, devoid of decency or perspective, proved that he had become a captive of his own imagination. Any war to aid the Jews, he reasoned, in Germany or elsewhere, was unthinkable, except perhaps in the minds of certain American "Jews" like William Bullitt and Henry Morgenthau. *Social Justice,* meanwhile, praised Mussolini for his concern with Italy's self-preservation, justified Germany's seizure of Czechoslovakia, and although critical of Hitler's treatment of German Catholics, named the *Führer* "Man of the Week."

Obviously Coughlin's remarks themselves were sufficient to make him a *bête noire.* But his abominable sense of timing also contributed to the opprobrium that surrounded him during the first quarter of 1939. George Gallup's statistics paled in significance as American supporters of European democracy embarked on a campaign to impugn the cleric's motives. Soon it became evident that although domestic opposition to administration foreign policy could be tolerated or even admired when conducted in a language Americans could understand, Coughlin's attacks, following closely his espousal of anti-Semitism at a time when German Jews were encountering Nazi terror, blurred in the national mind the fine line dividing the lawful right of dissent from slander and seditious libel. Thus the priest's enemies could find nothing to excuse his behavior, and the Catholic Church, historically defensive concerning its loyalty, now assumed the offensive in attempting to silence the clergyman.

Coughlin's extreme rhetoric so incensed Cardinal O'Connell of Boston and Cardinal Hayes of New York that both men informed the priest to stay away from their respective archdioceses. Archbishop Mooney manifested his displeasure by revoking his imprimatur, and after March *Social Justice* was published no longer "by permission of Father Coughlin's superior." Suggesting that the priest's diplomatic stance included a sense of mission only insofar as it supported passionately Nazi and Japanese foreign policy, the Reverend L. M. Birkhead of the Friends of Democracy emphasized the absence in the Royal Oak pastor's agenda of any appreciation for American history, the democratic process, and republican institutions. Alfred E. Smith, meanwhile, accused the cleric of bearing "false witness" to Americanism, while mystery writer Rex Stout was more forthright, stating his regret that he could not "take a gun and shoot the priest."

Other Americans of varied political and philosophical positions, including pacifist historian James T. Shotwell, New York priest Joseph N. Moody, and Walton E. Cole, a Unitarian minister in Toledo, also took exception to Father Coughlin's anti-Semitism, as did revisionist historian C. Hartley Grattan, who clearly recognized the necessity of distinguishing between his own isolationism and the priest's profascist disposition. Journalist Dorothy Thompson, an archenemy of Hitlerism, warned that the cleric's followers in New York had allied themselves with the German-American Bund; and even the United-Irish Republicans, American supporters of the terrorist Irish Republican Army, entered the verbal fray. When Coughlin attributed to Czech terrorists the responsibility for bombing six English cities, the leadership of the UIR denounced him and stated that, if necessary, the Irish would fight for full credit.

As the clergyman's opponents dragged Father Coughlin's name through the mud, President Roosevelt remained staunchly determined to place America's abundant resources at the disposal of those nations currently threatened by external aggression. In July, however, two months after proposing to remove the embargo, he discovered that senatorial isolationists still blocked his way. At a press conference following a crucial meeting at the White House, Senator William A. Borah of Idaho, the isolationist Lancelot, indicated that administration forces lacked the votes to secure repeal and predicted, moreover, that there would be no war in Europe "for some time." Accordingly, despite growing popular support for the President's position, Vice-President John

Nance Garner described the situation accurately with the terse remark, "That's all there is to it."

The administration's defeat on the embargo issue was a victory in disguise, because 123 solons who had voted for an arms embargo two years earlier now opposed the measure, a clear indication that the tide of isolationism was waning. But the retention of the embargo by Congress also afforded Adolf Hitler a chance to fulfill his ambition of negating militarily the clause in the Versailles Treaty that had created the "Polish Corridor" and made Danzig a free city. Although British and French leaders had signed a treaty in April 1939 guaranteeing Poland's territorial integrity, they failed to include in the negotiations, as they had at Munich, Joseph Stalin, who, having solidified his own power through a recent series of bloody purges, consequently commanded little respect and less trust in the West. This snub was duly noted in the Wilhelmstrasse, and on August 23 Hitler concluded with Stalin a treaty that was as earth-shaking as it was unexpected. The Nazi-Soviet nonaggression pact shocked American radicals and fellow travelers as much as it did Coughlin, William Dudley Pelley, and Fritz Kuhn; but at the same time the treaty confirmed the belief of most Americans that communism and Nazism were similarly evil and best avoided. In any case the effect of the agreement was soon manifest. Concerned no longer with the vulnerability of Germany's eastern frontier, the *Führer* readied his armies to attack Poland. On September 1 the *Wehrmacht* struck, and two days later, after futile appeals to Berlin, Britain and France retaliated by declaring war on Germany.

Four thousand miles across the Atlantic, after being awakened by a phone call from Ambassador William Bullitt in Paris, Roosevelt replied to the sad news: "It has come at last, God help us all." And within a few hours, most Americans had learned that for the second time in twenty-five years the lights had gone out in Europe.

In a fireside chat two days later, the President promised that as long as it lay within his power there would be "no blackout of peace in the United States." Yet while he issued the routine proclamation of neutrality on September 5, he realized that concerning the war most Americans would never adopt a spiritual impartiality. He himself considered the mandatory embargo potentially disastrous for Britain and France because the two nations were unprepared for war and the Polish army was proving itself totally mismatched. But the President could not act precipitately, for a frank revelation of his feelings would provide combustible ammunition for isolationists who perceived in Europe's upheavals no threat to American national security and who accepted a basic tenet of contemporary revisionist historiography that trickery alone would "get" the United States into war. The first priority in the mind of the Chief Executive, therefore, was to establish a national consensus that would approve his plan to transfer American power to the British and French. This was a delicate task, and to accomplish it Roosevelt turned to "the tricks of the fox to serve the purposes of the lion." While saying nothing specific about aiding the democracies, he sought to slow the Nazi juggernaut without destroying national unity. He would repeal the embargo, but the fateful step would be taken for the purpose of returning the nation to international law as a basis of its foreign policy.

In interpreting the President's oblique attack upon the sacrosanct isolationist principle of unilateralism in foreign affairs as a blatant attempt to maneuver the United States into war, Father Coughlin was substantially correct, albeit for the wrong reason. Because the radio priest assumed that German and Japanese policy in no way jeopardized the freedom and security of the United States, he could not comprehend the motivations underlying Roosevelt's intuitive, and as yet unarticulated belief that a Nazified Europe would pose a distinct threat to national safety. In fact, as historian Thomas A. Bailey suggested in his pioneering study of the impact of public opinion upon American diplomacy, the Chief Executive's repeated assurances that the administration wished to avoid war served a purpose similar to those of a physician, whose seriously ill patient had to be placed in a satisfactory state of mind before being informed of the gravity of his condition. Because Coughlin, no less than his fellow extremists, tended to see the hands of wicked men as determinants of all crucial events, he did not understand that it was not mendaciousness but, rather, a sense of urgent necessity that caused Roosevelt to proceed slowly and carefully in formulating the government's response to the European conflict. The President, to be sure, had become a Machiavellian statesman, but his cunning, born of good faith, illustrated his understanding of Samuel Eliot Morison's dictum that "the main object of foreign policy is not peace at any price, but the defense of the freedom and security of the nation."

Overly optimistic in assessing his own power, Father Coughlin reasoned that he occupied a strong position from which to fight repeal of the embargo. Although he boasted a record of having contributed to the defeat of three important New Deal measures, in his current endeavor he seemed to ignore the importance of several contrary signs. Since his blatant use of anti-Semitic propaganda, he had encountered adamant opposition from his immediate superior, Archbishop Mooney, and his national reputation had dipped to a new low, as reflected in the increasingly negative tone of the "Coughlin mail" sent the White House.   In addition, while testifying before the Dies Committee, Fritz Kuhn revealed with pride that the priest had been invited to several Bund meetings (he did not attend any), and that many Bundists were Irish- and Italian-Catholics who also supported the clergyman. Although Father Coughlin scorned the Bund and also attempted to separate himself from Gotham extremists like Joseph E. McWilliams of the Christian Mobilizers ("Joe McNazi" according to Walter Winchell), the priest's lack of success may be attributed to his own apostasy from his earlier principles, and to the outrageous activities of his organization, the aforementioned Christian Front. The combination of these two factors indisputably linked Coughlin's name with the menace of American Nazism and thus destroyed what effectiveness he might have had as a responsible spokesman for those Americans who opposed Roosevelt's diplomacy.

The Royal Oak pastor had called for the creation of a Christian Front more than a year earlier, and shortly before the WMCA affair in November 1938, such an organization appeared in New York. The following spring, under the leadership of John Cassidy, an arrogant law student who supported himself by working nights for Edison Electric, the group established its headquarters in the Manhattan rectory of the Paulist Fathers and moved quickly to enlist "all Christian citizens that are truly American in that necessary crusade against the anti-Christian forces of Red Revolution."

A hallmark of American extremists during the depression was their vagueness concerning the means through which the inequities of "the system" might be exorcised, but the young toughs of the Christian Front considered violence an end in itself and thus moved into the streets on random "guerrilla" missions. Of course, it was impossible to identify communists and internationalists solely by their physical characteristics, so the Fronters directed their hostility at Jewish-Americans. For New York's Jews, the Front was a nuisance if not a nightmare. The group was known by its program of parades, picketing, provocation, and the notorious *propagandamarsch,* a ploy which the Front initiated by stationing a group of men and a small child on a street corner. When the youngster spotted a Jew, he shouted suddenly: "That big Hebe hit me!" Immediately, the "innocent" bystanders would turn on the Jewish pedestrian, and an inevitable brawl would ensue.

Members of the Christian Front mounted soapboxes and hastily constructed platforms to harangue crowds that were certain to gather during humid summer and autumn evenings. Speakers made it a point to inform onlookers that the structures upon which they stood could be dismantled in ten seconds and their parts used for bludgeons. Angry denunciations of the Roosevelt foreign policy and world Jewry, and caustic references to "the lady in pink in Washington" and "Rosie Rosenfeld" split the night air. As disgusted spectators answered these self-avowed, countersubversive orators with rotten fruit, broken bottles, and rocks, Mayor Fiorello La Guardia, police officials, and concerned citizens discussed possible ways to prevent the discontented, usually unemployed, Irish-Catholic products of deprived backgrounds from turning Manhattan streets into battlegrounds.

The response to the Coughlinite guerrillas ranged from unequivocal dismay to humorous derision. Although the *New York Times* usually relegated reports of the incendiary gatherings to back pages, seeking to play down the issue, American Catholics, from George Cardinal Mundelein to former heavyweight champion Gene Tunney, termed the Front an outrage to decent citizens, while the St. Patrick's Council of the Knights of Columbus prohibited its members from joining the superpatriotic organization. Four young representatives of the Anti-Nazi League, meanwhile, ridiculed the Front when they appeared in Manhattan, wearing giant spectacles and carrying placards that stated, "Fight International Spectaclery!" and asked, "What is the Spectacle Menace?"   Also seeking to demonstrate the absurdity of Christian Front racial propaganda, an anonymous member of a Midwestern labor union offered the following doggerel:

> Are you scrapping with your wife
> So your in-laws give you strife?
> Are the bill collectors sore
> Is your job a doggone bore?
> Does your husband tend to guzzle
> Can't you solve that crossword puzzle?
> Here's the cure-all for the blues . . .
> Go out gunning for the Jews!
>
> Don't you like the county sheriff
> Do you want a higher tariff?
> Has the country a depression
> Or is it a mild recession?
> Did your party take a beating
> Do you retch from overeating?
> Don't your new shoes feel just right
> Is your corselette too tight?
> Did you blow another fuse?
> Sure, you guessed it, it's the Jews!

In July Mayor La Guardia moved to end the midsummer's excesses by dispatching details of from six to twenty-five patrolmen to each street conclave. Precluded from enjoining the anti-Semitic orators from speaking by a Constitutional guaranty of free speech, the embattled city father denied a charge by journalist James Wechsler that he was partial to the troublemakers and informed New York magistrates of an obscure municipal law that forbade the abuse of racial groups. By late October New York police had preferred charges against 238 rabble-rousers and had gained convictions in 101 cases. As two undercover agents wrote confidentially a month later, anti-Semitism in New York had been "reduced to a point no longer constituting an acute problem."

But while they continued, the pavement atrocities of the Christian Front accelerated the decline of Coughlin's reputation. For one thing, in addition to the men and women who joined the group because they believed in the priest's cause, the organization also attracted Bundists, Christian Mobilizers, Crusaders for Americanism, and sundry other self-proclaimed, antisubversive patriots. For another, the leader of the extremist American Nationalist Confederation, George Deatherage, announced in a widely publicized remark that even if the cleric could not become "the American Man on Horseback" (because of his Catholicism), he was still "a great, great American." With support being offered the clergyman by such individuals as these, it was not coincidental that at a general gathering of American anti-Semites in New York in May the name "Coughlin" drew resounding cheers every time it was mentioned.

Unwittingly, the priest had created a monster over which he could exert little control. At times embarrassed by the Christian Front, he never clarified the nature of his relationship with the group. The result was much confusion concerning his true position. In a radio sermon on July 30, for example, Coughlin admitted that criticism of the Front was well-founded and claimed to have had no role in fomenting incidents attributed to the group. Yet at the same time he added that the organization was prepared to solve the communist problem in America "in the Franco Way if necessary, with bullets instead of ballots." A day later, furthermore, a banner headline in *Social Justice* proclaimed, "CHRISTIAN FRONT CARRIES FIGHT INTO MORE STATES!" The accompanying article praised "the highly organized, rapidly growing, militant Christian Front" and its leader, John Cassidy. In an interview with Edward Doherty of *Liberty* magazine the cleric emphasized his admiration for "the average Jew," while admitting that the latter had been placed in jeopardy by his guilty leaders.

If the Royal Oak pastor acted at times like Mr. Hyde, he behaved at others like Dr. Jekyll. Four days after the *Liberty* interview he ordered New York *Social Justice* salesmen to cancel an impending anticommunist rally when it appeared that a concomitant, antifascist rally might spark violence. And in November, Coughlin even seemed to have resumed his first public role as an independent, humanitarian statesman when he publicly returned a check sent him by Joe McWilliams's Christian Mobilizers. Under no circumstances, Coughlin explained, would he be "tied indefensibly with the Mobilizers, and thence with the Nazi Bund." But in the American mind this is exactly what had happened. The priest's popular image had become that of a fascist, though this identification did not prove that he was an evil person; rather, it demonstrated that both as a tactician and strategist he had finally shown himself to be abysmally incompetent.

The latter criticism, obviously, could not be made of the troubled statesman in the White House, who in the month after the outbreak of war had accelerated his deliberate program of convincing the American people that their national defensive frontier extended into Western Europe. Summoning a special session of Congress, President Roosevelt hid his desire to extend to Britain and France as much aid as possible behind the statement that his sole wish was to stay out of war. In fact, the Chief Executive seemed to suggest that the munitions ban itself threatened peace, but it appeared more likely that he actually sought some sort of halfway agreement in which isolationists would accept his suggestion to repeal the embargo in exchange for a provision forbidding American vessels to enter designated "danger zones." Congressional opponents demurred on the grounds that the demand for repeal had come, in the words of Senator Borah, "from the warhounds in Europe." But the President's policy, a mixture of intervention and isolation, juxtaposed well with the current national temper. While desiring to abstain from the conflagration, most Americans nonetheless favored aiding the democracies to withstand totalitarianism. Consequently, after a bitter debate that reached across the land, Roosevelt achieved success. The Fourth Neutrality Law of November 4, heralding a significant reorientation of American diplomacy, lifted the embargo, renewed cash-and-carry, established danger zones for American vessels, restricted loans to warring nations, and prohibited American citizens from traveling on belligerent ships.

In view of his outrages during the preceding year, Father Coughlin's attempt to influence the neutrality debate could only be futile. Attempting once again to influence opinion by remote control, he argued that no principles were involved in the war, that the conflict was simply military competition between the respective forces of international capitalism and anticapitalism. To remove the munitions ban would thrust the nation into "a most unjust and un-Christian conflict which will only benefit international communism." Only a united America could resist being seduced by the warmongers in Washington, the cleric warned in a subsequent editorial in *Social Justice:* "Keep the arms embargo, keep neutrality, keep America out of war and the war out of America. Let America adhere even more strictly than ever to the policy of George Washington."

Yet antiadministration forces could not unite under a single banner. The war had caught most Americans psychologically unprepared, and it was this unpreparedness, more than any other single factor, that facilitated the administration's successful assault upon existing neutrality legislation. In fact, the two months following the German invasion of Poland were marked by the emergence of numerous antiwar and noninterventionist spokesmen and organizations, whose positions represented conflicting and sometimes antithetical points of view. In debating the best means with which to counter Rooseveltian diplomacy, these individuals and groups often discovered that their concern to avoid war and the American extremists were the only themes that unified them.

The editor of the *Nation,* for example, Oswald Garrison Villard, clearly hoped to avoid a recurrence of the Progressive nightmare of 1917 when he wrote appreciatively of America's historic mission and begged the President to avoid "the great power politics game in Europe." Quakers and pacifist organizations such as the War Resisters' League, *Pax,* the Fellowship of Reconciliation, and the New History Society also opposed repeal on principle, and leaders from these groups made it clear that under no circumstances would they join with "Machiavellian thinkers" like the radio priest, who, according to the *Conscientious Objector,* fought administration policy not because he loved peace, but because he sympathized with Nazi Germany.

From another angle of vision, Colonel McCormick of the *Chicago Tribune,* perhaps the most avid Roosevelt-hater in the entire country, found evidence in administration rhetoric that the Chief Executive had become a dictator who would not hesitate to destroy American democracy by engaging the nation in war. News analyst Boake Carter agreed with McCormick, displaying contempt for citizens who feared a possible Nazi invasion of the United States, and pointing out that even should Britain fall, America would remain an impregnable fortress. "Before making the world safe for democracy," he wrote in concluding a current best-seller, "we had better make democracy safe for the world."

McCormick and Carter personified the new stridency that characterized noninterventionist rhetoric, but even they seemed reticent when compared with thousands of American women who emerged suddenly as the most vocal advocates of maintaining the embargo. As Catherine Curtiss, national director of the Women's National Committee to Keep U.S. Out of War, informed Congress on October 3, never before had American women "been so aroused and determined to keep their country out of war." The ladies could not agree upon a precise program to counter administration policy, but they made noise and received much publicity. Dancer-playwright-aviatrix Laura Ingalls, for instance, "bombed" the White House with leaflets accusing "international money changers" of being responsible for the current crisis; Mrs. Pauline Revere Auerhamer, a descendant of the American patriot, began recruiting women for a march on Washington; members of the well-known Gold Star Mothers of the World, meeting in New York, passed a resolution against "sending our sons and grandsons overseas to fight and possibly die in this and any future war"; and the unrelated "Mothers of America" actually invaded the Capitol, denouncing supporters of repeal as "Jew lovers" shortly before the final vote.

Amid the highly emotional rhetoric employed by these and other antiwar and noninterventionist spokesmen and spokeswomen, therefore, the angry voice of Father Coughlin was not so much stilled as lost in an unorchestrated cacophony. Having occupied center stage in the anti-Roosevelt chorus for an extended period of time, the radio priest discovered during the neutrality debates of 1939 not only that his views were less newsworthy than before, but also that it had become exceedingly difficult to generate the excitement that had provided him personal sustenance throughout his earlier public endeavors. In short, 1939 was not 1935, and while the cleric definitely contributed to a tenfold increase in the volume of senatorial mail in September, American lawmakers no longer seemed to take him seriously.

In contrast, the American Catholic hierarchy and most noninterventionists could not dismiss the cleric so quickly. That Coughlin had become a pariah within the Church was stated unequivocally by the Reverend Maurice Sheehy of Catholic University during the latter's discussion of "The Challenge of Nihilism" on a national radio network. The views held by the Royal Oak pastor, Sheehy indicated, were shared by only a small group of Catholic malcontents, and although the Church had adopted no official position concerning the war, nine of ten American Catholics could be counted upon to support administration policy.

For the great majority of noninterventionist Americans, finally, the important task of saving the nation from war had just commenced, and this fact alone made problematic Father Coughlin's very presence at the fringes of the diplomatic debate. Because the priest's name was now synonymous with anti-Semitism and linked inextricably with the Christian Front, that presence was tantamount to a trump card available to the administration, to be played when the occasion warranted. At the conclusion of 1939 the time for concrete official action had not yet arrived, but within the respectable antiadministration camp there existed nonetheless a pervasive sense of unease, wrought by the realization that what Father Coughlin was currently saying was less important than what both sides in the foreign policy debate were saying about him. Moreover, any possibility of thwarting Roosevelt's policies depended upon the maintenance of an undeniable claim to untainted, patriotic motives. Yet with "friends" like Coughlin, Pelley, and Kuhn lending unsolicited aid to the cause, responsible noninterventionist spokesmen did not really need enemies.

11

Roosevelt's Unwitting Allies

★ ★ ★ Father Coughlin's decision to ascribe to an unseen Judeo-Bolshevik conspiracy responsibility for America's growing involvement in world affairs backfired with the initial advance of German Panzers into Poland. His dissenting views on United States foreign policy appeared to comprise part of a fascist-communist plot to lull the American people into acquiescing not only in Hitler's quest for *Lebensraum,* but also in whatever expansionist plans Joseph Stalin might have formulated. Long accused of being a Nazi sympathizer, the clergyman now discovered that many citizens also considered him an apologist for the Soviet Union.

While the Nazi-Soviet accord and the German attack made Coughlin's position more precarious, the outbreak of war held dire consequences for William Dudley Pelley and Fritz Kuhn. Publishing material sent him directly from Nazi propaganda agencies and thereby violating the terms of his suspended sentence of 1935, the Silver Shirt leader dropped from sight, led authorities on a frenzied chase, and then abruptly reappeared and disbanded his patriotic organization after explaining that the group had become superfluous in light of the splendid work of the House Un-American Activities Committee. Kuhn, meanwhile, the Yorkville *Bundesführer,* was jailed after Committee investigators and New York police discovered that among other things he had been helping himself to his organization's treasury.

The ignominy surrounding Pelley and Kuhn, like the opprobrium that smothered Father Coughlin, was a manifestation of the current crisis in German-American relations. By generating the fear that the United States might become involved in war, heightened tension between Berlin and Washington rendered comically counterproductive attempts by the two superpatriots to maintain their status. Striving to prove their devotion to American national-ism, the two men became instead flesh-and-blood antitheses of the very values and traditions they believed themselves to embody. Nevertheless, although their hysteria made it impossible for the two nativist-extremists to affect greatly the larger foreign policy debate, their activities and arguments com-prised an unsolicited and even more undesirable legacy for those responsible isolationists spokesmen to whom the yahoos were remotely, if at all related. Despite their protests to the contrary, Pelley and Kuhn were by early 1940 widely regarded as proponents of subversive ideas. And it was this popular view that eventually resulted in the two men becoming, even more than Fa-ther Coughlin, unwitting allies of the Roosevelt administration's slowly evolv-ing plan to identify all isolationists with the external forces threatening na-tional security.

Had Pelley been as acute an observer of American politics as he claimed to be in his published works, he might have taken advantage of the turmoil that wracked Europe to achieve the eminence he so coveted during the pre-ceding decade. The diplomatic and military success of Continental totalitari-anism, combined with President Roosevelt's assault upon the Constitution, had revived fears that dictatorial government might also emerge in the United States. So it was not surprising that by 1939 many of the subversive images that served the psychological needs of frustrated Americans during the Red Scare of 1919–1920 again assumed marked importance. As illustrated by a slowly rising rate of anti-Semitism, a noticeable increase in one-hundred-per-cent Americanism, and a reaction against the ethnic pluralism and cultural diversity of the New Deal, national unity and self-confidence had been se-verely shaken by coinciding external and internal problems.

Superficially at least, the Silver Legion seemed to profit from these circum-stances, for by September 1939 membership rolls carried over 5,000 names, and more than fifty national posts were again in operation. Sales of the four Silver Shirt "primers," the *Protocols, No More Hunger, The Hidden Empire,* and *The World Hoax,* were brisk, as was the circulation of pamphlets, avail-able from P.O. Box 1776, Asheville. These tracts continued to tell American patriots what they needed to know: *Dies' Political Posse* indicated that the Texas Democrat sought to make himself "a second Roosevelt," while *Our Se-cret Political Police* attempted to shatter the prestige of J. Edgar Hoover by revealing "what the American people think of the FBI." In *Jews Say So!* Pel-ley cited quotations from the Old Testament to prove once more the existence of a global conspiracy, a thesis he also stressed in *Is the United States Ruled by an Invisible Government?*

In view of his professed ability to see into the future, the self-styled mystic was somewhat embarrassed by Germany's advance into Poland. Two months earlier he had offered readers of *Liberation* "thirteen reasons why no war in Europe will occur this year," adding that there were actually closer to 150 reasons why "the Jews, through Roosevelt, Chamberlain, and Daladier cannot get a war going." But, of course, the issue suddenly became clear. Excusing his earlier myopia, Pelley scorned Americans who sympathized with the luckless Poles, announced that "the world's Israelites" finally had "their war against Hitler," and concluded that their attempt "to eliminate Nazism" would have momentous consequences. The European conflict, he concluded, amounted to nothing less than "the major struggle to test whether Judah shall dominate the world's future affairs unchallenged."

Immediately offering his moral support to the isolationist cause, Pelley warned Americans to avoid terming the conflict a "second world war," as such a designation could only give aid and comfort to "Semitic internationalists working overtime to see that it becomes such." Rather, the time had come for patriotic citizens to close ranks against a warhawk conspiracy dominated by "Jewish internationalists" in Congress, "trade-union dupes," and the "New Deal crackpot in Washington." Translating his fear into verse, the Silver Shirt commander composed "The Doughboy Blues," a ditty that described not only the reason why America would go to war, but also the song her soldiers would sing:

> *O haven't you heard the news?*
> *We're at war to save the Jews;*
> *For a hundred years they pressed our pants,*
> *Now we must die for them in France!*
>
> *So we sing the Doughboy Blues—*
> *It's a hellova fate to choose,*
> *To die to save the Jews;*
> *But the New Deal busted and left us flat,*
> *So this war was hatched by the Democrat,*
> *To end our New Deal Blues.*

But the final battle between patriotic America and the monster of Judah was not to be. Pelley's march toward Armageddon was hindered by the cumulative effect of his appeals to hatred and violence, prophecies of calamity, and stories of American impotence. Like the sorcerer's apprentice and Pandora, he had set free a demon that ultimately became his master. His anti-Semitism, unlike the sophisticated analysis of perhaps the only consistently intellectual American fascist, Lawrence Dennis, was built not upon a positive ideology but a group of interchangeable scapegoats that reflected not so much his own ideas as the hatred and anxiety of his followers. As such, Silver Shirt propaganda was designed not to convert potential followers, but to confirm the self-respect and individual worth of WASP anti-Semites, a majority of whom were already located within extremist ranks and felt threatened by the menace of diversity inherent in the New Deal's version of an open society. For these Gentile poor, the administration's hesitant yet deliberate movement in the direction of diplomatic involvement portended a global extension of the domestic quest for a pluralist society, and thus contradicted the nation's time-honored policy of aloofness from the immoral power politics of the Continent.

In a warped way William Dudley Pelley was lamenting the end of American innocence. In light of the fundamental goodness of her people, the nation would succumb to the blandishments of the English and French diplomatic establishment only through the skulduggery of self-serving, hypocritical leaders, whose control of national communications would enable them, together with representatives of the Judeo-Bolshevik cabal, to brainwash the unsuspecting populace. The strength of this argument, of course, lay in its simplicity. To the typical Silver Shirt, whose knowledge of foreign affairs was abysmal in the first place, the existence of an American *deus* or—in this case—*diabolus ex machina,* made understandable events that otherwise would have been beyond comprehension.

In fact, if the group was motivated to a large extent by real fears of the dislocations that war would bring to America, it often seemed that the Silver Legion was more a state of mind than a formal organization existing in the real world. Its members, who were probably more fatalistic than their leader, appeared to have faith in nothing save the inevitability of catastrophe. Rationally unable to face their own problems of status, let alone the diplomatic crisis now threatening the neutrality of the United States, the Silver Shirts preferred to minimize the tension wrought by their own suspicions and frustrations by taking it out on the Jewish communists, "in the mood of a man who, being afraid to stand up to his wife in a domestic argument, relieves his feelings by kicking the cat." By limiting the terms of the foreign policy debate to the workings of an omniscient domestic conspiracy, moreover, and even here keeping things on a symbolic level, Pelley and his supporters rendered unnecessary the need to confront directly the implications of the global events unfolding around them. Taking their cue from local, rather than cosmopolitan traditions and values, the Silver Legioneers reflected in microcosm the fears of a small-town America that had ultimately lost its bearings in a world of complexity and change.

These anxieties, which were manifested collectively in a countersubversive style of politics, were increasingly interpreted as evidence of the subversive intent of the organization. A report in May 1938, for example, that Silver Shirt commandos planned to assassinate President Roosevelt could not be confirmed but was nonetheless accorded page-two treatment by the *New York Times.* On two other occasions Martin Dies publicly condemned Pelley, once charging that a direct link existed between Asheville and Berlin, and later asserting that the Silver Legion commander ranked as "the greatest purveyor of hate in the country." In addition, the countersubversive group itself did little to enhance its public image. Touring the country in September and October, National Field Marshal Roy Zachary urged his audiences to stockpile ammunition in their homes. "They used bullets instead of ballots in Spain! When the time comes, the Silver Shirts will use guns, not votes, here in America!"

Incendiary statements like Zachary's received undue publicity, and it was understandable that by 1939 the pseudopatriotism of the Silver Legion had become for many Americans as distasteful as current Nazi anti-Semitism. Himself the recipient of several threats, Pelley sought protection from Asheville Police Chief C. W. Dermid; but shortly before midnight on March 10, as the Silver Shirt leader worked in his office, several "youthful Jewish hood-lums" (who else?) interrupted his labor by hurling rotten tomatoes against the façade of the building.

More than anything else, it was the tone of the propaganda emanating from Silver Shirt headquarters that proved most obnoxious to American opponents of Hitler. Designed to appeal to the basest of human passions, Pelley's journalism exhibited more than mere bad taste; indeed, *Liberation* was by 1939 an inflammatory compound of bigotry, innuendo, slander, and character assassination. In all fairness, most anti-Semitic hate sheets of this era could not match Pelley's craftsmanship and imagination, but his adversaries could not be certain whether his political pornography was designed only to stimulate the fantasies of individual anti-Semites (sitting in their bathrooms, with the door locked?), or, conversely, to serve as a clarion call for collective action against the established order. In this era of fear the choice was simple: the Asheville extremist appeared to be mimicking exactly the gospel of Aryan supremacy and consequently, it was the latter view that prevailed.

If the pursuit of subversive agents thus became for the Silver Legion an increasingly dangerous pastime, Pelley himself made things worse during the spring and summer when he leveled two new charges against the Roosevelt administration. Characteristically, the stories in which these allegations appeared dealt not with foreign affairs, per se, but with imagined manifestations of the omnipresent conspiracy. The most controversial article appeared under the headline "CRIPPLES MONEY!" and intimated that "reputable old-line Demos" had withdrawn support from annual Presidential Balls to raise funds for the National Foundation for Infantile Paralysis because the proceeds from this "racket" went directly into the Chief Executive's bank account where they were classed as "birthday gifts from the nation."

To Martin Dies the story was more appalling than Pelley's apologetics for Hitler, while another member of the House Committee on Un-American Activities, Representative Jerry Voorhis of California, also believed that it was high time to call the Asheville yahoo to the witness stand. Responding to these and other pressures, FBI Director J. Edgar Hoover dispatched special agents R. L. Morgan and J. B. Brown to Asheville to investigate Silver Shirt activities.

As the two federal investigators initiated their quest, Pelley was stepping up his crusade against communist infiltration. Accompanied by Miss Alice Lee Jemison, a representative of the extremist "American Indian Federation," he toured the Cherokee reservation located on the border separating North Carolina and Tennessee and returned to Asheville charging that New Dealers were fomenting communism among the Indians. Such an accusation, of course, was as absurd as linking the Kremlin with the Cincinnati Reds baseball team; the Cherokee were undoubtedly more "communistic" than any communists could ever be. Yet within the pages of *Liberation* and a specially prepared pamphlet entitled *Indians Aren't Red!* the Silver Shirt theoretician indicated in remarkable prose that the President sought outright "to instill

Communism among Indian Tribes," or "so outrage them that they would become natural allies of the Reds in case of a revolutionary showdown." The evidence? Elementary: in creating the Great Smoky Mountain National Park, the Interior Department had routed the Blue Ridge Parkway so adroitly that it was now, in Pelley's words, "the backbone of the entire plot to Sovietize these Indians into a model community for indoctrinating touring America with Communism."

Despite, or perhaps because of its absurdity, this allegation touched a sensitive chord. On August 20, in fact, Representative Zebulon Weaver of North Carolina went so far as to propose a full congressional investigation of charges that Pelley had interrupted the peaceful status of the local Cherokee reservation. Weaver, emphasizing that the inhabitants of western North Carolina had lived for decades in harmony with their Indian neighbors, did not wish to see "that fellow spreading doubt in their minds regarding who their friends are." Representative Noah Mason of Illinois and John Collier, United States Indian Commissioner, agreed with Weaver's sentiments, and after Collier's office concluded its analysis, the commissioner assured the North Carolinian that few Cherokee had ever heard about, let alone read, *Indians Aren't Red!* Yet if the affair ended without profit on the American side of the Atlantic, Pelley scored an unexpected victory when his pamphlet was subsequently appropriated by German-American Bundists, who sent it to Berlin where Nazi propagandists used it to demonstrate how the American government persecuted its minorities.

If, as Pelley indicated, the "great spirit" was displeased with Roosevelt's Indian policy, the grand sachem of the House Un-American Activities Committee was most unhappy with the commander of the Silver Legion. A vain man who was perhaps a bit too proud of his own efforts in protecting America against subversive ideas and agents, Martin Dies had encountered bitter opposition from liberals within the Democratic Party who, themselves the target of Committee criticism, had attempted to thwart the group by linking its anticommunist animus with the countersubversive campaign launched by the extremists. Thus far, Dies's enemies had proved unable to pin anything specific on their powerful adversary, so it was with no little glee that they greeted an embarrassing revelation on August 23. Six days after the Committee began public hearings into Silver Shirt activities, and the same day on which the Nazi-Soviet pact was concluded, Frazier Gardner, a resident of Washington, D.C., who had applied for a research position with the Committee, was exposed as Pelley's undercover agent.

Although testifying that he was not aware of the connection between Skyland Press and the Silver Shirt leader, Gardner admitted under cross-examination that for the previous six months he had received fifty dollars a week from the printing establishment. Dies was understandably piqued. Declaring that Gardner was part of a Silver Shirt conspiracy "to sabotage our work," the conservative Texas Democrat called agent Robert Barker to the witness stand, and on August 28 and 29 Pelley's financial manipulations, his publishing ventures, and, most important, his connection with various German propaganda agencies became a matter of public record. Now there could be no doubt that *Liberation* served as a Nazi transmission belt. Pelley's files, Barker asserted, bulged with materials sent him by the *Deutscher Fichte-Bund, Weltdienst,* and the *Volkischer Beobachter.* Citing passages from several Legion publications demonstrating that Pelley had plagiarized in spirit and fact from such Nazi theorists as Theodore Kessemeier, Alfred Rosenberg, and Robert Ley, Dies Committee counsel Rhea Whitley concluded that it was quite understandable that many Germans considered the Silver Shirt leader their American hero.

On August 29 the Committee terminated its investigation of Silver Shirt activities. Chairman Dies, while characterizing Pelley as "nothing more than a racketeer," believed nonetheless that he held sufficient evidence to indict the Asheville extremist as an unregistered agent of the Berlin government. To gain further information, therefore, Dies issued a subpoena to bring Pelley before the investigative body. But when sheriff's deputies arrived at Pelley's Asheville home, they found only a collection of rain-soaked, unopened letters; for good reason the Committee's prized quarry had dropped from sight.

Aggrieved by aspersions concerning his character, Pelley had attempted to secure an injunction against the subpoena on the grounds that the Committee's investigations were "theatrical and high-handed." His petition denied, he then filed a three-million-dollar libel suit against the tribunal for suggesting that his publications were un-American. Realizing that if he returned to Asheville he risked extradition to the nation's capital, on October 19 he also became a fugitive from North Carolina justice, when Judge Zeb Nettles, dismayed by Pelley's "unpatriotic propaganda and practices," ordered his arrest for violating the conditions of his suspended sentence of 1935. Hours later, with the goateed extremist conspicuously absent, police officers raided his headquarters and confiscated his ample files. On October 20, after special agent Barker returned to Asheville in an unsuccessful attempt to discover Pelley's whereabouts, it was clear that the Legion commander had for once decided that discretion superseded valor.

A headline in the *Washington Times-Herald* on October 29 indicated that Pelley had been captured, but Asheville authorities and spokesmen for the Dies Committee declined comment. A week later Asheville police circulated the following "wanted" poster to law-enforcement branches throughout the forty-eight states:

> William Dudley Pelley; 50 years appr.; 5–7, 130; black-gray hair; penetrating dark gray eyes; straight Roman nose and heavy eyebrows; wearing moustache and Van Dyke beard; nose glasses; distant looking, highly educated, good talker, interested in psychic research.

To describe Pelley was one thing; to capture him, quite another. Several residents of Asheville claimed to have seen him, and at various times he was reported in Washington, Texas, Michigan, and Massachusetts. He also seemed to be in constant touch with his publishers, as *Liberation* appeared at regular intervals, and the journal's style remained his. Indeed, Chairman Dies and Judge Nettles might well have wondered if their nemesis had not entered the spirit world of which he claimed to be a part. On November 3, a day before he planned to sell the Silver Shirt publisher's printing equipment to satisfy a tax lien, Asheville assessor William Swain mysteriously received a check to cover Pelley's delinquency during 1938 and 1939. Then, as Asheville police notified New York officials to double their vigilance, an editorial in the *Anti-Nazi Bulletin* hinted that "the man with the goatee" was hiding in the Black Hills of South Dakota, "the scene of many a cattle-rustler's hideout." Gossip columnist Walter Winchell added his voice to the growing clamor, reporting that Pelley had shaved his goatee, dyed his hair, and was in Yorkville, "in need of a physician to treat his fear and shock." Toward these and other rumors an editorial writer in the *Raleigh News and Observer* had one answer: "This *Fuehrer* business has ruined a pretty good magazine writer and created a first-class nuisance."

Were it not for a bizarre incident on Capitol Hill in January 1940, Pelley might never have appeared before the Dies Committee. On January 22, angered by the proclivity of Committee members to hunt for communists within the New Deal community, Representative Frank Hook of Michigan, a liberal Democrat, entered in the *Congressional Record Appendix* correspondence purporting to establish the existence of an understanding between the Silver Shirt commander and Chairman Dies. A week later, after a number of prominent American clergymen, educators, and civic leaders called for a full-scale inquiry, the Committee dropped its own bombshell when Dies announced that David Mayne, a Washington publicist and occasional associate of Pelley's, had admitted forging the correspondence to embarrass the investigative body.

As both sides traded angry charges, Representative Clare Hoffman of Michigan, a vociferous opponent of administration foreign policy, attempted to expunge the fabrications, but Hook refused, demurring until he could read a forthcoming Justice Department report on the matter. And, amid the uproar, there appeared a strangely familiar face. His goatee replaced by a growth of two-days' stubble, William Dudley Pelley had returned to confront his accusers and clear his name and that of his organization. Claiming that he had planned to return to Washington for some time, he explained his procrastination as a result of disgust at being "classed in the same investigative bullpen as Fritz Kuhn and Earl Browder." He had, he informed the Dies Committee, quietly gone about his business until the proper time arrived for an appearance that "properly conserved the dignity of the Legion of Silver Shirts." This remark, of course, was consistent with Pelley's general air of braggadocio; but a more pragmatic reason for his delayed appearance was that the statute of limitations on his suspended sentence would expire in twelve days. He was ready to testify, but would the Committee be kind enough to detain him until February 18?

For four days, from February 7 to 10, Pelley eagerly answered questions relating to his career as a countersubversive. Immediately it was apparent that he had changed his tune. Apologizing for his past indiscretions and denying any knowledge of the Gardner and Mayne affairs, he now expressed only admiration for the Dies Committee. In fact, as he told Acting Chairman Joe Starnes of Alabama, his countersubversive organization had itself become unnecessary. The Silver Legion had been founded "to propagandize exactly the same principles that Mr. Dies and this Committee are engaged in right now; in other words, antagonism to subversive influences in the United States."

This *volte-face* meant neither that Pelley had abandoned anti-Semitism nor that he embraced democracy. The Judeo-Bolshevik menace remained great; democracy was "the rule of the mob." Responding to a question asked by Representative J. Parnell Thomas of New Jersey, the Silver Shirt commander admitted that he felt "exactly the same as the Nazi Party in Germany in regard to the Jewish element in our population." When interrogated by Representative Voorhis, he stated that of every three Jews with whom he was acquainted, one was a communist. In another exchange, as Starnes criticized his "frequent praise, defense, and emulation of Hitler," Pelley shouted, "Right!" in a stentorian voice.

In an editorial that contrasted Pelley's current praise of the Committee with his earlier criticism, a writer for the *Asheville Citizen* explained that the tribunal "had looked upon him as an ogre of national dimensions, but for reasons satisfactory to himself, Pelley concluded it wise to deal with the Committee more in suavity than in contumacy. The members of the Committee will do well not to trust this Greek even when he comes bearing gifts."

The tribunal, to be sure, did not appreciate Pelley's sudden support. Itself accused of fascist proclivities by many American liberals, the Committee had a difficult time cleansing itself of the stigma left by Asheville's most notorious resident. As authorities stood ready to make their arrest, Starnes glared at Pelley: "You have frankly and unblushingly engaged in praise of Hitler; you have identified the purpose of your Legion with the Nazi Party; and the menace you speak of in defending yourself is largely the creature of your imagination. The record is clear. The Committee is through with you."

But Pelley had the last word, loudly reiterating his promise to disband the Silver Shirts because the Committee had rendered the organization unnecessary. Then, as police moved in, Starnes looked up from his desk, ordered the sergeant at arms to clear the chamber, and asked: "How can we wash our hands of this fellow?"

To this question an historian of anti-Semitism might well have answered, *"Es Vet Gornisht Helffin"* ("Nothing helps"). Indeed, Committee members had learned that all their logic could not prevail against the illogic of a confirmed anti-Semite whose belief cut like a sword through complex historical abstractions. With Pelley's appearance before the Dies Committee, the Silver Legion of America passed into oblivion. Yet the group's pro-Nazi activities brought into clearer focus the moral issue that loomed beneath the surface of the growing debate on American foreign policy. Many citizens who might otherwise have remained convinced that the war in Europe could not possibly affect the country's safety saw firsthand the obscenity of secular anti-Semitism as patterned on the Nazi model. In America Jews were guaranteed religious and civil liberty, and Pelley's assertion that their lives were worthless—a suggestion later carried to a horrible extreme in Germany—strengthened American resolve to aid England and France in resisting totalitarian aggression.

Pelley's attempt to join his name with that of an investigative body that commanded the respect of a majority of Americans reflected in microcosm the urgency with which the extremists now hastened to disguise their un-American inclinations. Nowhere was this endeavor so noticeable, or so absurd, as it was with Fritz Kuhn and his German-American Bundists during the six months preceding the initial German drive across Polish borders.

The date was February 20, 1939, and the scene a familiar one. Yorkville's Nazis had gathered to celebrate George Washington's Birthday, and for a short while Madison Square Garden took on the appearance of the Berlin *Sports-Palast*. An audience of more than 22,000 persons, many of them elderly, gazed on a huge portrait of the Father of his Country flanked by placards that read: "Wake Up America—Smash Jewish-Communism!" and "Stop Jewish Domination of Christian America!" Squads of uniformed *Ordnungsdienst,* sober and purposeful, paraded through the building, clicking their heels loudly on the cement floor. As approximately 10,000 persons outside the edifice protested the grotesque birthday party, a succession of speakers mounted the platform amid tumultuous applause. National Secretary James Wheeler-Hill denounced Roosevelt and Harold Ickes. George Froebose, leader of the Midwestern section, reviled "these confounded Jewish agitators, these CIO racketeers, these Barney Baruchs and Henry Morgenthau Juniors!" Guest speaker S. G. Van Bosse, a Philadelphia Lutheran minister, denounced the "internationalist serpents of intrigue" in Washington, and in a fitting denouement, predicted that "if Washington were alive today, he would be a friend of Adolf Hitler, just as he was of Frederick the Great."

As the celebration continued, Isadore Greenbaum, an unemployed plumber's helper, suddenly rushed to the platform as Fritz Kuhn railed against the subversive intent of Jewish-Americans. Screaming that he was not a communist, Greenbaum sprinted past startled guards to within six feet of the platform. Then, as the storm troopers pummeled him, police, disgusted onlookers, and Bundists joined in a general melee. When the battle subsided, Greenbaum stood proudly, *sans* shirt and pants, a scene that proved so provoking to New York theatregoers that newsreel shots had to be recalled.

Meanwhile, columnist Dorothy Thompson, wife of novelist Sinclair Lewis, was ejected from the press box for laughing too loudly at the scene unfolding before her. German citizens, she observed, listened complacently when Hitler made similar appeals to hatred, and she noted the absurdity of allowing the Bundists free speech, when she herself did not enjoy the right of free laughter.

The Bund's ostentatious obeisance to the symbol of George Washington, upon whose authority the organization justified its hatred of the democracy of the New Deal, did not improve German-American relations. Where Hitler and the professionals in the Foreign Ministry often spoke of the critical need to maintain calm on the American front, Kuhn and his cohorts, acting, he said, as American-Germans and not German-Americans, stirred a cauldron of hatred and contempt. Referring to the celebration, a writer for *Life* explained that "it was almost as difficult for an American to keep cool in the face of this display as it would be if—with exactly similar manners—a guest in the house were to scrawl obscenities on his walls and publicly proclaim his wife a trollop."

Although some Americans possessed sufficient perspective to agree with Senator Sheridan Downey of California, who defended La Guardia's decision to allow the rally and remarked that such meetings would amount to a lot less "if the opponents of Hitler would just ignore them," most people agreed with an editorial in the *New York World-Telegram* that asserted bluntly, "The more we see, the less we want."

For the first time in their respective careers, Father Coughlin and Herbert Hoover joined voices to deprecate the gathering. Residents of St. Louis and San Diego turned out to heckle Bund speakers at local Washington commemorations; the Council Against Intolerance in America sponsored a rally in protest against the Bundist appropriation of the first President; in Portland, Oregon, more than 1,200 newly naturalized citizens cheered Governor C. A. Sprague's admonition that "we want no half-loyal citizens here." Finally, Professor Percy Bridgman of Harvard announced that he had barred visitors from totalitarian nations from entering his classroom.

Indeed, for many individuals the time had come to stand up and be counted in the anti-Nazi phalanx. Representative John A. Martin of Colorado received resounding, bipartisan cheers from his colleagues when he stated that every person who sympathized with the mass meeting was a traitor. Senator John Bankhead of Alabama suggested concentration camps as a proper antidote to "these spreaders of un-American propaganda." A correspondent of Senator Key Pittman was despondent. "When I see in the press," he wrote, "that the leaders of this organization brazenly stood up and compared Hitler to Washington, it is time to decide whether Hitler and his propagandists shall run America, or Americans operating America for Americans." New York Justice Salvatore A. Cotillo made the same point in a radio speech, while a writer in the *Christian Century* wondered, "Must we permit our civil liberties to be used to destroy our democracy?" According to Dr. Guy Shipler, editor of the *Churchman,* the rally could well have dropped "the bomb that awakened America to a genuine and sinister threat."

The tone of much of this rhetoric was perhaps overly alarmist, but it was already a time for alarm. An historically vigilant people since Paul Revere's famous ride through the streets of Boston, or so they liked to believe, the American populace was, rather, more like a bear in hibernation, slow to awaken, but once aroused, a nasty beast with which to contend. And by 1939 the Bund's challenge to national unity had itself generated a substantial backlash. Angered most by the idea of aliens trespassing on that ritualistic preserve that symbolically united Elks in Decorah, Iowa, with Veterans of Foreign Wars in Brooklyn and Girl Scouts in Albuquerque, many American adversaries of German totalitarianism could no longer tolerate the Bund's schizophrenic nationalism. Reflecting this growing spirit of intolerance, the *Nation,* a journal that prided itself on its liberalism, offered a most illiberal remedy for the virus of domestic Nazism. Until the realization of "genuine economic democracy," at which time groups like the Bund would disappear from the fringes of American politics, the organization ought to be denied police protection, its members prohibited from wearing uniforms, and its "private army," the *Ordnungsdienst,* outlawed.

In proposing that constitutional guarantees of free speech and equal protection under law be denied the Bundists, the *Nation* epitomized the feelings of a growing number of Americans who had had enough of tolerance. Quite clearly, the significance of the Bund's observance of Washington's Birthday was its untimeliness in the context of German-American relations. The Reich's annexation of Austria, the conclusion of the Munich agreement, augmented anti-Semitism, and the simultaneous recall in November 1938 of German and American ambassadors had created in the United States a climate of fear and uncertainty that was itself exacerbated by concomitant litigation concerning the *Kingsland* and *Black Tom* incidents during the First World War. Not surprisingly then, national concern with the domestic Nazis had burgeoned to the point where the Wilhelmstrasse felt it necessary to inform Ambassador Hans Dieckhoff that in boasting of his friendly relations with Goebbels and Göring, "Herr Kuhn has—already on other occasions —consciously deviated from the truth in order to strengthen his position with his adherents."

Although Kuhn may have grown in stature with his sycophants, the professionals in the German Foreign Ministry worried lest the sensational publicity being accorded the Bund further darken the image of Germany in the American mind. In January 1939 this fear was heightened when the Dies Committee's initial report reached Congress. According to the Texas Democrat, evidence uncovered by his tribunal indicated that "unless checked immediately, an American Nazi force may cause great unrest and serious repercussions in the United States." Taking Fritz Kuhn's boasts at face value, the document established the existence of an alliance between the Bund and other extremist groups; discovered a direct line that connected Yorkville and Berlin; emphasized the training of German-American youth along the Nazi model; and suggested the probability that the Bundists were stockpiling arms for future use.

In addition to convincing the House of Representatives to appropriate funds to continue the investigation, the Dies Committee Report, itself the product of some very naive thinking by men who also prided themselves on their vigilance against potential subversion, illustrated the kind of publicity that resulted in the Bund's being perceived not as a noisy yet inconsequential group of hyphenated malcontents, but as a dangerous and well-organized Nazi fifth column. As a force in deteriorating German-American relations, it was this stereotyped illusion, not the less exciting reality, to which most Americans reacted.

Of course the Bundists themselves reveled in this adverse publicity, seeing in it a metaphorical platform from which to vent their displeasure with the Roosevelt administration's plan to repeal the embargo. Now very much in the limelight, they became, to the consternation of the diplomats in Berlin, even more hysterical in their denunciation of American policy makers. By September Bund publicists had prepared the faithful for the expected attempt by Jewish communists in Washington and London "to push us into war." The United States had reached the brink of disaster by allowing inferior races to immigrate freely, and the time had come to put an end to this dangerous practice:

> Oh Abie sails over the ocean;
> Und Izzy sails over the sea
> So the shrine of each patriot's devotion
> Has to take in the damned refugee!

> Go back, go back!
> Back where you came from across the sea!
> Go back, go back!
> And leave my own country to me!

> On each ocean liner they're coming
> By steerage and cabin and "first"!
> Great Britain and France get the best ones
> And send Uncle Sammy the worst!

> So Abie vill open a hock shop
> To lend Christian saps their own dough;
> Und Izzy should sell "high kless klothink"
> Then send off to Poland for Moe!

> My friends, there's no time like the present;
> We should have got wise long ago,
> Let's slam the door NOW in the faces
> Of Abie—und Izzy—und Moe!

With the actual outbreak of war Fritz Kuhn accepted fully the German claim that conflict began when Polish units attacked Gleiwitz, miles within the German border. At a rally in Sellersville; Pennsylvania on September 3, he further developed his position. The *Bundesführer* had proved unable to explain coherently the Nazi-Soviet pact, but now he was certain that it was Franklin Roosevelt's "fine political hand" that now guided the destinies of London and Paris. Denouncing Winston Churchill as the most despicable of world leaders (save FDR), Kuhn next interpreted the detention of the German liner *Bremen* by American officials as an unfriendly act, and then explained the sinking of the U.S.S. *Athenia* as yet another example of British machinations designed to drive the United States to war.

On September 14 Bund publicists declared their own war on the forces seeking repeal of the embargo. The *Free American,* seeking to alert readers to "the discredited, lying British atrocity propaganda which got us into the last war," charged that "the hate mongers of the radio press" did not understand that the war was "the direct and unavoidable consequence of the madness of Versailles." If approved, the pending neutrality measure would grant the President numerous "arbitrary, dictatorial powers"; the United States would head "straight for war on the side of England"; and American boys would "be slaughtered for Jewish shylocks and profiteers in the munitions trade."

In establishing itself as a bulwark against these possibilities, the Bund claimed to possess patriotic spirit and resolve: "The German element in the United States is as American as ANY OTHER and is not taking a back seat; this is our country, and it will not be made an appendage of the British Empire while we can help it."   But the notorious organization was powerless to affect events directly and was delighted to support more respectable American politicians and public figures who also sought to maintain a stringent neutrality. Among these individuals, none was so warmly applauded as Charles A. Lindbergh, whose praise of the German Luftwaffe, acceptance of honorary membership in the Order of Merit of the German Eagle, and association with Dr. Alexis Carrel, a racist French physician, had already made him a controversial international figure.

Emerging from self-imposed obscurity on September 15, the famed flier became a usable hero for the Bund, Coughlin, Pelley, and other extremists. Their anti-Semitism had stigmatized their reputations; Lindbergh's record was clean. Alone he had flown the Atlantic and thus, according to a peculiarly American tradition, was considered well qualified to analyze for public edification all kinds of important subjects. The hero had turned his back on the United States after the brutal kidnap-murder of his infant son, but his reappearance in 1939 reflected his deep concern with the state of world affairs. To the diplomatic debate he brought a naive, conspiratorial theory of historical causation, a curiously parochial vision of American mission, a strong belief in the superiority of Aryan peoples, and an abiding Anglophobia. But he also carried with him his reputation, and it was this force that the extremists, trapped like hitchhikers in an arid desert, hoped to ride to an oasis of respectability.

From their promontory on the political fringe the yahoos cheered as Lindbergh warned against an onslaught of British propaganda and stressed the need to ask "who owns and who influences the newspapers, the news pictures, and the radio stations?" Concerning the European conflagration itself, he argued that because no moral questions were at issue, sentiment and pity were irrelevant in determining American policy. "These wars are not wars in which our civilization is defending itself against some Asiatic intruder," he explained. "This is simply one more of those age-old struggles within our own family of nations." Thus the real challenge facing American policy makers was to remain aloof from the Continental madness while erecting "a western wall of race and arms which can hold back either Ghengis Khan or the infiltration of inferior blood."

Lindbergh's apparent espousal of pan-Germanic ideals earned for him the enmity of a large segment of the liberal press, but at least for the moment, as the incarnation of the American success ethic, he was protected against the implications of his words. The same thing could not be said of Fritz Kuhn and his cohorts who, until they packed Madison Square Garden in February, had impressed most observers as Dutch comics. Now, however, with the populace frightened by the uncertain state of international politics, the Bundists became a collective incarnation of antidemocratic values and were therefore subject to the wrath of the very forces with which they had identified in seeking to increase their mass support—the traditions, virtues, and laws of the United States.

The demise of Fritz Kuhn as an American *Führer* began in May, when reports of income tax evasion by one of his aides led Mayor La Guardia to initiate an investigation. Shortly thereafter, noticing a discrepancy between Bund books and bank accounts, District Attorney Thomas E. Dewey, already gaining a reputation as a mortal enemy of New York criminals, subpoenaed Kuhn and James Wheeler-Hill to testify before a grand jury. But the American Nazi leader refused to appear. He had encountered troubles with the law before, but only for disorderly conduct and unpaid traffic citations. This time the stakes were higher.

On May 25, under the careful surveillance of three New York City detectives, Kuhn and several aides left their Manhattan headquarters, their car heavily laden with luggage. After a frantic chase that ended when the *Bundesführer* stopped for gasoline in Krumsville, Pennsylvania, he and his associates were placed under arrest. Four hours earlier a New York County grand jury had indicted the Nazi pretender on twelve counts of grand larceny. In Dewey's words, the indictment demonstrated that Kuhn was "just a common thief"—but what a thief! He was charged with, among other things, absconding with nearly $9,000 from receipts garnered at the Washington's Birthday rally, $4,424 from funds collected to defend six Long Island Bundists convicted of violating New York's civil rights law, $565 to move the furniture of a blonde divorcée, Mrs. Florence ("Mein") Kemp of Los Angeles, to Manhattan, $151 to move the same furniture to Cleveland, $500 from proceeds set aside to reimburse a Bund lawyer, and finally, with falsifying records to cover his activities. Confronted with these charges, Kuhn denied guilt, explaining that he governed his organization according to the *Führerprinzip* that guided Nazi Germany and, after being set free on $5,000 bail, he departed for a speaking engagement in Milwaukee.

According to the *Nation,* Kuhn's arrest should have surprised only the innocent, and no one was shocked two months later when he again ran afoul of the law in Webster, Massachusetts. On July 20, after he and Russian National Fascist, "Count" Anastase Vonsiatsky, stumbled out of a local tavern and into the arms of waiting gendarmes, he pleaded guilty to charges of public drunkenness and profanity. Savoring the opportunity to incarcerate such a notorious personality, Webster Police Chief John Templeman remarked of the Yorkville yahoo, "He was just another wise guy who thought this was a hick town and that he could stage one of those beer-hall putsch things and be the dictator in it."

On August 16 Kuhn made his debut before the Dies Committee, and for two days he generated much heat but little new information concerning his organization's activities. The high point of his appearance occurred in an exchange with Representative Starnes of Alabama. After a good deal of verbal sparring, during which time the conservative Southern Democrat grew visibly tired of Kuhn's pomposity, Starnes asked his adversary if he proposed to establish a Nazi regime in the United States. Glaring at his interrogator, the *Bundesführer* shouted, "That's an absolute lie—a flat lie!" Immediately, his fists clenched, Starnes leapt forward toward Kuhn, and according to newsmen covering the scene, only the fortuitous intervention of Capitol Hill police prevented fisticuffs between the two self-styled, countersubversive patriots.

More damaging revelations came from Miss Helen Vooros, who fled the organization after members made "numerous wanton and unsuccessful advances" upon her at meetings. After describing "bundling" under the swastika, the excitable young woman concluded, "That's what they call pure. It disgusted me." Whether or not she realized it, Miss Vooros's remarks related directly to Kuhn as well as his subordinates. In addition to stealing and drinking to excess, the Yorkville extremist loved neither wisely nor well. Married and the father of two children, he was currently engaged in a torrid love affair with the aforementioned "Mein" Kemp. Although his love letters were marred by misspelled words and grammatical errors, the missives demonstrated that his interest in Mrs. Kemp was more than platonic.

Because Kuhn's testimony before the House Un-American Activities Committee had been sprinkled with contradictions, Chairman Dies announced on September 25 that he would seek the extremist's arrest for perjury and for failing to register as a German agent. Four days later, amid rumors that Kuhn, still free on bail awaiting trial in New York, would flee the country, a New York judge raised his collateral security to a prohibitive $50,000. Subsequently jailed in the famous New York prison known as the Tombs, Kuhn awaited eventual conviction on charges of larceny and forgery. His career as an American patriot having ended in ignominy, it was not surprising that Bund publicists accorded scant attention to the embargo issue after mid-September. Instead they related the tragic saga of their leader, a victim (of course) of "the desperate, international, hate-blinded Jew and his political slaves." On December 7, ironically, the *Bundesführer* marched off to Sing Sing to begin a five-year term, and the *Free American* lamented the fate of this "prisoner of war." What the journal failed to add was that with Kuhn's departure, the Bund had finally secured the title it deserved all along—the "Blunderbund."

To judge by the degree to which the patriotic pretenses of the extremists had been marred during 1938 and 1939, Hitler's diplomatic and military victories had succeeded in focusing public attention on the inverted nativists more directly than the preceding domestic crisis. Indeed, their vocabulary of countersubversion was now synonymous with the rhetoric of subversion. This transformation was portentous, for by narrowing the symbolic framework in which the diplomatic debate could occur, it contributed to a moral climate in which the patriotic motives of more respectable anti-interventionist spokesmen might also be tarnished by allegations of disloyalty to the Republic. To the credit of most national lawmakers, extremist propaganda that reached Capitol Hill during the embargo debate was generally dismissed as the work of "well intended though sadly misinformed individuals and organizations" that had "ignored, twisted, or misrepresented the facts." But other legislators had adopted a countersubversive semantical style that, when taken to an extreme, appeared to come directly from the text of the discredited yahoos.

Representative Hamilton Fish of New York, for example, co-chairman of the National Keep America Out of War Committee, exemplified the fear that conspiracies hatched in Washington and London would drag the United States into war. As "the world's last repository of representative government," he argued, the American people would do well to resist forces that "would involve us 'to save democracy' (we did that once before); 'to crush dictatorships' (by establishing them here); even 'to safeguard our neutrality' (by violating it)." Representative Clare Hoffman of Michigan was similarly convinced that "this administration and the Communists within its ranks, and its Communistic allies, are hamstringing the program for national defense." In fact, Hoffman concluded, the situation had become so desperate that "these New Deal pressure boys" now advocated "the overthrow of the Government of the United States by force."

But the most vehement speech during the embargo debate was one delivered by Representative John Rankin, the eccentric Mississippi Democrat, on November 3, the day before repeal. Explaining that the *Congressional Record* was "about the only free press left open through which messages could be transmitted uncensored to the American people," he unwittingly embraced both ends of modern anti-Semitism—joining the devil of capitalism with the devil of Bolshevism—as he insinuated that all voices would be silenced if a certain internationalist element, composed of communists, international financiers, and munitions makers, were able to secure removal of the arms embargo. Attempting to separate himself from the ranks of the extremists, Rankin also denied membership in "the Brown Shirts, Black Shirts, or the Silver Shirts." To prove, on the contrary, that he wore "a common white shirt, made in Mississippi," he praised the Dies Committee and, in words that might easily have appeared in Pelley's *Liberation* or Coughlin's *Social Justice,* predicted that its members would soon discover that "the elements in collusion with Moscow were financed by the smug international agitators in Wall Street who got rich out of the World War and who are now financing the propaganda to get us in the present conflict."

A similar emotionalism also inflamed the rhetoric of several isolationists in the Senate. Here, too, there were indications that supposedly responsible lawmakers were more concerned with internal conspiracies than diplomatic realities. Denying that Nazi Germany threatened the well-being of the American people, these solons instead turned to other issues. Senator Robert R. ("Bob") Reynolds of North Carolina, whose constituency included Asheville, founded his own countersubversive organization, the "American Vindicators," to protect citizens from foreign ideology and foreign war. Believing that repeal would place the United States in a position of "financing the world," he argued that England and France wished only to make good their war debts in refugees who in turn would take jobs away from native-born Americans. Senator Rush D. Holt of West Virginia, meanwhile, warned that the propaganda "for which England has always been famous," had become "a termite within America trying to break down American foreign policy." Another outspoken adversary of the administration, Senator Ernest Lundeen of Minnesota, resolved that the needle on the compass of American diplomacy should forever point to the "North Star" established in Washington's Farewell Address, lest subversives draw the country into war.

That comparable rhetoric also appeared in *Social Justice, Liberation,* and the *Free American* should not suggest that these and other isolationist spokesmen were located in the extremist camp; yet the similarities between the imagery employed by the yahoos and that used by several militant noninterventionists on Capitol Hill was the portent of a storm that would ultimately swamp all opposition to the Roosevelt foreign policy. Indicative of what lay ahead, on October 26, during the course of an address to the *New York Herald Tribune* Forum, the President offered backhanded gratitude to the countersubversives for allowing Americans to realize "the value of the democratic middle course," and to distinguish truth from falsehood, "no matter how often that falsehood is iterated or reiterated."   Looking for chinks in the armor of their respectable noninterventionist adversaries, the Chief Executive, members of the administration, and other ardent friends of European democracy had discovered a weakness. The fight to extend aid to Britain and France might indeed be won on the battleground of patriotism; and here, as the extremists had learned already, antisubversive activity sanctioned by the liberal establishment (and three centuries of accumulated history), could be far more effective than their own countersubversion, directed, as it were, from the bottom up.

12

Nineteen-forty-one: Lend-Lease, America First, and the Tragedy of Charles Lindbergh

★ ★ ★ By 1941, as a result of their own lack of restraint and the critical situation in Europe, the extremists' influence had reached its lowest point. The attack upon "brave little Finland" by the Soviet Union in December 1939, the invasion of Norway and Denmark by German armies four months later, and the fall of France in June hit the American people with the force of a jackhammer. European totalitarianism now appeared to threaten the existence of Great Britain and, in the minds of American interventionists, the national security of the United States.

Although most Americans might have supported a program of aid to the British, President Roosevelt still found it expedient to explain carefully his diplomatic course, insisting that it would not lead the nation into war. The Chief Executive was convinced that Germany menaced the Western Hemisphere, but he also realized that because noninterventionist sentiment remained pronounced, he could not lead a divided country into anything approaching a military alliance with London. To act effectively, he reasoned, the American people first had to understand both the danger posed by Nazi Germany and the necessity of accepting great risk and probable sacrifice in defending American security. However, his foreign policy already had been labeled militaristic by pacifists such as Oswald Garrison Villard and Norman

Thomas, and it was therefore not surprising that a certain deviousness marked his path toward an unprecedented third term in the White House. Since his famous "I hate war!" speech at Chautauqua in 1936, he had in fact been veering toward an increasingly internationalist position. Still, his explanation of the epochal destroyer-bases deal with the British as merely as extension of his Good Neighbor Policy and his promise to American parents that under no circumstances would their boys be sent to battle were necessarily equivocal. His approach, often interpreted as a sign of irresolution or even mendaciousness, was rather a manifestation of his oft-repeated desire to avoid any "irrevocable act" that might destroy the effectiveness of future policy.

Following his decisive victory over Wendell Willkie, the President shook the American people when he announced in a fireside chat that he would never approve a negotiated peace in Europe and, moreover, that the United States faced her gravest danger since Jamestown and Plymouth Rock. As German armies stood poised to invade Bulgaria and flames engulfed sections of London, Roosevelt announced that henceforth the United States would become an "arsenal of democracy" for nations opposing the dictators. A week later, with anger in his voice, he advised a joint session of Congress to beware of those who, "with sounding brass and tinkling cymbal, preach the 'ism' of appeasement." According to *Life* magazine, the gauntlet had been thrown down and "most of those who read it, concurred in varying degrees with the tough foreign policy set forth."

On January 10, 1941, with the introduction before Congress of symbolically numbered House Resolution 1776, Europe suddenly seemed much closer to the United States. For the first time American lawmakers and the man in the street were called upon to approve a measure that aimed directly at the defeat of Hitler and Mussolini and thereby heralded the abandonment of American neutrality.

To Father Coughlin, William Pelley, and the members of the German-American Bund, lend-lease was Armageddon. Yet any chance they had of preventing the enactment of the measure was smothered in the ignominy that surrounded them. Their allegations of Jewish conspiracies, British atrocities, and presidential mendacity had already proved troubling to responsible non-interventionists; and now, with the administration embarked on a policy of direct aid to Britain, the propaganda that most Americans earlier dismissed as the work of misguided individuals appeared more than ever the work of traitors to the Republic.

In such a context the eleventh-hour attempt by the extremists to influence their nation's destiny was as counterproductive as it was ill-advised. Each of the countersubversives only slid further into the mire. Father Coughlin, for example, had thrown his support to a hypothetical Willkie-Lindbergh ticket during the 1940 campaign, suggesting at the same time that FDR be impeached. When Willkie disavowed the support, remarking that he would rather be defeated than accept the aid of any movement "opposed to certain people because of their race or religion," *Social Justice* could retort only that the rebuff resulted from "Jewish pressure" placed upon the Indiana Republican. In 1941 the Reverend Maurice Sheehy called Coughlin an intolerable burden on the Church and Archbishop Mooney concluded that his ambitious charge was receiving propaganda directly from Berlin; contributions sent the Shrine of the Little Flower were one-seventh of what they had been two years before; and finally, the cleric failed late in the year to renew his regular broadcasting contract when several larger stations utilized a new NAB code to silence him.

If "powerful men in radio and other fields" had quieted Coughlin's radio voice, *Social Justice* strove mightily to offset the absence. Through his news organ the priest endorsed isolationist groups and spokesmen while denouncing in conspiratorial terms interventionists and other proponents of lend-lease. HR 1776, he charged, would endow Roosevelt with more power than possessed by either Hitler or Stalin. The "dictator bill" would reduce Congress to "the pygmy status of a peanut" and mark "the beginning of the end as we know it [sic]." Sarcastically praising the measure's proponents for initiating a new trend in American diplomacy, Coughlin wrote:

> One is no longer a patriot who is not a Britisher!
> He is no longer a Democrat who is not a Marxist!
> He is no longer an American who is not a New Dealer!
> God save the mark! God save America!

As debate on lend-lease continued, the clergyman's rhetoric grew hyperbolic. At one moment the measure was termed "a wolf in sheep's clothing"; at another, "a substitute of Karl Marx for George Washington"; at yet another, "the last and final attempt to bury 1776 and its traditions." Curiously, however, the ultimate passage of the bill caused *Social Justice* to adopt a more reflective view. "Ten years hence," the paper predicted, "FDR will prove that the man who occupied the presidential chair from 1933 to 1941 was superior to all his critics or—God forbid—the worst President ever inflicted upon this free country. Success is his vindication; failure is our vindication. Time alone will be the referee."

For the moment, however, the arbitral office fell to the United States Army. In March, with no explanation, military authorities prohibited the sale of the priest's journal on all posts. Unimportant in itself, this decision reflected a growing national distaste for dissent against establishment foreign policy. Coughlin's exegesis and criticism of the administration now had become tantamount to disloyalty. And a similar problem also confronted William Dudley Pelley, whose goal of halting America's inevitable march to war was further sidetracked by serious legal problems.

Following the Asheville *Führer's* riotous appearance before the Dies Committee in February 1940, Pelley escaped extradition to North Carolina by securing a writ of *habeas corpus*. When the document expired in April, North Carolina authorities remained unable to capture their elusive quarry. Pelley's case rocked along through appeal to the D.C. Court of Appeals, which hesitated until April 14, 1941, to order him remanded. But even then, his attorneys argued the case to the Supreme Court, and it was not until October 13 that the high tribunal ruled that he face justice.

During this period Pelley seemed to excite fear only from the excitable Representative Dickstein who, despite mounds of evidence to the contrary, held fast to his belief that the former Silver Shirt leader remained "the motivating force behind fascistic desires on the part of army men like General Mosley to lead a revolt against the government." Wildly implausible, this theory nonetheless emboldened Pelley because it kept his name in the public eye. And, printer's ink still surging through his veins, he determined to renew his crusade against the Jewish devils in Washington and London. In December 1940 sheriff's deputies, armed with a writ alleging that Pelley owed a former counsel $1,000, arrived at the Biltmore-Oteen building in Asheville just as moving vans were removing the former Silver Shirt leader's publishing equipment. William Dudley Pelley had escaped once again, this time to Noblesville, Indiana.

North Carolina officials did not pursue Pelley, but his reputation did; and by the first week in January Noblesville residents were described as "mad clear through" at his activities. Apparently the Asheville expatriate had slipped into town under an assumed name, attempted to purchase a weekly newspaper and publishing plant, and failed when owner Daily M. Hudler rejected his down payment of twenty $500 bills. Pelley was eventually able to purchase an abandoned box factory on the outskirts of the city, and he hired Carl Losey, an associate of a former Grand Dragon of the Ku Klux Klan, as president of his new press. By February two new journals, *Roll-Call* and the *Galilean,* offered readers material identical to that which had appeared in *Liberation.* But few Midwesterners now cared to read Pelley's anti-Semitic "metapsychics and esoterics," and an editorial in the *Asheville Times,* written immediately after his departure from North Carolina, provided a fitting epitaph to his career as a patriot defending American ideals: "Without regret Asheville says good-bye to Pelley Publishers. The very name 'Silver Shirts,' interpreted in the light of *Liberation's* tone and creed, suggests a secret society the opposite of fraternal or benevolent. The linking of Pelley's name with Nazi-Fascist agitators has made the sympathy of the vast majority of western North Carolinians with Pelley Publishers utterly impossible. *Liberation* did not represent liberty as North Carolina defines it, or as North Carolinians have died for it. *Liberation* has sowed discord, prejudice, hatred; it has reaped hostility to its avowed aims."

While Father Coughlin and William Dudley Pelley thus became victims of the kind of intolerance that at one time had sustained their own programs of countersubversion, the prognosis for the German-American Bund was by early 1941 as dark as the shadows cast by the Nazi swastika. Fritz Kuhn's arrest had purged the group of many members; James Wheeler-Hill had resigned in January 1940 after admitting that he swore falsely to being an

American citizen; in May a directive issued by the Works Project Administration sought to bar Bundists from employment with the agency; and at an Independence Day rally at Camp Nordlund, G. Wilhelm Kunze, Kuhn's successor, and two lieutenants were arrested for violating New Jersey's anti-uniform ordinance.

On August 18, while Ambassador William Bullitt spoke of the grave situation facing the United States during an address at Independence Square, Philadelphia, the Bundists held their own gathering, a joint meeting with the Ku Klux Klan at Camp Nordlund. Before fewer than one thousand persons, the two groups concluded what appeared to be a grotesque version of the Nazi-Soviet pact. Leaders from each organization proclaimed the other to be "pure American," and symbolizing the alleged union of interests, they celebrated a "wedding" of extremist groups. The Bund and Klan did not complete their merger, but their flirtation, a far cry from the days when New Jersey Ku Kluxers condemned the teaching of German in local high schools, attracted the attention of the contemporary custodians of Americanism, the members of the Dies Committee, who highlighted the rally in a series of open hearings on Bund operations in New Jersey.

In January 1941, however, the Committee dropped a bombshell of its own when it published a document which purported to be a Bund "official confidential manual," proving beyond doubt that the organization was absolutely militarized and "patterned after the ruthlessly efficient set-up which characterizes Hitler's regime in Germany." To hear the Dies Committee tell it, the Bund demanded total obedience from its members. And, according to the tribunal's final report issued in May, it was clear that the organization should be indicted, both as an agent of Berlin and as a means of introducing Nazi principles into the United States. These findings were exaggerated, for after Kuhn's incarceration a year earlier the German consul general in New York had advised the Foreign Ministry to discontinue once and for all its dealings with the group. Although this policy was adopted and continued until Pearl Harbor, the decision came too late to influence the Committee's conclusions. In the American mind the Bundists remained agents of Berlin, and this image contributed to the climate of fear and suspicion that surrounded debate on lend-lease.

German leaders had hoped that the more moderate and respectable noninterventionists in the United States would accomplish rationally what the Bundists and groups like them could never do—keep America out of war. But to their dismay the German-American extremists carried on a vicious propaganda campaign against the administration. A Bund journalist termed the President's "arsenal of democracy" speech incendiary, and in the main a rehash of the "long, current propaganda phrases that have filled the newspapers and have been roared out over the radio for a year or more." Roosevelt's announcement of the "Four Freedoms" to silence isolationist detractors was similarly dismissed as meaningless. Lend-lease, on the other hand, a creature of the Jewish conspiracy, placed the collective IQ of the American people on trial. "If it is passed," concluded an editorial writer in the *Free American,* "we shall conclude that the intelligence quota [sic] of the 1917 expeditionary force applies also to John Citizen and his wife—namely that the quota is not above the intelligence of ten-year-olds." But on March 11 the measure was approved, and the Bund was forced to steal a line from Theodore Dreiser: "The great American tragedy: sixty senators defy the American people: lend-lease bill gives the President a blank check to decide the fate of millions of lives!"

From the nature and tone of their rhetoric, it was clear that the extremists had shirked the primary responsibility that a democratic society imposes upon all dissenters from the majoritarian norm—that of educating the populace along some positive line of argument. But by the spring of 1941 the yahoos had indulged in a long orgy of agitation, undertaken for the sake of agitation and the edification of no one save themselves. If for no other reason, then, responsible adversaries of administration foreign policy should have been free of charges that their motives and sympathies were similar to those of the inverted nativists. Yet as the year progressed, anti-Semitism persisted as a moral issue and a source of controversy, while the great debate on American diplomacy became increasingly emotional and personal. And although the government in no way proscribed the right of dissent during this period, respectable noninterventionists learned, as the extremists had before them, that the price of vigilance against augmented American belligerency was measured in accusations of conflicting national loyalties and unpatriotic conduct.

The responsible lawmakers, organized pressure groups, and individual spokesmen were, to be sure, in large measure victims of external circumstances over which they had little, if any, control. The success of Hitler's military thrusts, combined with President Roosevelt's superb skill in allowing the times to educate the American people, made the anti-interventionist position at best precarious. There was, however, a more subtle and complex problem, the failure of the more important isolationists to fulfill an obligation thrust upon them by the very existence of an extremist fringe, and magnified by the latter's fervent support. In fact, the inability of several congressional isolationists, the American First Committee, and especially Charles A. Lindbergh, to demonstrate convincingly that their viewpoints reflected an abiding faith in democracy and the methods of rational discourse left them vulnerable to allegations by vocal American warhawks and defenders of the growing belligerency of the administration that, like the extremists, they too sought the destruction of the political system that made their dissent possible.

Most of this criticism was slander that American Anglophiles, emulating the countersubversive style of the extremists, justified in the interests of national unity and security. Yet the often unfair accusations were effective; and when evidence of appeasement, anti-Semitism, or pro-German sentiment was discovered in the noninterventionist camp, the isolationists found it difficult to maintain a claim to patriotic motives. This situation **was** pointed up by the

cases of Verne Marshall of Cedar Rapids, Iowa, a self-styled "wild man of
Borneo," and George Sylvester Viereck, a suave and indefatigable German
agent.

A "dark, hard-bitten veteran of World War I and numerous local causes,"
Marshall had earned a Pulitzer Prize in 1936 when, as editor of the *Cedar
Rapids Gazette,* he wrote a series of articles exposing crime within Iowa state
government. As an ambulance driver in France during the Great War, he had
seen the impersonal brutality of conflict and now, two decades later, as war
again threatened to engulf the United States, he felt that the President had to
be stopped. No admirer of the New Deal, Marshall formed his No Foreign
War Committee in New York on the same day that the Chief Executive announced plans to aid the British. Immediately removing $41,000 from the
Gazette treasury, the Iowa editor financed full-page advertisements in sixty
newspapers in forty-one states in an eleventh-hour attempt to prevent revision
of the 1939 Neutrality Law. The fiery journalist attempted to make it clear
that his group was in no way foreign oriented. "Let no man," he wrote in a
brochure describing the aims of his committee, "accuse us of being appeasers,
fifth columnists, pro-Nazis, pro-fascists, or of being anything save a group of
determined pro-Americans. We are ready for this fight, and I mean ready.
Behind us are legions of red-blooded, thoughtful, and brave Americans,
awaiting only the voice and leadership that have to date been denied them in
full volume."

Naming Lindbergh, Senator Bennett ("Champ") Clark of Missouri, commentator Boake Carter, Ida Connaway of the Mothers of America, Gladys
Lynn of the Mothers of American Sons, and Frances Sherrill of the National
Legion of Mothers as only a few of his admirers, Marshall claimed to have
wide support. In truth, however, the transplanted Iowan overestimated his
strength, and it soon became apparent that his efforts to sway public opinion
were as glandular as those of the foreign-oriented extremists with whom he
claimed to have no ties. Possessing little good will and less patience, he
showed neither concern for the preservation of American traditions nor
respect for the legal procedures that protected his countrymen from a jungle-
like existence. Acting like a man whose only interest was the vilification of
his opponents, he rechristened the Committee to Defend America by Aiding
the Allies the "Committee to Defend America by Destroying Itself," and
designated the group's respected founder, William Allen White, "the Char-
lie McCarthy of the interventionists." In fact, there was desperation in Marshall's tone of voice as he began his campaign against American belligerency.
"Unless somebody kills me," he informed a reporter from *Newsweek,* "I'll
stop the White Committee."

Like Coughlin, Pelley, and the Bundists, Verne Marshall was essentially an
onlooker at the diplomatic debate. Consequently he possessed a distinct initial advantage over the President and his advisors and diplomats. While the
latter were making decisions of great tactical and strategic importance, Marshall, beholden to no one, could second-guess the administration with impu-

nity and make promises without being overly concerned with their eventual fulfillment. An individual whose demagogic instincts were already well developed, he was in a position to capitalize on the overwhelming American desire for peace.

Late in December, warning that if Roosevelt should belittle his organization he would reveal numerous secret agreements allegedly concluded by the President with the belligerent powers, Marshall overreached himself. On December 27 he ordered the Chief Executive to halt the European conflict and three days later, revealing his own plan to end the war, he indicated that William R. Davis, an American millionaire, had brought to the White House from Hermann Göring a "just and honorable peace proposal" shortly after the demise of Poland. Although Roosevelt had completely ignored the plan, Marshall continued, the time was ripe to test the President's well-publicized desire for peace. Davis would make an excellent American representative at a general conference among belligerent powers. Yet when plans were made for Marshall to elaborate upon his strategy in a New Year's Eve radio address, the Iowan, "his head down and swinging," reverted to form and spent the time allotted him predicting catastrophe for adversaries of his committee.

As Marshall's attacks became more irresponsible, endorsements offered him by the extremists and their followers increased proportionally. And while Christian Fronters, Christian Mobilizers, and Bundists flocked in growing numbers to No Foreign War Committee meetings, spokesmen for more responsible noninterventionist groups deserted him. After a Nazi short-wave broadcast mentioned Marshall's utility to Hitler's cause, Charles Lindbergh, who already had withdrawn from a committee engagement when he learned that several anti-Semites were to be present, adopted publicly a policy of isolation toward the fiery journalist, of whom he was personally fond but who nonetheless disturbed him by "something about his attitude on life." That quality, undoubtedly, was Marshall's violent temper, a characteristic that combined with his desire to do things his own way, caused the resignation of his "field organizer," Orland K. ("O.K.") Armstrong, after the latter criticized his handling of relations with the press.

In mid-January, with the No Foreign War Committee treasury $45,000 in arrears, Marshall resigned as editor of the *Gazette,* declaring that with the passage of lend-lease, "national socialism will replace democracy and the United States will go to war." Yet if the Iowan's meteoric career thus reached its apogee well before the crucial vote on lend-lease, his visceral style and intemperate insistence upon a negotiated peace nonetheless had a strategic effect. Writers in the *Nation* and *New Republic* now termed Marshall America's leading appeaser; William Allen White disdained his bigotry while stressing the need for rational discussion of honest differences of opinion; and the Reverend L. M. Birkhead of the strongly interventionist Friends of Democracy argued that his resignation from the *Gazette* placed him "alongside salesmen of *Social Justice,* Christian Mobilizers, and Bundists." It was with good reason, therefore, that "Champ" Clark of Missouri, a leading senatorial opponent of lend-lease, remarked on more than one occasion that Marshall was "hurting the cause."

Verne Marshall lost his battle to prevent the enactment of lend-lease, and by May his No Foreign War Committee had disbanded, its avowed purpose of "provoking increased public discussion" having been served. Although in its "What Ever Happened to . . .?" column, *Newsweek* reported that Marshall had dropped from sight, he had simply returned to Iowa. Yet his activities left still another albatross draped around the necks of responsible noninterventionist leaders.

In contrast to Marshall, George Sylvester Viereck preferred to work behind the scenes. A complex man whose vanity and egotism verged on narcissism, he was driven by a neurotic need to develop and embellish his own reputation. And in the years preceding Pearl Harbor, he attempted singlehandedly to counteract damage done to German-American relations by the Bund by organizing two isolationist committees, founding a publishing house, and directing a propaganda ring that received outright support from several isolationist solons and unwitting aid from others.

The son of German immigrants, Viereck graduated from New York City College in 1906 and pursued a literary career until 1914, when he launched the *Fatherland,* a weekly journal that informed the German-American community of developments in the European theatre of war. Highly critical of the Treaty of Versailles, he readily embraced Hitler's New Germany and in 1933 became a German public relations counsel in New York. In March 1939 he convinced Dr. Frederick Auhagen, professor of German Literature at Columbia, to assume leadership of the American Fellowship Forum, a group of prosperous German-American businessmen that sought to achieve "the greatest possible cultural and material well-being of a happy and enlightened America." In other words Viereck hoped to affect prevailing American sympathy for Great Britain by creating a sympathetic awareness of German conditions, and to this end the Forum sponsored public meetings and published a journal, *Today's Challenge.* At the initial gathering of the organization, American fascist Lawrence Dennis discussed "America and Germany— Contrasts without Conflicts," while in the first edition of *Today's Challenge* Auhagen argued that the Munich Agreement signified "the most hopeful beginning of the New Europe that should have come twenty years ago."

Although the Forum disbanded shortly after the outbreak of war, its appearance marked a new departure in hyphenated isolationism. A naturalized American citizen who never became a member of the Nazi Party, Viereck was neither a fanatic nor an anti-Semite. His apartment walls may have been graced by pictures of Hitler and Goebbels, but photographs of Albert Einstein and Sigmund Freud were also present. His chosen task, that of ameliorating American objections to Nazi ferocity and the hysteria of the Bund, was ultimately impossible; but his organization did make a literate appeal to upper social classes and to intellectuals.

There was more to Viereck than mere altruism, however. According to a recent biographer of the German-American militant, he looked to the supermen of the Third Reich "to restore his power and influence on his own home ground." In this pursuit he worked tirelessly, spending most of his time as a publicist for the German Library of Information in New York. When American newspapers ceased printing official Nazi press releases in 1938, the library emerged as the primary outlet for such propaganda. Viereck, happy to be "interpreting German events to my own countrymen," served as editor of the library journal, *Facts in Review,* which reached 20,000 "interested persons" in 1939 and five times that number by 1941.

With the outbreak of war in Europe, Viereck's activities seemed to increase geometrically. First he attempted to strengthen isolationist sentiment and revive lingering resentment against the Allies by founding the "Make Europe Pay War Debts" and "Islands for War Debts Defense" Committees. Then he acquired a small publishing house in Scotch Plains, New Jersey, and quickly transformed it into an important center for the production and distribution of anti-Roosevelt and Anglophobic tracts. By the end of 1940, under the imprint of Flanders Hall, Viereck had published a dozen virulent pamphlets and books, a fact that caused an official in the German Consulate in Washington, to designate the firm as "our publishing house." One of these volumes, *We Must Save the Republic* by Representative Stephen A. Day of Illinois, was subtitled "A Flanders Hall America First Book" and illustrated Viereck's larger purpose of attaching his own views to those of the America First Committee. Thus, although directors of the most important noninterventionist organization disavowed any connection with Flanders Hall, readers of Day's volume, and others; would readily identify it as a work sanctioned by America First.

Yet committee work and pamphleteering were not enough, and Viereck turned directly to Capitol Hill, where, with the help of George Hill, a press clerk for Representative Hamilton Fish, and Prescott Dennett, a German agent and director of the Columbia Press Service, he secured thousands of congressionally franked envelopes in which he mailed reprints from isolationist speeches and articles that had appeared in the *Congressional Record.* So successful was this enterprise that during a six-month period in 1941, the franking ring deluged the nation with more than 500,000 reprints that had been secured under false pretenses from the Government Printing Office.

It was thus for good reason that the seemingly ubiquitous German factotum earned the reputation of being the Reich's "most valuable liaison agent in the Foreign Office." Viereck's tactical sophistication on one occasion led Senator Gerald P. Nye, who earlier had refused his request for a large number of speech reprints, to assent after Dennett convinced him that he would be aiding the "Make Europe Pay War Debts" Committee. The North Dakota Republican complied, failing to realize that the committee in question was named George Sylvester Viereck. However, Viereck too undermined isolationist unity, although in a more subtle way than the extremists. A government investigation of foreign propaganda that began in September 1941 revealed the names of several isolationist lawmakers whose franks had been misused, and subsequent election losses by Nye, Senator Wheeler of Montana, and Senator Rush D. Holt of West Virginia indicated that most Americans had not adopted a foreign-oriented, noninterventionist stance.

As if the troublesome legacy of the discredited yahoos, the antics of Verne Marshall, and the cunning of George Sylvester Viereck did not present enough problems to noninterventionist leaders, the debate on lend-lease, one of the most dramatic in American history, confronted the isolationists with a twofold dilemma—the administration's control of the decision-making process on the one hand and the urgency of the moment on the other. Heralding the end of twenty years of aloofness from international commitment, lend-lease increased the pace and vehemence of the noninterventionists' battle against the prevailing national sympathy for the valiant fight being waged by the British people.

The problem with lend-lease was that it left unanswered the question of the degree to which the United States would aid Great Britain, and it was this uncertainty that led many noninterventionists to interpret the measure not as a reasonable step toward nonbelligerency but as a giant leap toward war. This sense of foreboding helps explain why, for example, Senator Clare Hoffman of Michigan entered in the *Congressional Record* a particularly vicious radio address by the well-known, professional anti-Semite, Gerald L. K. Smith, who predicted as early as 1936 that Roosevelt sought to engage the nation in a war to communize Europe. In 1940, condemning the President for his dealings with "Reds, Pinks, and Radicals," the former lieutenant in Huey Long's Share-Our-Wealth movement envisioned the day when his organization, the Committee of One Million, would seize the government by force. In the speech cited by Hoffman, Smith emphasized the impossibility of preparing America "as long as Communists are permitted to throttle defense activities," and termed lend-lease a choice between "atheistic communism and Christ-inspired Americanism."

According to several leading noninterventionists, in fact, the conspiracy of warmongers already had taken command of executive decision making. In a confidential letter to the editor of *Liberty* magazine, Senator Arthur H. Vandenberg of Michigan wondered "how much hell Mr. Stalin could raise if he just gave the word to all his dupes in the United States," and "whether we have any adequate conception of the extent to which they occupy strategic positions in our social and economic life." Senator Reynolds of North Carolina, meanwhile, the only Southern senator to vote against lend-lease, clung to the belief that alien immigrants had sabotaged national defense. This view, together with the legislator's continued praise of Nazi economics and militarism, identified him in the eyes of many North Carolinians as "the most prestigious friend the fringe of American fascists had." Senators Nye, Wheeler, and D. Worth Clark of Idaho also employed the *Congressional Record* to insinuate that the administration had betrayed the cause of peace, a view that was seconded by Representatives Day of Illinois, Fish of New York, and Bernard Gehrman of Wisconsin.

But the most extreme statement of the debate came from Wheeler while he analyzed lend-lease on Theodore Granick's popular "American Forum of the Air." Convinced that the measure would bring war to America, the Montana Democrat termed HR 1776 the New Deal's "Triple-A foreign policy to plow under every fourth American boy." Wheeler immediately regretted having spoken such harsh words, but there was no way to retract them; and on the following day he and other opponents of the administration grimaced as the President termed his remark "the most untruthful, the most dastardly, unpatriotic thing that has been said in public life in my generation." Again in February the arch-isolationist left himself open to accusations of rhetorical irresponsibility when during a speech to the Senate he attempted to demonstrate that a financial oligarchy had captured control of diplomatic decision making. After necessarily professing to abhor all bigotry and prejudice, he produced as evidence of his allegation a list of bankers who were predominantly Jewish. In fairness to Wheeler, his imagery harked back to the 1890s and the Populist cry against unrestricted immigration, international finance, and urban sophistication; but in early 1941, with Hitler assailing all liberalism, the Montana politician's conclusion could not help but appear un-American. That Wheeler was also an outspoken critic of Nazism was all but forgotten, as was his willingness to help Great Britain if aid could be extended without involving the United States in binding commitments.

Political expediency dictated President Roosevelt's postponement of a full-scale debate on American diplomacy until late 1940, when it became clear that Britain alone could not rebuff Hitler and that Germany threatened the security of the United States. The passage of lend-lease on March 11, after two months' discussion, constituted an "irrevocable commitment" to the British and the longest step toward war taken by Washington before Pearl Harbor. Roosevelt's triumph did not, as one government official intimated, leave the battle against aid to Britain in charge of "a national political alliance of crackpots," or "the fanatic fringe," but the Rubicon had been crossed. To confront administration policy, a person now risked being identified with antidemocratic forces. To the extent that isolationism thus became an obscene word in the lexicon of American politics, the extremists had contaminated the people they so admired.

Against the background of what presidential aide Robert Sherwood has properly termed an Anglo-American "common-law alliance," the travail of American isolationists became more acute and apparent. By midsummer, in an effort to cope with Nazi submarine warfare, the administration moved to repeal restrictive provisions in the 1939 Neutrality Law, while several incidents on the high seas, notably those involving the *Greer, Kearny,* and *Reuben James,* intensified the drive to arm American merchantmen for defensive purposes. On November 13 the vital provisions of the 1939 law were finally jettisoned; and although the vote against repeal was significantly greater than had been the division on lend-lease, the noninterventionist cause had in fact been lost two months earlier.

The final decline of isolationist respectability gathered momentum on June 4 when Mississippi's John Rankin charged in a ringing speech on the House floor that "Wall Street and a little group of our international Jewish brethren are still attempting to harass the President and Congress into the European war unprepared." Responding to this invective, Representative Michael Edelstein of New York bitterly pointed out that "the fact of the matter is that the number of Jewish bankers in the United States is infinitesimal. I deplore the idea that anytime anything happens, whether it be for a war policy or against a war policy, men in this House attempt to use Jews as their scapegoat. I say it is unfair and un-American."

Five minutes later, Edelstein died of a heart attack. His death brought the issue of anti-Semitism within Congress to public attention, as persons who had heretofore dismissed the rantings of the extremists expressed dismay that demagoguery had invaded Capitol Hill. The *Chattanooga News-Free Press* expressed alarm that "a totalitarian spirit existed within national legislative halls," and indicated that this "basic Hitler principle" menaced the unity so important to national security. A writer for the *Hartford Courant* termed the statement a "mischievous utterance" by a man attempting to fasten responsibility for American foreign policy upon a small minority. By naming the Jews as scapegoat, as the countersubversives had done all along, Rankin could then shift the blame onto that group should the United States go to war.

If Rankin's comments implied the existence of a link between the discredited extremists and isolationist forces in Congress, the troubles encountered by Senator Wheeler in July were equally suggestive of such a connection. Sincere in his opposition to Rooseveltian diplomacy, the Montana Democrat had utilized the franked postcard as a means to counter what seemed to him an American *carte blanche* to Britain. The postcards, which had been purchased by America First, carried Roosevelt's pre-election pledge to refrain from sending American troops to foreign shores, a promise, Wheeler wrote, that was broken when the President sent 4,000 soldiers to Iceland. "Write today to President Roosevelt," the card concluded, "that you are against our entry into the European war." Instead, several servicemen had written their congressmen demanding to know where Wheeler's loyalty lay. And at a press conference on July 25, Secretary of War Henry Stimson charged the Montana Democrat with conduct "coming very close to the line of subversive activities against the United States, if not treason."

Although agreeing with Stimson that Wheeler had acted unwisely, Roosevelt refused to allow any member of the administration to engage the Montanan in a direct confrontation. Fearing that such a move would cause the Great Debate to deteriorate even more into a battle of personalities, the Chief Executive was content to let Wheeler's "venomous instincts" lessen his effectiveness. Shortly thereafter, Wheeler revealed that he had not intended to send the postcards to American troops, and Stimson, retreating from his earlier attack (he might have been helped by thirteen isolationist senators who denounced his attempt to "smear" their colleague), noted that only 200 cards had actually reached American soldiers and, moreover, that he regretted his original accusation. "So far as official Washington is concerned," wrote an editorialist in the *Ellicott City Times,* "the affair is probably considered closed."

But for many Americans the affair not only remained open; it provided a sounding board for anxieties and emotions only remotely connected to specific foreign policy issues. Noninterventionists embarked on a symbolic crusade, praising Wheeler as a "great American," a "true American," and a "patriotic American." Supporters of the administration, meanwhile, were equally unable to defend the President's policy on its merits. In fact, only one of Roosevelt's correspondents even mentioned Wheeler's misuse of the franking privilege. Advocates of American aid to Great Britain attacked the Montana Democrat in very personal terms. An Oakland woman, inquiring rhetorically, "What is a Wheelbergh?", provided a succinct answer: "A Wheelbergh is a birdman of the ostrich family, also related to the dodo family. The Wheelbergh's favorite trick is to bury its head in the sand. Naturalists think it may be due to a dislike of looking at anything that doesn't resemble itself." Other citizens placed Wheeler in the Nazi camp. A resident of Atlantic City remarked that "England had her Moseleys. We have Wheeler. It is high time he was tracked down." A Dallas man wondered how the government could "tolerate the un-American activities of Senator Wheeler to wreck the country."

A man whose integrity precluded any dealings with organized prejudice, Wheeler was revolted by "professional hate groups and other crackpots who for their own unwholesome reasons supported the America First movement." On many occasions he publicly condemned the racial and religious policies of the Third Reich and in one instance rejected outright a suggestion by an unnamed Kansas anti-Semite to "take out after the Jews." Yet following the postcard controversy, his role as a leading isolationist spokesman became onerous. To read an Oregon editor's description of the Montanan before he was to make a local address in mid-September, one would think that the images employed would better fit William Dudley Pelley or Father Coughlin:

Senator "Bunco" Wheeler—Jew-baiter, Roosevelt-Hater, Oath Violator. . . .
    Wheeler will bark, snarl, undt yelp like a Hitler hound. . . .
    Political Jackal Wheeler should be jailed for taking $12,000 a year from Uncle Sam to work as a Senator while touring the nation for the "Hun-America First CUR-MITTEE. . . ."

Years later, recalling that climate of suspicion and personal vindictiveness, Wheeler wrote bitterly of the "tolerance" demonstrated by liberals in 1940 and 1941. If a man was interventionist, he remembered, he was "automatically welcomed with open arms as a 'liberal.' " But if a man was noninterventionist, he was "ipso facto considered a reactionary, and probably pro-Hitler as well."

Nowhere, though, was the alleged resemblance between foreign-oriented extremism and respectable isolationism more significant than in the case of the America First Committee and its principal spokesman, Charles Lindbergh. The brainchild of R. Douglas Stuart, a college student whose father was an executive with the Quaker Oats Company, America First appeared in September 1940 and quickly became the paramount isolationist organization in the country. Its national chairman, Robert E. Wood, was an idealistic businessman who supported FDR in 1936 but broke with the administration three years later on the issue of foreign policy.

Committee leadership and financial backing were conservative, but the organization appealed to all persons who shared a sincere desire to avoid war. Prominent Americans who joined the group included pacifist Oswald G. Villard, industrialist Henry Ford, novelist Kathleen Norris, New York lawyer Amos R. E. Pinchot, Mrs. Nicholas Longworth, Chester Bowles, and liberal journalist John T. Flynn. The members of America First held to the belief that even if Britain fell, a prepared United States could withstand Hitler. America, with her system of free labor, could compete successfully with National Socialism because totalitarian systems arose from internal economic distress. Thus President Roosevelt might prevent such an occurrence by initiating improvements at home rather than by waging war abroad.

But from its inception America First was severely handicapped. For one thing, the Committee did not become well known until mid-1941, and by that time the Axis threat had substantially increased interventionist sentiment throughout the nation. Although Germany's invasion of the Soviet Union on June 22 suggested that the organization might yet win its battle against intervention, America First did not escape the implications of its dismissal of the significance of a Nazi victory.

Ignoring the sincere motives of Committee leaders, defenders of the administration acted as if they faced a deliberate conspiracy aimed at circumscribing the President's freedom of action. The polarization of American politics was evident as Roosevelt himself condemned Committee spokesmen as "unwitting aids of the agents of Nazism" who "preached the gospel of fear." Interior Secretary Harold Ickes predicted that they would make terms with Hitler "at the expense of this country's welfare," and also observed that "their subtle arguments and pretended willingness to sacrifice themselves for the common good" were calculated "to bring about divided counsels until the harm they do is irreparable." Presidential speech-writer Robert S. Sherwood suggested that they desired to see "America become Hitler's next victim."

This type of criticism played havoc with the truth, but such charges were predicated upon enough evidence—circumstantial and real—to leave the impression that the Committee was only slightly more honorable than the Christian Front or the German-American Bund. The extremists, to be sure, had faded in importance during the debate on lend-lease, but they saw in the organization a means to secure respectability. *Social Justice,* for example, revealed that Father Coughlin would have become an active spokesman had he the liberty to join. And on May 1 the *Free American* carried a front-page editorial imploring readers to "join the America First Committee and continue to bombard your representatives."

The Committee was actually infiltrated by a number of men and women seeking to use its platform to legitimize their own pro-Nazi arguments. The *Beacon Light,* published by Atascadero anti-Semite William Kullgren, was distributed at a number of San Francisco meetings, a fact that led the editor of the *Western Journal of Education* to conclude that attendance at these gatherings was composed "preponderantly of local Nazis." Laura Ingalls, later indicted as a paid German agent, spoke frequently for the organization, and on one occasion told a southern California chapter that the group ought to adopt as "an American symbol of unity" the outstretched left arm. "This is the old Indian salute, and therefore purely American," she explained, "and no one can accuse us of being Nazis, for Nazis use the right arm."

There were other embarrassments. Christian Fronters packed Brooklyn America First meetings. Nazi agent Walter Schellenberg made his last public appearance in the United States seated on an America First speaker's dais on May 22. S. A. Ackley quit the Committee to form his own Anglo-Saxon Confederation. The chairman of the Pontiac, Michigan chapter allegedly served as a liaison between the Committee and anti-Semitic groups in the Chicago area, including the German-American National Alliance. The name of the editor of the blatantly anti-Semitic, Lake Geneva (Wisc.) *Herald,* Douglas M. Stewart, was easily, and deliberately, confused with that of R. Douglas Stuart of America First.

Committee leaders neither solicited such aid nor countenanced political partisanship and anti-Semitism. In fact, as their manual explicitly stated, the Committee excluded "persons with leanings that place the interests of any foreign country or ideology ahead of those of the United States." To this end the Committee hierarchy rejected the endorsement of Father Coughlin and the Christian Front; informed chapter leaders to have no dealings with Gerald L. K. Smith or Edward James Smythe; and scorned Bundist approval because of that group's aping of "the philosophy, the aggression, and the methods of Hitler's Germany." At an America First rally at Madison Square Garden on May 23, moreover, John T. Flynn, New York Committee leader, publicly berated Christian Mobilizer Joe McWilliams, who was present with many followers to hear Lindbergh.

These gestures did not alter the assumption by many American hawks that the Committee was a branch office of Berlin. A cartoon in the proadministration *New York Evening Post,* depicting Hitler with his arm around Senator Wheeler, put the matter in black-and-white terms. America Firsters were akin to Benedict Arnold. If they did not find things satisfactory in America, their adversaries reasoned, they could leave. The Archbishop of Dubuque,

Francis J. Beckman, lamented what seemed to him a growing intolerance. Archbishop Beckman, himself an ardent isolationist, explained that even if "Christ Himself were this moment to return and confront these modern Herods and Pilates—He too would be crowned by them a Bundist."

Although there was no direct connection between Berlin and America First, an implicit link did exist in Hitler's desire to let responsible isolationist leaders achieve the basic goal of Reich diplomacy—keeping the United States out of the war. This fundamental cornerstone of German foreign policy was, however, based on the erroneous assumption that noninterventionist strength was strong enough to shape Washington's course.

On September 11, shortly after Roosevelt had issued "shoot on sight" orders to American convoys, Hitler's hopes, and those of noninterventionist Americans, evaporated as Charles Lindbergh addressed an overflow America First gathering in Des Moines, Iowa. Considering the degree to which the former flying ace had come to personify isolationist hopes, it was with a strange insensitivity, in fact almost a cold-blooded disregard for the explosiveness of human emotions, that he spoke. The speech was crucial not only to Lindbergh's career; it also marked the *Dies Irae* for the cause of respectable isolationism. To comprehend its significance and the interventionist reaction to it, its author must be understood.

A man of paradox, Lindbergh despised publicity but faced huge crowds wherever he went. At war with American newspapers after his epochal trans-Atlantic flight, he nonetheless championed a free press and free speech against an asserted conspiracy to silence him. Counseling Roosevelt to be cautious in handling American diplomacy, he himself epitomized the active, spontaneous life. A man who once considered forsaking American citizenship, he attracted supporters whose basic pride lay in their patriotism. Most ironically, by 1941 the man who had quickened the spirit of internationalism so greatly by flying the Atlantic had emerged as the country's leading noninterventionist.

The sources of Lindbergh's isolationism were varied, but the intolerance accorded his radical father during the First World War seemed to have left the most lasting impression. A candidate for governor in Minnesota in 1918, the elder Lindbergh endured much harassment because of his distrust of Eastern capitalism. Conservative opponents often refused to let him speak, tore down his banners, and tarred and feathered his supporters. In addition, the flier's own personal experiences—especially the hysteria surrounding his son's kidnapping and murder—had left him disappointed with democracy. Married to the former Anne Morrow, heiress to a Wall Street fortune, he shared her family's distaste for the Soviet Union and its deep suspicion of New Deal liberalism. Concomitantly, however, this scion of small-town America was full of wonderment and admiration for the efficiency and military prowess of Hitler's Germany. These feelings led him to justify the German search for *Lebensraum,* or "living space," in Eastern Europe.

Emerging from a period of personal isolation in 1939, Lindbergh swiftly became the premier spokesman for the noninterventionist cause. In a series of speeches and articles he argued that because the war was not a contest between right and wrong, but a battle between differing conceptions of right, a negotiated peace would be a sensible solution. Germany, able and virile, had begun to expand at the expense of France and England, while the latter countries sought to maintain their current possessions and historical ethical systems. Where the British possessed organization without spirit, the French retained spirit without organization. Germany reflected both qualities. The flier thus believed that the United States could do little to prevent what he considered an inexorable process in which the forces of the present were somewhat mystically ranged against the forces of the past. The cost of constructing planes to aid the British, for example, would be prohibitive; the number of possible targets too large; and the potential of American military effectiveness too small. As he warned a Keep Out of War rally in Chicago in August 1940, European problems could not be solved by American intervention; American frontiers did not lie in Europe; American destiny would not be decided on foreign soil.

Drawing support from a heterogeneous group of Americans, including respectable business leaders, disappointed liberals and old Progressives, and men and women who sincerely wished to avoid war, Lindbergh received such strong backing that political scientist Max Lerner considered him to be "far more formidable than any of the German sympathizers or native patrioteers." Yet in his naive interpretation of global politics Lindbergh left himself and the cause for which he labored open to criticism. Almost immediately, interventionists argued that his sincerity was devoid of moral concern. Liberal journalist H. R. Knickerbocker questioned his "shameless declarations that the United States should quit Great Britain, watch her fall, then trade with Hitler and make what we can out of the defeat of civilization." A writer for the *New Republic* asked, "Which is more dangerous, *Mein Kampf* or Lindbergh's mind?" Senator Key Pittman, a staunch advocate of administration policy, concluded that the flier was "an inexperienced young man, totally unfamiliar with our country, its statesmanship, and its military matters."

For a man who disdained controversy, Lindbergh fared poorly in 1940 and early 1941. Doubts concerning his true intentions mounted, and rather than clarifying his positions on moot issues in American diplomacy, his statements tended to polarize opinion concerning the famed flier himself. While testifying on lend-lease, he displayed contempt for the American defense effort and apathy toward the outcome of the European conflict. These views were equated with appeasement by many observers, such as the members of the Roosevelt-Wallace Democratic Club of Detroit, who censured him for effecting "discord and disunity in the American defense effort, and lending moral aid to the Axis powers." An editorial writer for the interventionist *Salt Lake City Tribune* analyzed "Lindbergh's Adaptations of Hitler's Hated Harangues," and concluded that the "obvious purpose" of his statements was a negotiated peace "which had been Hitler's hope from the first."

Disregarding this criticism, Lindbergh plunged ahead. His "Letter to Americans," which appeared in *Collier's* in March, was endorsed by such prominent Americans as Alfred M. Landon, former Illinois Governor Frank Lowden, architect Frank Lloyd Wright, commentator Boake Carter, novelist Kathleen Norris, "Believe It or Not" columnist Robert Ripley, and historian Arthur J. May. Driven by an honest desire to prevent the nation from wrecking her ideals on the shoals of foreign adventure, Lindbergh joined the America First Committee in April and informed a Chicago rally that lend-lease had failed to affect the trend of the war and could only intensify the European blood bath. A week later, in New York, he reiterated his belief that Roosevelt's convoy proposal was useless. "A nation's ideals must be backed by the hard logic of military practicality," he reasoned, and America's were not.

Lindbergh's arrival quickly augmented America First membership, but the flier's presence also incited further censure by interventionist spokesmen who felt that his appeal "could only obstruct unity and weaken us as a nation." That advocates of American participation in Britain's struggle would not tolerate the flier's dissent was illustrated by an editorial in the Meriden (Conn.) *Record* which linked him with pro-Nazi extremists by referring to his "Bund address" and argued that, his sincerity notwithstanding, his brand of isolationism was "dear to the heart of Hitler." Senator William H. Smathers of New Jersey announced that the time had come for Lindbergh to cease trying to "sell the American people on the false doctrine of German invincibility," while the Reverend L. M. Birkhead called upon Committee leaders to repudiate what he termed the flier's pro-Nazi supporters. Similar opinions were filed by Wendell Willkie, Mayor La Guardia, Mrs. Eleanor Roosevelt, financier James P. Warburg, mystery writer Rex Stout, and the strongly interventionist Fight for Freedom Committee. The volume of the Great Debate had become thundering indeed.

Lindbergh could not see that in the eyes of his adversaries he had become, however unwittingly, a forceful purveyor of German propaganda, and he was shocked and saddened when President Roosevelt took note of his activities during a press conference on April 25 and in a masterpiece of invective labeled him "a Copperhead" and a "modern Vallandigham." The analogy, which linked the flier spiritually to an Ohio representative who had been accused of treasonable utterances during the Civil War, convicted by a military tribunal, and banished, became for Lindbergh an affair of honor. Deeply anguished by the Chief Executive's implications concerning his loyalty, motives, and personal character, the noninterventionist leader concluded that Roosevelt believed him "no longer of use to this country as a reserve officer." And, after discussing his feelings with friends, he decided to answer the charge by resigning his rank of colonel in the United States Army Air Corps Reserve.

The resignation was a thunderclap in an already stormy sky, and the flier's partisans quickly loosed a torrent of mail on the White House. Amos R. E. Pinchot, an Eastern lawyer who fought with the First New York Volunteer

Cavalry in the Spanish-American War and was now an outspoken America First leader, condemned Roosevelt for singling out Lindbergh when in fact many responsible and sincere men and women had made similar comments regarding Britain's bleak future. Representatives Charles Tobey of New Hampshire and Clare Hoffman of Michigan made the same point, as did a sympathetic writer in the *Christian Century*.

But Lindbergh's support was more than offset by American Anglophiles who seized upon his exchange with the President to step up their campaign to impugn the noninterventionist's patriotism. Presidential Press Secretary Stephen Early wondered if the flier had returned the medal German leaders bestowed upon him in 1938; a New York aviator suggested that he be conscripted as an instructor or aviation mechanic; and a San Francisco woman proposed to send him to Germany, "where he belongs." It was the belief of the *Newark Star-Ledger* that he deserved a promotion, "from Hitler!" The Tampas brothers of Valdosta, Georgia, changed the name of their restaurant from "the Lindbergh" to "the Roosevelt," while a correspondent of Representative Mike Monroney of Oklahoma suggested that Lindbergh be made commanding officer at the emergency landing field at Ti, Oklahoma—population six.

Lindbergh's predicament was also assessed poetically:

> Lindy used to be a hero;
> Now his stock is down to zero.
> Badly has he got in Dutch—
> Just because he talked too much.

> Fear not good Lindy, even if thy heart be faint
> Or overburdened with the pretty baub
> That Hitler hung with thy coat, on other side,
> From that, thy liver, now so purely white.

Following his resignation, Lindbergh's private life became even more guarded; he saw fewer friends and had little contact with America First rank-and-file. Embittered by Roosevelt's insult, he confided to his journal that the administration, conspiratorially supported by American intellectuals, international financiers, British agents, and "Jewish interests" in the communications industry, "seems to have 'the bit in its teeth' and [is] hell-bent for war."   This analysis was essentially correct: Roosevelt and his advisors had identified Britain's cause as America's own and made clear their intent to accomplish all they could to prevent Germany from achieving total hegemony in Europe. Yet the apparent affinity between Lindbergh's views and official Nazi press releases remained a major problem. The flier would not allow himself to be intimidated by anyone, and he seemed at times even to take a perverse pleasure in the imputed resemblance. Consequently observers questioned the manner in which he saluted the American flag at a rally in Madison Square Garden on May 23. One eyewitness, terming Lindbergh's outstretched left hand treasonous, compared the gesture with earlier wartime opposition: "Then, no man dared to *Goose-Step* down Broadway; no man dared to stand in Madison Square Garden and salute our flag with a *Nazi salute;* and by the eternal, *No* man has the right to do it today and remain a citizen of this country."

To a great extent the flier's own prognostications were sufficient reason for the increasing censure. On May 29, for instance, he announced that if the American people followed Roosevelt, the country would be plunged into "a war between hemispheres that may last for generations." It was the President, and not Hitler, who sought world domination. Americans should turn to new policies and to new leadership. Comments like these drew bitter rejoinders. On June 6 the *New York Times* reported that Japanese bombers had dropped reprints of Lindbergh's speeches in bombing raids on Chungking, China. The city fathers of Charlotte, North Carolina, renamed Lindbergh Avenue, while leaders in Little Falls, Minnesota, struck the name of the isolationist leader from its water tower. Chicago's "world's tallest beacon" was no longer "the Lindbergh Beacon." Even Carl Sandburg had had enough of the former hero. Comparing him with another self-made man, Abraham Lincoln, Sandburg regretted that the flier's speeches contained "no hint of the passion for freedom and equality of opportunity that shook Lincoln." And there were always the cheerful postcards sent by Briton Harold Nicolson after each particularly heavy shelling of London: "Do you still think we are soft?"

Support for Lindbergh exploded anew in mid-July after Secretary Ickes, who had long distrusted the flier, branded him "a Nazi mouthpiece" and "Knight of the German Eagle." But Ickes's comments also drew the isolationist leader into the open; and in a letter to the White House released to newsmen before it reached Roosevelt, Lindbergh disavowed alleged Axis sympathies, sought a congressional inquiry of Ickes's charges, and demanded an apology. Ickes and the President remained silent, however, and the noninterventionist spokesman's "letter to teacher" had backfired. He was in a position where he would be damned if he returned the German medal and damned if he did not. He had been placed on the defensive and, as Ickes confided to his diary, "that is always a weak position for everyone."

Ickes was quite correct; though Lindbergh remained the chief spokesman for America First, his position had weakened considerably. If the de facto, Anglo-American alliance constituted the primary reason for his predicament, another problem was that by the middle of 1941 he had become for the American extremists "a symbol of rugged, patriotic virtues," perhaps even America's "man on horseback."

In fairness Lindbergh did nothing to encourage the yahoos; yet he did nothing to repudiate them either. And in the long run it was this omission that proved important. Lauded by *Social Justice,* Lindbergh was also named to Pelley's "patriotic honor roll." The vice-president of the German-American Bund, meanwhile, August Klapprott, agreed with a lesser functionary, Hermann Schwarzmann, in hoping that the former flying ace would become *"Führer* of our great political party"; the *Free American* commended him for giving the American people "a douche of good, American common sense"; and the *Christian Front News* supported his battle against vast armies of the night, composed of "war mongers, political parasites, financial shylocks, and munitions moguls." Every countersubversive, it seemed, was climbing aboard the Lindbergh bandwagon, and further support was also lent by Park Avenue fascist John B. Snow, Boris Brasol, and Count Anastase Vonsiatsky. In Berlin, understandably, the official word praised Lindbergh as "the most potent enemy" of American Jews.

Burdened by these endorsements and his own naiveté, Lindbergh delivered responsible American isolationism a mortal blow at Des Moines when he singled out "the British, the Jewish, and the Roosevelt administration" as the primary forces drawing the nation toward war. Although this accusation was in no way the product of any deep-rooted anti-Jewish prejudice, the controversy surrounding Lindbergh had reached the point where any intimation of anti-Semitism could easily be equated with Nazism. Accepting the full responsibility for his words and denying that he had attacked the Jews on the basis of race or religion, the flier explained that he had worded his Des Moines address "carefully and moderately," mentioned the Jews only in two paragraphs, and, moreover, had pointed to the groups generally believed to be the most interventionist in their thinking. "It seems," he wrote in his journal on September 15, "that almost any problem can be discussed today in America except the Jewish problem. The very mention of the word 'Jew' is cause for a storm." With the exception of John T. Flynn, chairman of the New York unit of the Committee who felt that any mention of the "Jewish problem" was inadvisable because of its emotional connotations, other isolationist leaders concurred with Lindbergh, explaining that their favorite orator had been victimized by the excerpting of "garbled fragments" by the interventionist press. What the America First leadership failed to realize the significance of, however, was the inappropriateness of Lindbergh's timing.

The reaction to the address was overwhelming; the damage to the isolationist cause, irreparable. That many Americans were now arguing less about foreign policy issues than about the proper responses to such problems became clear as Presidential Press Secretary Early discovered "a striking similarity" between Lindbergh's statement and "the outpouring from Berlin in the last few days." F. H.. Peter Cusick of the Fight for Freedom Committee noted that the flier's prestige had "descended even more quickly than Hitler's dive bombers about which he talks so admirably." Lewis W. Douglas, chairman of the Policy Group of the Committee to Defend America by Aiding the Allies, warned: "Anti-Semitism, implied in Lindbergh's speech, is one of the characteristics of Nazism wherever it has stuck up its ugly head." Wendell Willkie termed the address "the most un-American talk made in my time by any person of national reputation."

Across the United States resentment soared. Interventionist congressmen, remembering Representative Edelstein's death, flooded the *Record* with speeches and editorials; Senator Claude Pepper of Florida termed Lindbergh an internal enemy of the United States; and the Texas State Legislature passed a resolution opposing his proposed visit to the Lone Star State. Billboards in Los Angeles sported "Adolf Loves Lindy" signs. A St. Louis advertising executive sent Roosevelt a bumper-sticker bearing the legend: "TO HELL MIT LINDBERGH!" Correspondents of the Chief Executive described the flier as a "a homegrown rattlesnake" and "the budding *Führer* of America." Columnist Dorothy Thompson interpreted the speech as final proof of his hatred for "the present democratic system, and his desire to emerge as America's savior with a new party along Nazi lines behind him." The Reverend L. M. Birkhead issued a pamphlet entitled, *Is Lindbergh a Nazi?* A preacher in Hayward, California, warned his listeners: "On American soil the beast of Berchtesgaden stirs. Anti-Semitism is on its way. Is this an effort to start in our midst the wave of the future?"

Lindbergh and America First also drew fire from the liberal press. A writer for the *New Republic* noted that "the thing that is dangerous about America First is that it has become the effective general staff of all the fascist, semi-fascist, and proto-fascist elements in America. It has become the focal point of anti-Semitism. Let in the light. We have a right to know where the money comes from." In a memorandum to Attorney General Francis Biddle two months later, President Roosevelt asked the same question. His doubt reflected the fears of many of his countrymen, and for the moment, as revealed in several opinion polls, Charles Lindbergh had eclipsed the German-American Bund as the most renowned steward of anti-Semitic propaganda in America. Citizens who for the previous decade had either ridiculed or feared Coughlin, Pelley, and the Bundists, now fastened their attention on the flier. The fear of countersubversion had come full circle; the isolationist bloc both in and outside of Congress had lost its solidarity; and noninterventionists were everywhere on the defensive, explaining that they were not Nazis.

Paradoxically, men who claimed to be superpatriots had unwittingly helped attach the stigma of un-Americanism to perhaps the most "American" American of the twentieth century. Lindbergh served his country with distinction during the Second World War, but he never lived down the tarnished image that resulted as much from the work of the countersubversives as it did from Hitler's atrocities, Nazi military success, and the flier's own poor judgment.

More than a year before the Des Moines affair, Father Coughlin had utilized a Biblical metaphor in pleading with the noninterventionist leader to disregard the Philistines who sought to impugn his motives. "The Winchells who poured vinegar into your wounds," wrote the radio cleric, "are the same puppets who danced before the Annases, the same puppets who poured vinegar upon the lips of the crucified Christ. Today you are scourged, spat upon, crowned with thorns. Tomorrow you may be wending your way to Calvary, there to be crucified by court order between thieves. After Calvary there is always an angel to roll back the stone under which your enemies think they have buried you. Millions in days to come will hallow your name. . . ."

Figuratively, Lindbergh had indeed ascended the hills of Calvary, and he had also been crucified among thieves—the inverted nativists. But the "angels" of which Father Coughlin spoke were nowhere in sight. Nor were there any heavenly spirits to save the extremists from the consequences of their own excesses. Having applauded Lindbergh for attacking the conspiracy they had so long believed in, they enjoyed a fleeting moment of respectability. Yet as Ralph Waldo Emerson so wisely observed, the borrower runs in his own debt. Their protests to the contrary notwithstanding, the extremists had imitated a movement without roots in the American past. Their inverted nativism, though cloaked in patriotic rhetoric and imagery, was as American as the *"Horst Wessel Lied."*

In October Pelley surrendered to Asheville officials. Subsequently convicted for sedition, he served eight years of a fifteen-year sentence before returning to the study of psychic phenomena. In 1965, at the age of seventy-five, he began a somewhat longer than seven-minute stay in eternity. Father Coughlin remained an adversary of American diplomacy until the middle of 1942, when the Church hierarchy and the United States government joined forces to relegate him to a life of silence—a silence broken only by infrequent interviews and, ironically, by an occasional blast at contemporary "New Left" clerics seeking social justice. The German-American Bund, finally, received even shorter shrift. Outlawed by the government shortly after Pearl Harbor, by 1942 the Bund had become only a bad dream disturbing the sleep of particularly fitful New York Jewish-Americans.

EPILOGUE

Extremism
and the Historical Process

★ ★ ★   But there is more to this story than the troubled sleep of American Jews during World War II. That raucous critics of the emerging New Deal political and global order should be historically designated as "extremists" underlines their position both as losers in the Great Debate before Pearl Harbor and avatars of a tradition deemed inimical to the national interest in the postwar era. Through the mechanism of guilt by association—specifically the identification of prewar noninterventionists with extremists, and thence with European Nazis and fascists—Franklin Roosevelt and his interventionist colleagues foreshadowed much of the style and substance of postwar debates on loyalty, subversion, and patriotism. Given the state of permanent emergency that became the basis of the Cold War globalism, advocates of limits on foreign policy—no matter their political persuasion—came under suspicion as subversive conspirators against the safety of the nation.

Such opprobrium owed much to the victory of the interventionists in the Great Debate—as it did to the continuing impact of the surprise Japanese attack at Pearl Harbor and to the memory of the ill-fated Munich conference of September 1938. In retrospect, these two events generated a dominant world-view very different from the paradigm that had guided Washington policy-makers during the interwar period. The nation's searing experience with Nazism, followed almost immediately by the similarly alarming Cold War with the Soviet Union, fed pervasive distaste for any political activity that might be equated with totalitarianism.

The equation of fascism with communism heavily influenced postwar domestic security and foreign policy. It also influenced many American historians and social scientists. In the postwar era, Americans who did not hew to what Arthur M. Schlesinger, Jr., termed "the vital center" became "extremists" on either the left or right. Because the American Communist Party was moribund after 1948, and because antiwar radicals and popular-front advocates of the wartime anti-fascist alliance found themselves in full retreat shortly thereafter, the notion of extremism became by the late 1950s an epithet directed primarily at such rightist groups as the reborn Ku Klux Klan, the John Birch Society, the Minutemen, and other organizations and individuals who did not abide the New Deal order.

Nor did the generation that assumed the mantle of vital-center liberal pluralism and wrote consensus history in the 1950s and 1960s address the 1930s on its own terms. They exhibited little empathy with those Americans who challenged the liberal center. Just as the Roosevelt administration had sought to delegitimize its isolationist and noninterventionist critics before Pearl Harbor, liberal historians and social scientists advanced theories of status politics, authoritarian personalities, and the "paranoid style" in American politics to point up the dangers of ideology to the civil, pragmatic, and "reasonable" mainstream. Ideological critics of the political mainstream were located on the fringe—usually the "lunatic fringe"—of society.

Liberal pluralists inherited and refined a paradigm similar to that which had guided most mainstream defenders of the New Deal's domestic and foreign policies since the late 1930s. Hence consensus historians did not care to notice that in the decade preceding Pearl Harbor the political mainstream featured a conspiracy theory of dissent no less important than the pervasive "devil theory" of war. The devil theory, a staple of 1930s debate over intervention, laid responsibility for U.S. entry into World War I at the feet of a powerful cadre of financiers and munitions makers. Interlocking visions of devils and conspirators pervaded the political landscape of the 1930s, reflecting and affecting the course of that very "center" that Schlesinger would celebrate in 1948, let alone the views of Americans far removed from the exercise of power. Both theories proved problematic in coming to terms with global realities; both assumptions shaped the Great Debate on prewar foreign policy. Variations on the devil theory informed the work not just of imputed extremists but of writers from Ernest Hemingway to Charles Beard, Harry Elmer Barnes, and other historians who had considered intervention in World War I a dreadful mistake. The theory also influenced the neutrality legislation of mid-decade, the Nye Committee investigations, and the abortive Ludlow Amendment of 1938, which would have added a constitutional amendment to subject a declaration of war to national referendum. And, as we have seen, America First and Charles A. Lindbergh made the devil theory of war a major theme in their battle to prevent FDR from taking the nation to war for the second time in a quarter-century.

But conspiracy fears bulked even larger in the Roosevelt administration's drive for national unity—an undertaking that assumed prime importance after 1939 as the President and Congress competed in stalking potentially subversive groups. As FBI records reveal, questions of loyalty became an integral part of mainstream foreign policy issues. Indeed, questions of security exerted a huge impact upon the ways American leaders formulated their policies. Loyalty and security concerns did not cease with Japan's attack on Pearl Harbor; the tension between alleged subversion and national safety grew stronger, becoming a central theme in Roosevelt's wartime leadership and ultimately a permanent feature of American life during the Cold War.

In November 1939 the FBI began assembling a "custodial detention index" of persons with "strong" Nazi or communist "tendencies" whose liberty during war "would constitute a menace." The next year Congress passed the Smith Act which required aliens to register with the Attorney General and made it a federal crime to advocate the violent overthrow of the government. This law, probably the most drastic restriction on peacetime free speech in American history, signaled that a majority of congressmen and the President believed that the time had come to check persons whom Attorney General Robert Jackson described as "ready to give assistance or encouragement in any form to invading or opposing ideologies."

As institutional precursor of the postwar vital center, the Smith Act in effect outlawed ideologies that might be deemed "un-American." By mid-1940 the fear of fifth-column activities comprised a moderate red scare, uniting intellectuals like Lewis Mumford, the editors of *The Nation*, Roosevelt, and J. Edgar Hoover. After the Nazi-Soviet Nonaggression Pact of August 1939, which linked communism and fascism in American minds, concern with subversive intrigue grew markedly. With Representative Martin Dies's House Committee on Un-American Activities decrying leftist influences in the White House, the loyalty issue became partisan, and all the more important to FDR. Despite his Attorney General's dissent in May 1940, the President approved Hoover's surveillance of "persons suspected of subversive activities," a directive that quickly encompassed the right to open suspicious mail entering or leaving the country. In September, after passage of the Smith Act, Attorney General Frank Murphy (generally regarded as a friend of civil liberties) agreed. "Unless we are pudding-headed," he asserted, "we shall drive from the land the hirelings here to undo the labors of our fathers."

Roosevelt was sensitive to the potential for abuse inherent in antisubversive activity, recalling the excessive American vigilantism of World War I. Yet his administration's dilemma—reconciling its determination to defend civil liberties with its dedication to checking internal subversion—ultimately proved intractable in a world where the exercise of brute force seemed the sole test of survival. What historian J. Woodford Howard termed "the symbolic prosecution of foreign agents," like American Communist Party leader Earl Browder, became analogous to the denunciation and harassment accorded noninterventionists. Here, as we have seen, Roosevelt's drive to unify the nation in support of Great Britain emphasized and exaggerated the danger of anti-Semitic domestic fascists led, ultimately, by Charles Lindbergh. Well before Pearl Harbor the administration's conspiracy theory of dissent proved more formidable than the devil theory of war—and of FDR himself—promulgated by noninterventionists.

The administration's conspiracy theory of dissent, made urgent by Germany's threat to subdue Europe, no doubt strengthened the interventionist cause and lent unity to the war against Hitler and the Japanese. The interventionists' linking of Lindbergh and noninterventionists with Nazi anti-Semitism underlines two points: that American campaigns against subversion have not been confined to a single ideology, political party, or social class; and that these crusades have not held a monopoly on morality. When Lindbergh named the Jews as one of the three main groups seeking intervention, the outraged response of interventionists seemed to draw a distinct ethical barrier between a tolerant Roosevelt administration and its bigoted, extremist opponents. Yet as White House policies toward Jewish refugees from the European conflict indicate, this view is at best misleading. While denouncing glandular anti-Semites like the Bundists, Pelley, Coughlin, Gerald L. K. Smith, and—allegedly—Lindbergh, pre–Pearl Harbor interventionists either could not see, or more likely found it impolitic to admit, that their own house was permeated by a powerful, albeit genteel, anti-Semitism.

Recent scholarship demonstrates that fully one-third of the American populace was prepared to approve anti-Jewish immigration measures, hardly astonishing in a nation still confronting economic woes. The fate of the Wagner-Rogers Bill in February 1939 indicated that two-thirds of Americans polled opposed the measure to admit twenty thousand additional Jewish refugee children beyond the annual quota of twenty-seven thousand persons from Germany and Austria. Skeptical Americans saw the bill as "a wedge for thousands more" while several Jewish leaders worried that passage actually would strengthen anti-Semitism.

Even more important in shaping the State Department's restrictive immigration policy after 1938 was the fear shared by Roosevelt, Hoover, and Under Secretary of State Breckenridge Long that Jewish refugees might themselves be part of a fifth-column recruited to serve Hitler's interests in the United States. Long personally disliked Jews, and he and the President were known to share a chuckle at anti-Semitic jokes. In private moments FDR exhibited some dubious views on racial issues, including thoughts of crossbreeding Europeans and Asians to subdue the delinquent traits of the Japanese. On one occasion he told Treasury Secretary Henry Morgenthau that "you either have to castrate the German people or you have to treat them in such a manner that they can't just go on reproducing people who want to continue the way they have in the past." Roosevelt also disdained the Burmese as "dislikeable," and he told Joseph Stalin at the Yalta Conference in 1945 that the Vietnamese were "a people of small stature...and not warlike." On another occasion, as he discussed with associates the Puerto Rican birthrate, the President insinuated, jokingly, the need to use "the methods which Hitler used effectively," in this case an electric current, "very simple and painless," that would "sterilize subjects in about twenty seconds."

Similar attitudes and assumptions informed national policy toward Japanese Americans after Pearl Harbor. The removal of 127,000 Nisei and Issei from the West Coast, and their incarceration in wartime "relocation" camps, also exposed the intersection of imputed racial and ideological motivations in American security planning. The decision to confine this tiny minority of loyal citizens, defended in terms of "military necessity" in Executive Order 9066, involved all three branches of government and evoked scant opposition, even from traditional defenders of civil liberties.

Ironically, as the United States fought a total war to eradicate Nazi racial theories, ideas of Anglo-Saxon superiority also served to consolidate American and British cooperation in the Pacific. Here FDR's correspondence with Dr. Alex Hrdlicka, an idiosyncratic anthropologist at the Smithsonian Institution, commands more than passing interest. Hrdlicka long had considered Japanese leaders "utterly egotistic, tricky, and ruthless" men, "working toward the exclusion of all, and particularly the white man, from the Pacific and Eastern Asia." Roosevelt did not embrace Hrdlicka's extremism, but during the early weeks of the war the President did ask him to undertake a study of race-crossing of Asian and European stocks. If the Japanese could be driven back to their islands, FDR thought, possibly their aggressive characteristics might be bred out of them.

Franklin Roosevelt was clearly no political cousin of the Beast of Berchtesgaden, but the President's racial views—and at least two American policies— amplify D. W. Brogan's observation that "in the years between the wars, the United States was only outdistanced by Germany as a market for race theories, some of them crude enough to have suited Hitler." In this context, making an issue of extremist anti-Semitism both before and after Pearl Harbor was at least as pragmatic as it was ethical. Genteel anti-Semitism expressed by Long and others in the administration suggests as well that the picture of the 1930s as an era of ethnic liberalism marked by the assimilation of Jews and other minorities is exaggerated.

Equally clear, demands for patriotism, loyalty, and unity contained within the administration's conspiracy theory of dissent exacted a price. "Rarely," the historian Wayne S. Cole observed in 1973, "have any movements or public figures been more thoroughly discredited than were isolationism and the isolationists." Indeed, calumnies heaped upon peace advocates before Pearl Harbor impeded the desire and ability of the nation's leaders after the war to consider alternatives to globalism. Events during the 1930s, catalyzed by the Great Debate into huge moral generalizations, cast dark shadows upon the landscape of postwar foreign policy and affected the ambience of the Cold War in a variety of ways. When the communist menace replaced the fascist peril, the government knew how to deal with imputed domestic subversion. A foreign policy based upon power and demands for internal loyalty, rather than on the domestic airing of sincerely held policy differences, became a basic theme of bipartisan foreign policy after 1945.

Here Roosevelt's cunning diplomacy (admittedly inspired by the divided state of public opinion) and several decisions he made in 1941 impaired the country's long-term chances for peace. In September 1941, for instance, he explained the *Greer* incident as a German submarine attack upon that American destroyer; yet a later investigation showed that ultimate responsibility for the attack was unclear. Presidential manipulation of public opinion was nothing new in 1941, of course, but as Senator J. William Fulbright observed in 1970 (as he lamented the growth of the imperial presidency and the blank check which Congress had given Lyndon Johnson after the Gulf of Tonkin "incident" in 1964), "FDR's deviousness in a good cause made it easier for LBJ to practice the same kind of deviousness in a bad cause."

Augmented ties between the presidency and the nation's intelligence establishment also figured prominently in postwar security considerations, especially in the 1950s when the Central Intelligence Agency began its long career of exceeding its mandate as a mere gatherer and interpreter of intelligence. In light of numerous secret CIA attempts to destabilize foreign governments and undercut domestic dissent during the Cold War, FDR's order to FBI chief Hoover in September 1941 to investigate congressional attitudes toward his foreign policy assumes alarming import. Several legislators had indeed misused their franking privilege in distributing anti-administration materials, but their transgressions betrayed only their wish to keep the United States out of war—not Hoover's conviction that they were Nazi agents. Nor did the trial of numerous alleged "seditionists" in 1944 clarify security matters; that event became a bizarre circus.

If interventionist charges of noninterventionist disloyalty, and noninterventionist accusations of executive perfidy, both became self-fulfilling before Pearl Harbor, notions of guilt by association and executive tyranny did not die with the end of the war. After 1945 revisionist historiography resurfaced, with a hostility befitting advocates of a point of view relegated from center- to backstage in the previous decade. Beard, Barnes, and Charles Callan Tansill, among others, wrote new books which revived earlier noninterventionist arguments. But where these writers had elicited some sympathy before 1939, their postwar revisionism encountered a climate similar to the hostile environment of 1941. As the Cold War deepened, there was no room in the academy for their criticism of Roosevelt's diplomacy.

Even more interesting was the reappearance in the early 1950s of a fusion of interventionist tactics with substantive arguments employed by noninterventionists during 1939–1941. Within the McCarthyite crusade against alleged communist subversion in government between 1950 and 1954, one confronts a strategy that combined an anti-elitist thrust with the charge that recent American global reverses reflected treason by national leaders. This accusation demonstrates the fickleness of history, as liberal interventionists who earlier had tarnished the noninterventionist cause with the tincture of fascism now discovered that they themselves comprised what Alistair Cooke termed *A*

Generation on Trial. The Yalta Conference, the "loss" of China, the spy cases, and the Soviet detonation of an atomic bomb suggested that Harry S Truman's containment policy and his internal security program not only had failed but had facilitated the emergence of the Soviet Union as a world power and a threat to American safety.

As the nation's experience with fascism at home and abroad had influenced debate on foreign policy in the late 1930s, foreign and domestic confrontations with communism and the McCarthy phenomenon in the early 1950s strengthened liberal internationalists in their conviction that earlier noninterventionist assumptions were dangerous to national security. This was unfortunate because it placed advocates of disarmament and conciliation even further on the defensive, outside the emerging, elite-dominated, pluralist consensus. Opponents of the foreign policies of containment (and intervention) pursued by both the Truman and Eisenhower administrations became the antithesis of this consensus, and were often tarred with the "extremist" epithet.

Senator Joseph McCarthy's demise in 1954 might have relieved liberals, but it did not transform either official or popular perceptions of the communist menace. Indeed, the Soviet threat remained the prime motif of a succession of presidents seeking popular support for their policies. In focusing their counter-charges on McCarthy himself, furthermore, liberals failed to see that they might actually weaken the potential of congressional challenges to executive authority in foreign policymaking. The absence of this balancing factor assumed significance during the Johnson and Nixon years especially, when critics of American intervention in Southeast Asia echoed complaints by Lindbergh, Beard, and other noninterventionists about executive secrecy and deception, the erosion of congressional prerogative in foreign affairs, and the dangerous growth of the presidency. Lyndon Johnson's decision in 1968 not to seek reelection, and Richard Nixon's Watergate, provided evidence of how counterproductive the conspiracy theory of dissent had become by the late 1960s. These developments, however, provided little consolation for liberals and radicals whose sincere criticism of American Vietnam policy and the apparently unrestrained global exercise of national power now earned them the opprobrium traditionally accorded a treasonous minority. For citizens who opposed this war, history had moved 180 degrees—against them. They were now the extremists.

Since the 1930s the terms "extremism" and "extremist" have been used so often in American politics, in such diverse contexts, and by so many disparate people and groups as to render them at once protean—and meaningless. Yet from Roosevelt's New Deal through the presidency of George Bush, the notion of extremism has figured prominently as a subtext of politics and of foreign and security policy debate. Liberals who used the epithet of extremism in condemning prewar noninterventionists, and in the 1950s and 1960s McCarthyites and the Far Right, stressed the unreal and subversive character of these groups' oversimplified, moralistic, and antipolitical warnings against heinous internal conspiracies. But if liberals found the notion of extremism a useful political weapon, the modern idea of extremism carries still greater significance. For as the fate of many pre–Pearl Harbor liberal interventionists during succeeding decades suggests, trading on conspiracy fears can be tricky business, as likely to backfire as to achieve desired goals. Extremist politics based upon conspiratorial accusations have generated long-term failures which more than offset short-term successes.

Perhaps the strangest aspect of extremism after 1950 is the journey taken by those pluralist scholars who originally advanced the idea of a politics of unreason during the era of liberal ascendancy. By the early 1970s this group—heir to the tradition of intervention before Pearl Harbor and liberal internationalism after World War II—had embraced the very political characteristics they earlier deemed irrational and extremist. After the social and cultural upheavals of the late 1960s, many disillusioned liberals became neoconservatives, providing many of the ideas (and even the personnel) that facilitated the emergence of the New Right of the 1980s. Having played a key role in defining in retrospect the derogatory paradigm describing critics of the New Deal, and then leading the battle against the extremist New Right beginning in the late 1950s, this intellectual cadre proceeded to develop and institutionalize the positive image of the current political right. In so doing the neoconservatives helped shift the mantle of political extremism to the Democratic Party, where it now rests (encapsulated by the well-known "L" word), and to those Americans whose critiques of the current free-market order designate them as cultural and social subversives, or "politically correct."

The postwar notion of extremism emerged primarily as a shield for vital-center liberalism, which sought to parry conservative Republican and neo-isolationist critiques of the New Deal order and the nation's new Cold War internationalism. Liberal academics extolled the genius of interest-group politics as the New Deal defined them, and their consensus view of history depicted the nation's past as devoid of significant conflict and dissent. Americans were "born free," and dissent had no place in a country whose inhabitants demonstrated overarching agreement on political and economic fundamentals. Americans had differed, certainly, but only over the best means to improve capitalism and strengthen the nation's democratic institutions. The 1950s were thus influenced by the assumption that fundamental criticism of the status quo was illegitimate. Consensus history and social science reflected not only the perceived need for unity in the face of the Soviet challenge, but also postwar prosperity, the overlapping of Democratic and Republican foreign and domestic policies, and the political fallout generated by McCarthyism, a phenomenon that confirmed elite groups in their desire to be rid of ideology and in their feeling that demagogues and mass democracy threatened national unity and must be contained. Ignoring their own complicity in the rise of McCarthyism, anticommunist Democrats and Republicans embraced bipartisanship in foreign affairs and their own form of political correctness, and they determined to avoid the ideological traps that had produced totalitarianism in Europe.

After delegitimizing the left in 1948 by linking Henry Wallace's Progressive Party with the Soviet threat, the liberal pluralists discovered a radical, neofascist potential lurking within the domestic and foreign policy programs of the McCarthyite wing of the Republican Party and other rightist groups. Consistent with Daniel Bell's description of the 1950s as the decade that marked "the end of ideology" (if not history itself), social scientists and historians developed several strategies to prove that ideology and politics comprised a dangerous, un-American mix. This campaign reached its height during and after the McCarthy era, when writers like Bell, Edward Shils, Seymour Martin Lipset, Nathan Glazer, Talcott Parsons, and Richard Hofstadter, among others, joined to employ insights drawn from contemporary sociology and psychology to criticize those aspects of American politics that did not "fit" the New Deal urban-liberal paradigm.

More pointedly, these scholars decried what Hofstadter and others later termed "the paranoid style" and "pseudoconservatism" of the American right. They defined the radical right primarily as an expression of status anxieties; worried about "authoritarianism" within American labor and other perceived defectors from the New Deal coalition; and discerned within McCarthyism a dangerous mass politics similar to European fascism. They explained the right's criticism of welfare capitalism and of containment—domestic as well as foreign—as irresponsible and potentially ruinous. As this critique went, McCarthyites (and their Goldwaterite successors) weren't really conservative. They and groups like them were radicals who would risk nuclear annihilation and undo the humane and civil practice of politics established in the 1930s and 1940s. Furthermore, the extremists' monistic, simplistic, moralistic, and populist (antipolitical) temper excluded them from mainstream life. From this perspective liberal academics rewrote much American history, criticizing groups that challenged the status quo as nativist, racist, and out of touch with reality, usually because of changes in their status.

These liberal pluralists rejected analyses of class in favor of assessments of American affluence. They argued that interest-group politics best served the nation in its determination to combat communism. Interest-group politics alone allowed for economic growth and military strength, respective guarantors of domestic tranquility and world peace. Interest-group politics was a forum where middle-class groups of like-minded citizens (and in the early 1950s nearly all white Americans seemed middle-class, or about to become so) could organize to decide who got what, and how. The federal government served as a benign broker in this process, ensuring that no single interest would become too powerful. John Kenneth Galbraith celebrated this system in two 1950s best-sellers, *American Capitalism* and *The Affluent Society*, even as he criticized the inequalities and wastefulness of corporate capitalism.

The 1950s and early 1960s marked the pinnacle of liberal-pluralist influence. Despite a Republican president and two sharp "Eisenhower recessions," economic growth nourished unprecedented prosperity. The Republican Party embraced the New Deal welfare state as well as the need to exert power internationally in defense of the "Free World." The liberal-pluralist elite, which came to include national security managers, social planners, and "experts" in such diverse fields as civil defense, education, and baby and child care, appeared to preside over a society that, though admittedly not perfect, might become so. When Massachusetts Senator John F. Kennedy became the youngest and first Catholic president in American history, liberals rejoiced at a blow dealt traditional anti-alien nativism, and looked forward to a political "Camelot."

During these years liberals in government and the academy accelerated their warnings of a growing antidemocratic peril from the right. In the early civil rights movement they pointed to the scurrilous rhetoric and violence of the trice-born Ku Klux Klan, the White Citizens Councils, and other anti-black groups. They also exposed, analyzed, and denounced the ultra-anticommunist John Birch Society, the paramilitary Minutemen, fundamentalist minister Billy James Hargis, and American Nazi leader George Lincoln Rockwell. Assessments of these and other extremists continued to stress their "paranoid" (unreal) characteristics as evidence of a dangerous "thunder on the right" which would undercut the nation's commitment to an open society. The welter of charge and countercharge that followed the Kennedy assassination (and persists to this day) augmented popular apprehension about connections between ideology, extremism, and conspiracy.

In this atmosphere Senator Barry Goldwater's nomination in 1964 as the Republican presidential candidate became a godsend—and something of a self-fulfilling prophecy—for liberal pluralists. Goldwater was an extremist and hence a veritable death knell for the GOP. His politics, liberal Hubert Humphrey joked, rendered the handsome Arizonan a potential actor "for Eighteenth-Century Fox." Fiscally prudent, Goldwater disdained big government and its heavy tax system as well as other federal intrusions. He aimed harsh words at the New Deal and at conventional interest-group politics as conducted by Democrats and the conspiratorially aligned, apostate, Eastern liberal wing of the Republican Party. Goldwater was also a militant anticommunist whose campaign proposal that the United States use low-yield nuclear weapons to defoliate Vietnam raised the specter of nuclear Armageddon. His was a platform of conscience, not compromise. "Extremism in the pursuit of liberty is no vice," he told the Republicans' San Francisco convention, "and moderation in the pursuit of justice is no virtue." Goldwater extolled individual responsibility, explained that there was "no substitute for victory" against the communists, and then ran a curious campaign during which he denounced unions in Detroit, medicare in Florida, and the Tennessee Valley Authority in Knoxville.

Goldwater suffered one of the most resounding electoral defeats in American history. During the campaign he drew unsolicited support from groups like the Birchers, the Klan, and Dr. Fred Schwarz's Christian-Anticommunist Crusade. Although Goldwater took great care to separate himself from these dubious supporters, his liberal opponents gained much from their practice of guilt by association. His foreign policy views seemed doubly dangerous because he stood outside the national security establishment. As with Joe McCarthy's wild accusations of communists in government, the Republican Party had forfeited its claim to acting responsibly in foreign affairs.

Lyndon Johnson's image during the campaign was that of a man of moderation and peace. His huge plurality suggested that on the national level, at least, the right-wing conspiracy against the New Deal and liberal pluralism had been quashed. The Republican Party itself seemed moribund, a victim of ruinous ideology and an opponent who apparently relished the role of Bela Lugosi.

But liberals who rejoiced might have been less sanguine. Goldwater did win twenty-seven million popular votes. There remained a huge body of Americans dissatisfied with the failure to win the Cold War, the power of the federal government, the strength of labor unions, the influence of the liberal communications empire, and the tone of modern culture itself, especially the spiritual costs of rampant consumerism. Although Kennedy-Johnson liberals themselves worried about growing "soft" in an age of materialism, about juvenile delinquency and related family pathology, and—it seemed at times—about the very problem of "problemlessness," they did not realize that a growing segment of the populace considered *them* part of the problem. Since the mid-1930s Republican anticommunism had focused its energies inward, as the young William F. Buckley observed, upon problems of laxness in high places, on declining national morality, on the "sin" of modernism, or "rottenness" in society. The Goldwater candidacy circulated a similar critique. And through direct mail and television the Republicans created a far larger financial base than the Democrats.

Yet as long as interest-group pluralism commanded mainstream politics, the establishment could repulse these sorts of challenges as extremist politics. As long as the Democratic Party coalition held together, the center could ward off attacks from both left and right as evidence of sociological and/or psychological maladjustment. Although both McCarthyite and Goldwater critiques utilized mainstream political channels, with mainstream political leaders serving as hunters and quarry, the liberal pluralists missed these points.

But prevailing definitions of extremism soon changed. For within the next decade the seemingly impregnable liberal-pluralist fortress crumbled—first reeling from a blow by the left, then dropping from a counterpunch from the right. This combination destroyed the New Deal coalition, supplanted interest-group pluralism with a political agenda of cultural and social issues, and heralded a national political shift no less portentous than the leftward swing that had occurred three decades earlier.

Expediting this change, many from the pluralist academic elite that had fashioned notions of extremist politics as late as the mid-1960s abandoned the liberal ship to become neoconservatives, members of a "counter-establishment" which became in turn the intellectual vanguard of a conservative political resurgence. Curiously, their new politics was fueled by a conspiracy theory reminiscent of the old Trotskyite critique of Stalinist Russia as "a degenerated workers' state." For many disillusioned liberal-pluralists like Glazer and Lipset, and newcomers like Norman Podhoretz, Irving Kristol, and Midge Decter, "populist" and "authoritarian" laborers no longer seemed as ominous as they had in the 1950s. On the contrary, these old antagonists now appeared to be allies against a greater enemy—an internal New Class which neoconservatives equated with the managerial bureaucracy that betrayed the proletariat when it seized leadership in the Soviet Union after 1917. For the neoconservatives, as for the subsequent New Right, the notion of the sinister New Class figured as prominently a foil in political debates after 1975 as had the "radical right" for liberal pluralists during the 1950s and 1960s.

An explanation of this transformation is complex, but it includes Lyndon Johnson's dubious overextension of his 1964 mandate on both domestic and foreign fronts; the radicalization and alienation of the civil rights movement as two presidents parried its quest for integration; and the growth of an overlapping counterculture and radical student movement which parodied America's materialistic culture and challenged the nation to live up to its democratic promise. In the backlash wrought by these events, exacerbated by an economic decline that began in the early 1970s, class issues emerged within the political arena for the first time since 1945. For in postwar America, liberal pluralists in and out of government had repudiated as irrelevant (and dangerous) the notion of class, with its implications of stratification, inequality, and (God forbid) imperfection.

Yet even before the convulsions of the 1960s Americans had discovered significant pockets of domestic poverty—and an underclass. This discovery struck liberals as the cause that might elevate the country from the miasma of materialism by providing the sort of challenge that "old" trade-union liberalism could not. If the Soviets worshiped "godless materialism," Arthur M. Schlesinger, Jr., quipped, Americans had embraced "godly materialism." By fostering anxious and continual consumption, this materialism undercut masculinity, demoralized women, and threatened the future of American children and the nation itself. Consumer values threatened to swamp the ethics of the producer culture that Americans identified with national greatness—character, self-sacrifice, frugality, and the ability to save for a rainy day. One problem with this perception lay in its myopia, its inability to allow for the possibility that working-class poor might not share the liberal, middle-class contempt for so-called materialism. Another problem with this view was that it projected onto the poor those very values of consumerism that so troubled the liberal-pluralists. In the pluralist view, success demanded work, but work could not be considered a certain ticket to material success. Rising material expectations notwithstanding, there was no place for a policy of entitlement for have-nots.

The civil rights movement and Michael Harrington's *The Other America*

(1963) put a human face on poverty and energized the liberal commitment to action. But the ensuing campaign against poverty was less noteworthy for its attainments than for descriptions of the poor that accorded have-nots blame for their own misfortune. America's poor, it seemed, were infantile, unable to defer gratification, prone to mental illness—denizens, in short, of a "culture" of poverty. This picture, ironically, owed something to previous liberal-pluralist criticism of the "Beat" generation, whose constituents also condemned the obsessive materialism of the "straight" world but who *chose* to live lives of poverty and consequently were denounced as self-indulgent adolescents unwilling to cope with reality. In a manner similar to the pluralists who castigated the Beats, and to liberal scholars who explained the unreal culture of political extremism through constructs like status politics and the "paranoid style," liberal social planners who conceived the war on poverty focused much attention upon a deviant culture. In this way Johnson administration liberals censured a powerless group for its own misfortunes, helped undermine the war on poverty before it began, and, as Barbara Ehrenreich suggests, provided a definition of poverty to service a more conservative era.

For when it came to relinquishing and redistributing wealth and power, the liberal establishment proved not only peevish but downright hostile. Equality of opportunity was one thing, equality of condition quite another. Middle-class liberals assumed that poverty might be vanquished at little cost to anyone. But radical programs—especially at the level of community organizing—contained negative implications for social harmony and political consensus. "Keep out the crooks, Communists, and cocksuckers," LBJ told his incoming head of the Office of Economic Opportunity in 1964. The President might also have advised keeping out poor people for, soon after, when community organizers articulated their desire to use the OEO to promote real social change, Johnson's war on poverty became a conflict declared but never fought. Most important, many liberal pluralists recoiled from the new black anger, withdrew support from civil rights, and condemned this murky yet dangerous underclass and its advocates, with their demands for equality of condition. Longtime allies in the liberal-Democratic coalition, blacks and middle-class Jews parted company in the late 1960s, a rift widened beyond healing by the bitter 1968 New York teachers' strike, and by the emergence of Black Power.

If the war on poverty proved stillborn, the war in Southeast Asia did not. By 1965, on college and university campuses, principled opposition to the conflict emerged, soon escalating into teach-ins and increasingly visceral condemnations of "Johnson's War." For antiwar protesters, many of whom had earlier risked their lives in the civil rights movement, the conflict in Vietnam sharpened questions about the nation's institutions and the liberal-pluralist elite's commitment to democracy. They turned to such disparate critics as J. D. Salinger, Herbert Marcuse, Paul Goodman, and Joan Baez to discover what had happened to democracy's promise. The motley counterculture, meanwhile, rejected even that question.

Even more than disputes attending the war on poverty, discord over Vietnam fractured liberal elites and the middle class generally. After initial hesitation, many liberal internationalists joined this protest, finding the idealism of the young morally persuasive, or embracing the realist argument that the United States lacked the means to "win" the war within conventional definitions of "victory." By the mid-1970s, in fact, the liberal establishment revealed numerous defectors, including former CIA agent Daniel Ellsberg, former Secretary of Defense Robert McNamara, and nuclear strategist Bernard Brodie—men who had forsaken anticommunism, the Cold War, and deterrence.

But the war and the protest against it became a different sort of Rubicon for many other liberal pluralists. Dealing with a "paranoid" right of hicks, kooks, and bigots had been one thing. John Birch Society campaigns proved nettlesome on local levels, but they were too idiosyncratic and overstated to exert national impact. Attacks on fluoridated water and sex education in the schools, attempts to impeach Earl Warren over the issue of school prayer, and Birch Society founder Robert Welch's assertion that Dwight Eisenhower had been a "card-carrying member of the Communist party" had generated more disdain than fear.

But mass civil disobedience and violence by the nation's youth were more difficult. Middle-class intellectuals, once liberal on issues of poverty and race, recoiled from student challenges to the meritocracy and hierarchy that governed universities, and to the standards that governed culture generally. They loathed the counterculture and its anarchic quest for liberation through communal living, spiritual questing, drugs, and sexual experimentation. Rather than blaming the young participants for this unprecedented assault on civilization (they were deemed incapable of serious political discourse), the pluralists fingered parents and "experts" like Dr. Benjamin Spock—advocates and practitioners of middle-class "permissiveness"—for creating this utopian monster with its condemnation of the military-industrial complex, corporate power, and cherished institutions. By 1968 radical students had fashioned a serviceable image of "fascist Amerika" while academics like Bell, Lipset, Glazer, Shils, Sidney Hook, Lewis Feuer, and Bruno Bettelheim responded in kind, with derogatory references of their own, linking war protesters to *fascisti* and to the "totalitarianism" of Hitler, Lenin, and Stalin.

This backlash crested in the early 1970s, and it marked the second major ideological flight for many liberal-pluralists—first, in the 1940s, from communism, and now, from liberalism. Much irony accompanied this passage: the group that had stressed sociological and psychological insights in its critique of earlier right-wing extremism now found itself on the wrong side of Democratic Party reforms. Democratic efforts to mollify dissenters within the party in 1968 had the effect of eliminating the pluralists from their honored status as party intellectuals. Their anger at the excesses of the children of affluence and the party that seemed to coddle them was sharpened by the tradition of economic scarcity that many neoconservatives had endured during the 1930s and 1940s. A large number were first- and second-generation immigrants, often Trotskyites in the Old Left of the 1930s. Adamant critics of

Stalinism, they became after 1945 ardent supporters of the Cold War. Many were also of secular Jewish descent, emphasizing the need for the United States to continue as global policeman lest Israel's security be jeopardized. The neoconservatives were clearly united by their unwavering anticommunism.

Yet if psychosocial considerations help explain the metamorphosis of many liberal-pluralists into neoconservatives, these hypotheses say little about that part of neoconservatism that became so potent in the early 1970s. The nub of the neoconservative critique stressed the importance of limits to the federal bureaucracy and to its policy promises and the expectations these generated. Although neoconservatives never comprised a political party, they brought to the political process an updated abhorrence of the extremist threat posed by mass politics—a version that now encompassed student protesters, the counterculture, and their mentors in academia and the professions. In defining this disparate lot as a conspiratorial New Class, the neoconservatives hastened the breakup of the New Deal coalition and its paradigm of interest-group politics. This vindictive form of class-consciousness also fueled Alabaman George Wallace's presidential aspirations, facilitated the emergence of a politics dominated increasingly by social concerns, and expedited the resurrection of Richard Nixon—as well as the Nixon administration's divisive rhetoric and dubious actions on behalf of "national security."

The theme of liberal "permissiveness" provided the catalyst for these shifts. From neoconservative and conservative ranks there erupted bitter condemnations of liberal elders who had contributed to their offspring's self-indulgence and desire for immediate gratification. Bettelheim's call to "punish" the protesters and dropouts and to instill "fear" within them provided a key reference point for Republican vice-presidential nominee Spiro Agnew, who offered himself as the "strong father" whom the young lacked. "A society which comes to fear its children is effete," Agnew explained. "A sniveling, hand-wringing power structure deserves the violent rebellion it encourages." Responsibility for the student movement rested with "those who so miserably failed to guide them . . . the affluent, permissive, upper-middle-class parents who learned their Dr. Spock and threw discipline out the window."

In the Bettelheim-Agnew text, a large segment of middle- and upper-middle-class America seemed to have rejected the core values of character, discipline, and thrift. This message proved congenial to white working-class men and women, often ethnic and often youthful themselves, who could not ignore these values. They saw the radicalism of the blacks and poor, the antiwar demonstrators, and women's liberation as the rejection of everything they affirmed—the work ethic, patriotism, monogamy, and religion. Younger Americans in the work force may have incorporated permissive attitudes of the counterculture in their own lives, but the inflation of the late 1960s—which produced the largest wave of strikes since World War II—sharpened their self-image as unjustly disadvantaged to that portion of the middle-class that had raised such ingrates.

Working-class support for George Wallace in the Midwest and North reflected strong support for his friendly views on economic and labor issues, and for his repeated attacks upon those professionals who, he argued, facilitated black advancement by federal fiat. Wallace's antipolitical fury appealed to class antagonism even more than it did to racial prejudice. When he denounced "the liberals, intellectuals, and long-hairs [who] have run the country for too long," and "the over-educated ivory tower folks with pointed heads looking down their noses at us," he spoke for "the little people" who agreed that "social engineers" and "phonies" in Washington would be better off in the Potomac River. His strong showing in 1968 signified that an influential part of the middle class itself—most notably employees of private business—shared this view. For the Wallace constituency, the basic problem of politics was sociocultural as well as economic. The threat to the nation's welfare came not from the grass roots. Rather, Wallace echoed portions of the McCarthy and Goldwater critiques against Eastern elites—and the accusation of executive and federal perfidy levied by many noninterventionists before Pearl Harbor. Like his predecessors, Wallace defined the enemy conspiracy as internal. It was headquartered in Washington and New York, and it involved the liberal elite that oversaw such programs as welfare and busing, as well as their allies in the university and the media.

Nixon also found this theory congenial. An old hand in fashioning accusations of conspiracy—indeed, he credited the Alger Hiss cases as assuring his political career—he honed his skills further in his "new" incarnation. Promising to heal national divisions, he ended his aborted second administration deepening them as no president before or since. During his first campaign he too made class antagonism his central strategy to cut into traditional Democratic Party strongholds. The evil of "permissiveness" loomed even larger in his strategy of class polarization than it did in Wallace's.

Nixon's distaste for intellectuals did not deter him from using class analyses which soon would be advanced by neoconservative writers like Norman Podhoretz and Daniel Patrick Moynihan. Nixon focused administration malice upon the youthful, *déclassé* extremists of the radical left and upon the myriad groups and individuals he considered their confederates. As the president's "enemies list" and his attempts to link indigenous protest to foreign sources made clear, he felt that radical sympathizers were just as dangerous, if not more so, as the radicals themselves. These foes lurked everywhere and included Fidel Castro, Jane Fonda, Joe Willie Namath, and the Kennedys—as well as the liberal media, university professors, and even those sectors of government that would contest his leadership.

Advanced as a weapon to discredit mass politics on the right in the 1960s, the "paranoid style" now characterized the Nixon administration's campaign against the left. Donning a hard hat to make symbolic common cause with laboring men and women who still had "character and guts and a bit of patriotism," Nixon combined overt appeals to the traditional values of the producer culture (which he identified with the middle-class "silent majority") with covert moves against the left and those he perceived as its allies—actions that went far beyond the law and executive accountability. Administration attempts to circumvent, if not destroy, competing power centers in Washington went hand in hand with illegal FBI and CIA campaigns to subvert the left and its supporters. Liberal pluralists who had left the Democratic Party to support Nixon in 1968 added condemnations of his enemies—advocates of Black Power, leaders of the drive for women's rights, "radical liberals," and (always) their supporters.

It was but a short step from the war against the left to the illegal activities aimed at the Democratic Party and its New Class allies before the 1972 election that became known as Watergate. Here was a political "monism" far more dangerous than the radical right's program which the old liberal-pluralists had denounced two decades earlier. Here too was a president seeking to short-circuit the democratic process even as he sought to solidify what he saw as a coalition of cultural conservatives, ready to direct its anger at black violence, radical militancy, drugs, and sexual liberation. Would America be led, Agnew inquired, by "a majority of the American people, or [would] it be intimidated and blackmailed into following the path dictated by a disruptive radical minority—the pampered prodigies of the radical liberals in the United States Senate?" Here, finally, was a lever to sunder what remained of the old New Deal coalition. And here was legitimation for a new political alignment of blue-collar workers, ethnics, conservative Catholics, Southerners, and residents of Sunbelt states.

Nixon's criticism of busing, his opposition to abortion, and his commuta-tion of the life sentence accorded Lieutenant William Calley after the My Lai incident in Vietnam indicated the timeliness of conservative readings of social issues. The President angered neoconservatives (and conservative Republi-cans) with his pragmatism, especially his policy of Vietnamization and attempts to achieve détente with the Soviet Union and to normalize relations with Beijing. But Nixon's 1972 campaign endorsed neoconservative views on the need for harsh rhetoric and measures to restore domestic tranquility. No less than the campaign and election of 1964, the contest in 1972 centered on questions of ideology, patriotic symbol, and rival conspiratorial perceptions. But if all this worked to Republican Goldwater's disadvantage in 1964, by 1972 the Arizona senator seemed an avuncular GOP statesman while Demo-crat George McGovern was the extremist.

Like Goldwater, McGovern rejected "centrist" descriptions of his candi-dacy and thus played into the hands of Republican Party strategists. He wanted to confront poverty directly by redistributing wealth. To fund a thousand-dollar cash grant to all American citizens, he proposed a $30 billion cut in the defense budget and an end to all support for South Vietnam. Equally important, the Democratic platform revealed how far reform within the party had proceeded in four years. Positions on the war, busing, and abortion all suggested New Class influence. In Boston, especially, as historian Ronald P. Formisano shows, busing created deep grassroots resentment among the white working classes against this absentee elite. The Nixon camp found it easy to depict McGovern (who also supported decriminalization of marijuana, even as his daughter was arrested for possession during the campaign) as the candidate of the irresponsible, self-indulgent counterculture—of those persons who favored "ass, grass, and amnesty." And the revelation that McGovern's initial choice for vice-president, Senator Thomas Eagleton of Missouri, had undergone electric-shock therapy to combat depression, added the problematic image of the Democratic leadership as emotionally unstable and dependent on psychiatry—another putative New Class connection.

Within the year, of course, questions of psychology and electoral morality—as well as concern about leftist, extremist politics—became moot. Nixon's self-inflicted ruin (and Agnew's demise) allowed citizens to ponder the politics of social and cultural resentment and gave them the opportunity to create a new interest-group politics which might embrace the reformist impulses that had transformed the Democratic Party since 1968. The electorate appeared to do this in 1976, the nation's bicentennial, when it chose Jimmy Carter of Georgia. For a year or so, Carter addressed the problem of reviving the old Democratic coalition—of winning back ethnic voters, working men and women, and Southerners who had jumped to the Republican fold. Economic issues were uppermost in the minds of most voters, especially after the energy crisis of the early 1970s, defeat in Vietnam, and other new realities suggested limits to American global power. But if Americans looked closely at themselves in their bicentennial year, they also would have seen a society dividing increasingly into wealthy and poor. Whether evaluated by race, class, or gender, inequality threatened the nation's social cohesiveness.

Carter failed to restore an interest-group politics based upon the earlier model. The upheavals of the previous fifteen years had undercut American faith in politics as a means to achieve change. If feminists, environmentalists, and other reformers gravitated toward the Democratic Party, this did not produce old-style coalition politics. Carter himself ran as an outsider. Like Wallace he represented the "little man," but unlike Wallace he was a Bryanesque populist who sought positive ways to rectify the "betrayal" of the people. A born-again Christian, like millions of Americans in this era of declining earthly expectations, he revealed his own frailty in *Playboy* by admitting that he had violated the Fifth Commandment by "lusting" for women other than his wife. His critique of the American "plutocracy," meanwhile, included promises to plug tax loopholes for the rich, halt corporate crime, and end economic and racial discrimination. He also wore a plain business suit as he traversed Pennsylvania Avenue on Inauguration Day, asked Americans to turn down the heat to conserve oil, and made it a point to stay with "average" families when visiting town meetings across the country.

Carter may have appointed a record number of women and blacks to federal posts, but he failed to revitalize either the old Democratic coalition or interest-group politics. His administration's brave rhetoric of the first six months gave way to internal confusion, wrangling, and the inability to deal constructively with two critical problems—energy and the Iran hostage crisis. Carter also swung markedly to the right on issues of finance, national defense, and the need to reassert traditional values to redress the country's malaise.

Carter's politics of moral gesture and austerity opened the door for another self-styled populist, Ronald Reagan, backed by the secular and fundamentalist/evangelical New Right. Reagan's 1980 triumph, and the permanent transfer of the label of extremism to liberal Democrats, owed much to a powerful politics of symbolism which built on—and extended—Carter's avowal of the importance of traditional values. Reagan also spoke of simple verities, but he did so to resurrect the values of the bygone producer culture, offering Americans a last chance to recapture the self-reliance, individualism, and confidence they had squandered since the terrible 1960s. The United States would once again "stand tall" against its adversaries, especially the "evil empire" of atheistic communism. Reagan also seemed to profit from his ability to blur divisions between economic and social issues, translating the former in terms of the latter.

But whether Reagan's landslide win marked the permanent fixture of a Republican majority (as political observer Kevin Phillips had forecast twelve years earlier), or whether Reagan was a quick-fix solution (another pretty product in the era of consumerism) to ameliorate American frustrations, remained debatable. Millions of citizens from the working and service classes stayed away from the polls in 1980. A mere 28 percent of the potential electorate gave Reagan his landslide victory, and political analysts began to study the alienated, nonvoting "party."

By most accounts, between 1965 and 1980 the Democratic Party brought on its own demise when it abandoned the economic interests of its traditional constituents in favor of contentious positions on social and cultural issues like busing, the Equal Rights Amendment, abortion, and the environment. But a major force in the shift of Democrats to the Republican Party were neo-conservative arguments, later appropriated by the New Right. Through sophisticated computer technology for fund-raising and recruitment, the New Right harnessed the anger of a large group of disgruntled citizens whom political scientists called "middle-American radicals." Many of these people came to politics through single-issue organizations. But increasingly—under the prodding of direct-mail wizard Richard Viguerie—they coalesced in behalf of the virtues of traditional personal morality, the importance of the nuclear family, the right to life of the unborn, and the need to increase the place of religion—especially evangelical and Fundamentalist Protestantism—in American life. By the late 1970s the national religious revival that began after World War II had crested. Its television cadre, headed by the Reverends Robertson, Bakker, Swaggart, and Falwell, focused upon the power of born-again Christianity to rescue the nation from its wicked obsession with secular humanism. Although these men often denounced their political counterparts and the Reagan administration for moving too slowly (if at all) in translating their religious agenda into political achievement, the connection of born-again

Christianity and born-again Americanism helped both them and the president.

By the early 1980s the liberal-pluralist view of a nefarious, right-wing conspiracy had been turned on its head. What had been labeled extremist in previous years—Joe McCarthy's anti-elitist anticommunism, Barry Goldwater's militarism and his attacks on the federal government designed to unshackle "free enterprise," George Wallace's angry denunciations of "pointy-headed" highbrows, the Birch Society's fear of a secret group of intellectuals and cryptocommunists bent on world domination, and the zealous condemnation of atheistic Marxism, pornography, rock music, and sexual permissiveness by religious crusaders like Schwarz and Hargis—had by 1980 become important components of a broad cultural consensus. Open appeals to racism, to traditional anti-alien themes, even to anticommunism were less important parts of the conspiratorial notions that nurtured this transformation. In place of the traditional sites of alleged conspiracy stood the federal government itself. In the view of liberal-pluralist defectors to neoconservatism, government was now in the hands of the conspiratorial New Class, with its desire to unleash the aforementioned evils upon the nation through its proxy "reform" movements. The foe, ultimately, was no secret organization; it was the huge federal bureaucracy and its allies—the national political leadership, the courts, liberal or "moderate" politicians of all persuasions, "special" interests, labor "bosses," corporate leaders who traded with the Soviet Union, major universities in thrall of secular humanism, the "liberal" media, and the National Endowment for the Humanities, to cite only the short list.

In their critique of the mass politics of the 1960s in the pages of *The Public Interest*, *The Present Danger*, *Commentary*, and the *Wall Street Journal*, the neoconservatives played intellectual midwife to the New Right and provided the right a theoretical bludgeon to use against these adversaries and another, hidden, internal enemy. For the more important foe and policy victim of neoconservative and New Right politics in the late 1970s and early 1980s was the increasing number of economically deprived, politically frustrated, and increasingly black and female Americans who qualified as the nation's poor.

Far more than the neoconservatives, the New Right detested the welfare state and looked to the Reagan administration to dismantle it. In pursuing this goal the Right updated an old Jacksonian notion of conspiracy to link the excessively ambitious and the exceedingly shiftless. In the view of the New Right strategist William Rusher, society was divided into two groups. The "producers" consisted of a coalition of working men and women who through their own physical effort "made" things, along with American capitalists who generously provided necessary wages. The "non-producers," meanwhile, included that burgeoning population that made nothing tangible. Both the New Class (the "verbalist elite") and the poor were symbiotic parasites who threatened to become a permanent political fixture, sapping the vigor of the country. In Rusher's view, "businessmen, workers, and farmers had a common economic interest in limiting the growth of this rapacious, new, nonproducing class."

Although Reagan never came close to demolishing the major features of the welfare state, his unprecedented popularity reflected the success of his rhetorical appeal to the traditions of the old producer culture. That code was clearly obsolete in an era whose most powerful citizens wholeheartedly embraced the values of free-market consumerism. But if Reagan's rhetoric was fraudulent, it was marvelously orchestrated and extremely effective. Ironically, the permissiveness and licentiousness that neoconservatives and the New Right claimed to discover on the left became, in turn, justification for the rapacity and permissiveness that dominated administration policy and so much of public life in the 1980s. Supply-side economics, privatization, and deregulation all served as a mask for privilege, much lawbreaking, and the further entrenchment of wealthy elites. Reagan's economic policies did little for middle-class Americans except increase their anxiety about falling to a lower echelon. The sharp decline in middle-class interest in aiding the poor and homeless over the last decade mirrored administration attitudes. And George Bush's promise of a "kinder, gentler America" remains mockery.

Further hypocrisy accompanied this dynamic. Corporate America itself embraced sexual themes in advertising which far outstripped in explicitness the despised sexual revolution. More ominous for the New Right, numerous televangelists succumbed to big sins of flesh and pocketbook. One prominent New Right fund-raiser, a closet gay, died of AIDS. And then there were Ollie North and the Iran-Contra affair, followed closely by the coming of Mikhail Gorbachev, the end of the Cold War, and a chilling recession which reminded citizens of the 1930s. The New Right failed to make the Reagan administration its Trojan Horse and by mid-decade found itself paralyzed by financial disarray and disabling factionalism. A final irony in this decline lay in the financial rescue of much of the right's own new-class infrastructure by the Reverend Sun Myung Moon, leader of the infamous "Moonies." As journalist Sidney Blumenthal points out, "the movement that had crusaded against un-Americanism became, in part, a financial dependency of a foreign power with a hidden agenda."

In the fifty years since Pearl Harbor, warnings of nefarious conspiracies and charges of extremism have exerted substantial impact upon the course of American history. Most striking, however, during this half-century these warnings and charges appear to have moved 180 degrees on the political spectrum. In the years before Pearl Harbor, liberal interventionists targeted a "lunatic fringe" on the right—a taxonomy that included not only self-promoting mass dissenters like Coughlin and Pelley but also well-intentioned and sincere noninterventionists who warned of the danger to American liberty that lay in participation in total war. Although battered by McCarthyism in the early 1950s, liberal pluralists held to their view that the age of ideology had ended, and despite their own complicity in federal encroachments upon civil liberties, they emerged victorious in the anticommunist debate after the

Wisconsin senator's collapse in 1954. During the 1950s these liberal pluralists identified political extremism (especially its "neofascist" potential) with notions of class, with working men and women, with politically oriented preachers, and with populism. But over the next thirty years many liberal-pluralists became neoconservatives. In making this transition they altered conventional wisdom about extremism and "normalcy," reflecting their own disillusion with the social and cultural upheavals of the late 1960s and early 1970s. By the mid-1980s most neoconservatives had come to defend as positive features on the political landscape those categories which they had earlier defined as extremist.

In retrospect this shift indicates the existence of new enemies by the 1980s; it does not suggest a new theoretical construct to explain conspiratorial dangers to the nation's welfare. Yet these developments do clarify anew the weakness of liberal-pluralist critiques of radical right extremism in the years preceding Pearl Harbor as well as during the 1950s and 1960s. For in their warnings about thunder on the far right, liberal pluralists failed to anticipate—or acknowledge—the growth of a broad-based conservative movement after World War II, a movement that contained politically savvy groups like the Young Americans for Freedom, Buckley's *National Review*, and middle- and upper-class Goldwater partisans. By conflating radical right and conservative politics generally, the liberal-pluralists ignored the conservatives' continuing intellectual and organizational development—an evolution that achieved significant progress by the time of liberal-pluralist disenchantment with Great Society redistributive programs, the Democratic Party's waning commitment to anticommunism, and the disaffiliation of so many Americans from the values of the producer culture. Since World War II, the old liberal-pluralist view of extremism notwithstanding, conservative politics remained centered in the Republican Party, drew key support from a wide range of businessmen and business-related foundations, and exerted its strongest appeal within the upper middle class. Conservative politics were not, nor had they ever been, merely an eruptive politics of malcontent, evidence of a diffuse malaise. The conservative journals, think-tanks, and other organizational matrices to which many liberal-pluralists fled after 1970 existed well within the established political order. Even the Birch Society exhibited these characteristics.

Most interesting in the liberal-pluralists' journey to neoconservatism and beyond was their continuing dependence on an enemy to clarify their own definition. Their transference of extremism from the right to the left (and from the political fringes to the mainstream) reveals their own doubts about the promises of democracy and their unwillingness to confront the tough policy choices those promises raised. As neoconservatives they recoiled from questions raised by the left, the young, and the poor about the established Cold War order, and they found solace with a politics that defined these questions as the work of a subversive, even revolutionary, force. Adherents of the liberal consensus, who had defined and defended the promise of democracy since the

1930s, ultimately proved unwilling to confront that challenge themselves.

Right-wing hate groups are still out there—more than twenty-two thousand such organizations now exist in the United States according to one estimate. But one hears comparatively little these days about the neo-Nazis, skinheads, survivalists, and their myriad cohorts as a unified political threat. Perhaps this is a measure of how attitudes and behavior once scorned as extremist have become normal parts of our lives. The theme of "divide and conquer" is now central to American political campaigns; hence former Klansman David Duke's candidacy for governor in Louisiana came as no surprise. Far from a fringe phenomenon, Duke's theme of "us against them" also figured prominently in George Bush's campaign for president in 1988, when he used the furlough of convicted murderer Willie Horton to depict Democrat Michael Dukakis as a partisan of black criminals. This motif continues as an important theme in the battle sweeping American campuses over the issue of "political correctness"—which seems in many ways an extension of the neoconservative and conservative condemnation of the New Class and its allies during the 1970s and 1980s.

In the last half-century, in short, there appears a direct line connecting "un-American" communists, fascists, and Nazis during the 1930s with the radical right of the 1950s and 1960s, with the New Left and counterculture of the late 1960s and 1970s, and with the New Class and the "politically correct" in recent years. Perhaps it is in the nature of American liberalism-become-neoconservatism to concoct terrible, abstract enemies in order to maintain its self-image as a vanguard of American exceptionalism in a mediocre and increasingly unruly and threatening world. If nothing else, events during the past fifty years underline anew the limited usefulness of extremism as a descriptive term, as well as its problematic use in the hands of political and social elites.

A Note on the Sources

The historian who analyzes nativist extremism during the 1930s faces several problems. In the first place, because many writers on the subject reflect the liberal bias of the Roosevelt years, he must exercise care lest his judgments be a priori in nature. Secondly, he should attempt to avoid another pitfall common to liberal, pluralist historians who received their training in the 1930s and 1940s—this being the tendency to place too heavy an emphasis upon socio-psychological concepts and interpretations and consequently to make conspiratorial fears the monopoly of the so-called "lunatic fringes" of society. Rather, the observer ought to place himself in the shoes of his protagonists and try to view the world as they did, not as he himself would like to see it, or as other commentators have interpreted it. In his quest the historian must assess critically and, to the extent possible, dispassionately, extremist polemics and those of their adversaries. This task is a difficult one, for if there is one characteristic that dominates literature on the extremists, it is the failure to take seriously their criticism of American life and Roosevelt's diplomacy.

By far the best analysis of the New Deal era is William E. Leuchtenburg, *Franklin D. Roosevelt and the New Deal, 1932–1940* (New York, 1963), a volume of prodigious scholarship and valuable insights. The multivolume *Age of Roosevelt* (Boston, 1957–1960) by Arthur M. Schlesinger, Jr., is also helpful, especially *The Politics of Upheaval* (1960). Paul K. Conkin's *The New Deal* (New York, 1967) is a concise, critical synthesis. Also noteworthy are two volumes by James M. Burns, *Roosevelt: The Lion and the Fox* (New York, 1956), and *Roosevelt: The Soldier of Freedom* (New York, 1970). Burns's studies comprise the best political biography of FDR.

On extremism generally, the reader should consult Seymour M. Lipset and Earl Raab, *The Politics of Unreason: Right-Wing Extremism in America, 1790–1970* (New York, 1970). Although prone to excessive generalizing, the authors break new ground in combining sociological and historical methods. Two helpful works of a more theoretical nature are John H. Bunzel, *Anti-Politics in America: Reflections on the Anti-Political Temper and Its Distortions of the Democratic Process* (New York, 1967), and David Spitz, *Patterns of Anti-Democratic Thought* (New York, 1965), while portions of Michael Parenti's *The Anti-Communist Impulse* (New York, 1969) illuminate the "respectability of American anti-Communism." A new, stimulating series of readings may be found in Richard O. Curry and Thomas M. Brown, eds., *Conspiracy: The Fear of Subversion in American History* (New York, 1972). For the 1930s, meanwhile, the best overview of domestic extremism is provided in Donald S. Strong, *Organized Anti-Semitism in America: The Rise of Group Prejudice During the Decade 1930–1940* (Washington, 1941), which provides detailed analyses of important nativist groups during the depression. Gustavus Myers's *History of Bigotry in the United States,* ed. Henry Christman (New York, 1960), also contains material on the subjects discussed in this book, but Myers's study is marked by a heavy emphasis on detail and a dearth of interpretation. The volume also lacks an index. O. John Rogge's *The Official German Report: Nazi Penetration, 1924–1942: Pan-Arabism, 1939–Today* (New York, 1961), is filled with undigested facts, while John Roy Carlson (pseud.), *Under Cover: My Four Years in the Nazi Underworld of America* (New York, 1943), reads as if it were written by a secret agent. It was, and is unreliable (if exciting). Michael Sayers and Albert Kahn, *Sabotage! The Secret War Against America* (New York, 1942), is similar in tone but more trustworthy.

There are several good dissertations that analyze extremism during the 1930s. The author has depended heavily upon Morris Schonbach, "Native Fascism During the 1930s and 1940s: A Study of Its Roots, Its Growth, and Its Decline," UCLA, 1958, which traces the response of government authorities to the extremists, and Victor C.

Ferkiss, "The Political and Economic Philosophy of American Fascism," Chicago, 1954, a noteworthy intellectual history. In "Right-Wing Extremism During the Nineteen-thirties," master's thesis, Texas, 1962, Larry Newell devotes a chapter to William Dudley Pelley and the Silver Shirts, and in another section emphasizes the uncritical usage of the term "fascism" by many persons during the mid-thirties. The author has made use of material from both chapters. A dissertation that takes a broader view is Rodger Allen Remington, "The Function of the 'Conspiracy Theory' in American Intellectual History," St. Louis, 1965.

Because Father Coughlin's papers are unavailable to scholars, a situation that is not likely to change, investigators must depend on other sources for an understanding of the priest's career. The best assessment of his political activities before 1936 is David H. Bennett, *Demagogues in the Depression: American Radicals and the Union Party, 1932–1936* (New Brunswick, N.J., 1969). A model of scholarship, the book is especially worthwhile for its concluding chapter, "Yesterday's Radicals and American History." In *Father Coughlin and the New Deal* (Syracuse, 1965), Charles J. Tull analyzes skillfully the priest's relationship with President Roosevelt, his role in forming the Union Party, and the emergence of the Christian Front. Ruth Mugglebee's *Father Coughlin of the Shrine of the Little Flower* (Boston, 1933) provides the best analysis of the cleric's early life but borders on hagiography.

Several articles also illuminate Coughlin's activities. Peter A. Soderbergh assesses the priest's rise to power in "The Rise of Father Coughlin, 1891–1930," *Social Science*, XLII (1967), 10–20, while James P. Shenton, in "The Coughlin Movement and the New Deal," *Political Science Quarterly*, LXXIII (September, 1958), 352–373, analyzes the content of correspondence in the Roosevelt Library and the Father John A. Ryan Collections to distinguish the characteristics of ardent Coughlinites. Shenton's "Fascism and Father Coughlin," *Wisconsin Magazine of History*, XLIV (Autumn, 1960), 6–11, discusses the priest's later career and notes the widespread use of "fascism" as a scarehead during the late 1930s. Craig Newton, "Father Coughlin and His National Union for Social Justice," *Southwestern Social Science Quarterly*, XLI (December, 1960), 341–350, analyzes the failure of the Union Party in 1936.

Two studies of American Catholicism during the depression discuss the priest and his followers. These are George Q. Flynn, *American Catholics and the Roosevelt Presidency, 1932–1936* (Lexington, 1968), and David J. O'Brien, *American Catholics and Social Reform: The New Deal Years* (New York, 1968). Gary T. Marx advances a sociological interpretation of Coughlin's rise and fall in "The Social Basis of the Support of a Depression Era Extremist: Father Charles E. Coughlin," University of California, Berkeley, *Survey Research Publications, No. Seven* (Berkeley, 1962).

Dissertations and theses that treat various aspects of the priest's career include Nick Masters, "Father Coughlin and Social Justice: A Case Study of a Social Movement," dissertation, Wisconsin, 1955; Eleanor W. Paperno, "Father Coughlin: A Study in Domination," master's thesis, Wayne State, 1939; Myles Platt, "Father Coughlin and the National Union for Social Justice: A Bid for Political Power," master's thesis, Wayne State, 1951; and Edward C. McCartney, "The Christian Front Movement in New York City, 1938–1940," master's thesis, Columbia, 1965.

In addition to the aforementioned sources, a sifting of the Coughlin correspondence in the Franklin D. Roosevelt Library at Hyde Park, New York, can be most enlightening. Official File 306 and President's Personal File 2338 contain immense amounts of material. Also rewarding are selections from the Father John A. Ryan Papers, available on microfilm from Columbia University, and material relating to the Christian Front in Box 2539, Folder 85, of the La Guardia Papers at the New York Municipal Archives and Record Center. The priest's weekly journal, *Social Justice*, is available at most good university libraries.

The most valuable source concerning Pelley and his Silver Shirts is the text of his sedition trial in 1942. This volume, together with attached documents, is available in

State of North Carolina vs. William Dudley Pelley of the Silver Shirt Legion, Superior Court of Buncombe County, January Term, 1942 (Asheville, 1942). Pelley's convictions are presented in his own works, including his newspaper *Liberation;* "My Seven Minutes in Eternity," *American Magazine,* CVII (March, 1929), 7–9; and three "scholarly" volumes—*Nations-In-Law* (Asheville, 1935), *No More Hunger* (Asheville, 1936), and *The Door to Revelation* (Asheville, 1939). Arthur Graham, meanwhile, presents an interesting portrait in "Crazy Like a Fox: Pelley of the Silver Shirts," *New Republic,* LXXVIII (April 18, 1934), 264–266, as do Johann J. Smertenko, "Hitlerism Comes to America," *Harper's,* CLXVII (November, 1933), 660–670, and Samuel D. McCoy, "Hitlerism Invades America," *Today,* I (April, 7, 1934), 3–6, 26–29. An article by Jean Burton, "The Silver Shirts," *Modern Monthly* (February, 1934), 18–24, is also helpful. Finally, a doctoral dissertation by Donnel B. Portzline, "William Dudley Pelley and the Silver Shirt Legion of America," Ball State, 1965, is the only full-length analysis of the Asheville *Führer's* philosophy and career.

The importance of the German-American Bund as a factor in the deterioration of German-American relations is an underlying theme in several recent studies, these being Alton Frye, *Nazi Germany and the American Hemisphere, 1933–1941* (New Haven, 1967); James V. Compton, *The Swastika and the Eagle: Hitler, the United States, and the Origins of World War II* (Boston, 1967); Saul Friedlander, *Prelude to Downfall: Hitler and the United States, 1939–1941,* tr. Alice B. and Alexander Werth (New York, 1967); Klaus Kipphan, *Deutsche Propaganda in den Vereinigten Staaten, 1933–1941* (Heidelberg, 1971); and Hans L. Trefousse, *Germany and American Neutrality, 1939–1941* (New York, 1951).

Both Gerhard Weinberg, "Hitler's Image of the United States," *American Historical Review,* LXIX (February, 1964), 1006–1021, and Joachim Remak, "Germany and the United States, 1933–1939," dissertation, Stanford, 1954, suggest that, like the Bundists, Hitler himself thought that the United States had fallen into the hands of a Jewish-communist conspiracy. The attempts of German diplomats to convince the Chancellor that this was not the case and the embarrassment provided them by the Bund may be traced in the U.S. Department of State, *Documents on German Foreign Policy, 1918–1945,* Series C, 5 vols. (Washington, 1957–1966); and Series D, 12 vols. (Washington, 1949–1956). This source is essential.

The best published analyses of the German-American Bund include Joachim Remak, " 'Friends of the New Germany': The Bund and German-American Relations," *Journal of Modern History,* XXIX (March, 1957), 38–41, and Leland V. Bell, "The Failure of Nazism in America: The German-American Bund, 1936–1941," *Political Science Quarterly,* LXXXV (December, 1970), 585–599. Evelyn Knobloch, "The Nazi Bund Movement in Metropolitan New York," master's thesis, Columbia, 1961, provides useful material on the Bund's role in city politics. Bundist activities are covered in depth in the *New York Times,* while Official File 198A in the Roosevelt Papers contains much material relating to American Nazism generally. Boxes 758, 2544, and 2564 in the La Guardia Papers contain documents pertaining to the Yorkville extremists, and the Bund's journal, the *Free American,* is an indispensable source. Another news organ, the *Anti-Nazi Bulletin,* is also helpful, but must be used with care. These references will be augmented next year with the publication by Cornell University Press of Sander Diamond's *Germany and the Bund Movement in the United States.*

On the problem of anti-Semitism, a good introduction is Melvin Tumin, *An Inventory and Appraisal of Research on American Anti-Semitism* (New York, 1961). Gordon W. Allport offers valuable insights into the psychology of bigotry in *The Nature of Prejudice* (New York, 1958); Arnold Buss provides perhaps the most satisfactory analysis of "scapegoating" in *The Psychology of Aggression* (New York, 1961); and T. W. Adorno *et al., The Authoritarian Personality* (New York, 1950), and Edward Shils, *The Torment of Secrecy* (Glencoe, 1956), also discuss aspects of the psychology of extremism. In addition to these works, the author has used concepts discussed by Eric Hoffer, *The True Believer: Thoughts on the Nature of Mass Movements* (New York, 1951), and Hans Toch, *The Social Psychology of Social Movements* (Indianapolis, 1965). Norman Cohn's book, *Warrant for Genocide: The Myth of the Jewish World Conspiracy and the Protocols of the Elders of Zion* (New York, 1967), is an excellent study of the documents that provided the countersubversives of the 1930s with much of their ammunition.

The author's analysis of status politics depended heavily upon two essays by Richard Hofstadter, "The Paranoid Style in American Politics," and "The Pseudo-Conservative Revolt," in Hofstadter's *The Paranoid Style in American Politics and Other Essays* (New York, 1965). In *The Protestant Establishment: Aristocracy and Caste in America* (New York, 1966), E. Digby Baltzell describes the social upheaval of the 1930s from the viewpoint of WASP America, while George Wolfskill analyzes ultraconservatism during the same period in *The Revolt of the Conservatives: A History of the American Liberty League, 1934–1940* (Boston, 1962). A first-rate study of the importance of status politics during the New Deal years may be found in Otis L. Graham, Jr., *An Encore for Reform: The Old Progressives and the New Deal* (New York, 1967). Two useful sociological studies are Reinhard Bendix and Seymour M. Lipset, eds., *Class, Status and Power* (Glencoe, 1953) and Seymour M. Lipset, *Political Man: The Social Basis of Politics* (Garden City, 1960).

The role of the House Un-American Activities Committee in popularizing the menace of domestic "fascism" is accorded scholarly treatment in August R. Ogden, *The Dies Committee: A Study of the Special House Committee for the Investigation of Un-American Activities, 1938–1944* (Washington, 1945). Walter Goodman's book, *The Committee: The Extraordinary Career of the House Committee on Un-American Activities* (New York, 1968), contains an appendix listing every published report made by the illustrious organization.

Although American diplomacy before Pearl Harbor has been analyzed in a number of good studies, no historian has yet indicated the importance of the extremists for an understanding of the developing debate on foreign policy. Nevertheless, Wayne S. Cole, "American Entry into World War II: A Historiographical Appraisal," *Mississippi Valley Historical Review*, XLIII (March, 1957), 595–617, is a model bibliographical essay. Two books by William L. Langer and S. Everett Gleason, *The Challenge to Isolation, 1937–1940* (New York, 1952) and *The Undeclared War, 1940–1941* (New York, 1953), are standard monographs. Donald F. Drummond, *The Passing of American Neutrality, 1937–1941* (Ann Arbor, 1955), is an underrated study of America's march toward war. Selig Adler, in *The Uncertain Giant, 1921–1941: American Foreign Policy Between the Wars* (New York, 1965), assesses the interplay between domestic politics and foreign affairs in the interwar period. Robert A. Divine presents a balanced account of cash-and-carry neutrality in *The Illusion of Neutrality* (Chicago, 1962), and the same author discusses the hesitant efforts of the Roosevelt administration to engage the United States in the world crisis in *The Reluctant Belligerent: American Entry into World War II* (New York, 1965). The President's personal determination to place American resources in the hands of the British government is the subject of T. R. Fehrenbach's *F.D.R.'s Undeclared War, 1939–1941* (New York, 1967), while the administration's efforts to convince the American people of the danger posed to national security is emphasized in Richard W. Steele, "Preparing the Public for War: Efforts to Establish a National Propaganda Agency, 1940–1941," *American Historical Review*, LXXV (October, 1970), 1640–1653. Warren Kimball, meanwhile, presents a solid analysis of lend-lease in *The Most Unsordid Act: Lend-Lease, 1939–1941* (Baltimore, 1969). A volume that stresses the significance of ardent American interventionists, especially in 1941, Mark L. Chadwin's *The Hawks of World War II* (Chapel Hill, 1968), reaches conclusions that are similar to the author's.

On isolationism, Manfred Jonas's *Isolationism in America, 1935–1941* (Ithaca, 1966) is an admirable intellectual history. In *The Isolationist Impulse: Its Twentieth Century*

Reaction (New York, 1957), Selig Adler assesses from an internationalist's viewpoint the impact of isolationist propaganda and pressure groups. The complexity of twentieth-century isolationism is the subject of Alexander DeConde's "On Twentieth-Century Isolationism," in DeConde, ed., *Isolation and Security: Ideas and Interests in Twentieth-Century American Foreign Policy* (Durham, 1957), pp. 3–32. Bernard J. Fensterwald, Jr., uses sociological and psychological data to explain isolationism in "The Anatomy of American Isolationism and Expansionism," *Journal of Conflict Resolution*, II (June and December, 1958), 111–139, 280–309. A suggestive intellectual analysis of the roots of American antitotalitarian feelings is offered in Les K. Adler and Thomas G. Paterson, "Red Fascism: The Merger of Nazi Germany and Soviet Russia in the American Image of Totalitarianism, 1930s–1950s," *American Historical Review*, LXXV (April, 1970, 1046–1064.

The standard work on the America First Committee is Wayne S. Cole's scholarly *America First: The Battle Against Intervention, 1940–1941* (Madison, 1953). *The Wartime Journals of Charles A. Lindbergh* (New York, 1970) is now the most important source for the development of the controversial flier's views. Lindbergh is also the subject of two popular biographies, Kenneth S. Davis's *The Hero: Charles A. Lindbergh and the American Dream* (Garden City, 1959) and Walter S. Ross's *The Last Hero: Charles A. Lindbergh* (New York, 1964). The famed aviator's place in the battle against intervention is emphasized in Lowell R. Fleischer, "Charles A. Lindbergh and Isolationism, 1939–1941," dissertation, Connecticut, 1963. Lindbergh's travails and those of America First may be traced in correspondence in the Roosevelt Papers, Official File No. 92, and in the papers of Amos R. E. Pinchot, Files 87–89, in the Manuscript Division of the Library of Congress.

Finally, the student of American extremism during the 1930s must consult the *Nation, New Republic*, the *Christian Century*, and *Commonweal*, although these sources must be used with care. The *Appendix* of the *Congressional Record* is also helpful in revealing attitudes held by American senators and representatives concerning foreign policy issues.

Bibliographical Note
to the Revised Edition

Since the publication of *To Save a Nation* in 1973, the liberal consensus that had so much to say about American political extremism during the preceding forty years has all but disappeared. This consensus was supplanted, for a short while, by a left-radical historical interpretation which emphasized the central role of internal, self-aggrandizing groups like the Power Elite and the Military-Industrial Complex in determining American domestic and foreign policy. With the decline of the New Left in the mid-1970s, another explanatory paradigm emerged, termed neoconservatism, which exhibited an outlook similar in many essentials to the earlier liberal stance, but which converged with—and contributed to—the increasingly conservative mood of many Americans.

Neoconservative writing on extremism within the last fifteen years suggests the outlines of a new (old) orthodoxy, in which "liberals" have supplanted communists, fascists, and the radical right of the 1960s as overarching menaces to national greatness. But the current, bitter debate on "political correctness" suggests a crucial dichotomy in dialogue. Here one cannot ignore the continuing fallout from Vietnam and Watergate and the questions and doubts these epochal experiences unleashed. During the late 1960s, after all, many young people rebelled against authority of all kinds, while beginning in the 1970s citizens generally began to rebel against big government. Within these revolts, set against the paradox of declining national economic growth and increasing consumer aspirations, one encounters an increasing peevishness among the electorate, often expressed in mean-spirited opposition or apathy on questions of public policy. In other words, if the former rebellion faded, the second rebellion persists. And despite the Reagan "restoration" and the second proclamation in forty years of "the end of history," matters remain unsettled. Clio apparently will continue to march ahead, not always in step with prevailing—or contending—ideologies. On this point readers may wish to compare Daniel Bell, *The End of Ideology: On the Exhaustion of Political Ideas in the Fifties* (1960, rev. ed., New York, 1965), which played a signal role in defining right-wing "extremism" in the 1960s; and Francis Fukuyama, *The End of History and the Last Man* (New York, 1992), which seems similarly related to the designation of left-oriented "political correctness" as an extremist position.

The best recent overview of the long history of American political extremism is David H. Bennett, *The Party of Fear: From Nativist Movements to the New Right in American History* (Chapel Hill, N.C., 1988). Bennett avoids taking on the paradigms that have informed students of extremism and conspiracy theories, but this does not detract from his thorough research and discerning synthesis. Another overview is George X. Johnson, *Architects of Fear: Conspiracy Theory and Paranoia in American Politics* (Boston, 1983). Most helpful in treating the 1930s on its own terms, Leo P. Ribuffo's *The Old Christian Right: The Protestant Far Right from the Great Depression to the Cold War* (Philadelphia, 1983) exhibits uncommon historical empathy and raises many good questions about the influence of current events upon intellectual attitudes. The winner of the 1985 Merle Curti Prize, Ribuffo's book is now the starting reference point for anyone who would understand "extremism" from the late 1920s onward. Ribuffo also offers interesting historiographical insights (including a solid critique of *To Save a Nation*) in "Fascists, Nazis, and American Minds: Perceptions and Preconceptions," *American Quarterly*, XXVI (October 1974), 417–433.

Three overviews of the prewar, war, and postwar eras, respectively, perceptive in analysis and tracing the centrality of conspiracy theories and the continuing impact of the anticommunist crusades of the late 1940s and early 1950s, are John Patrick Diggins, *The Proud Decades: America in War and Peace, 1941–1960* (New York, 1988); Richard M. Polenberg, *One Nation Divisible: Class, Race, and Ethnicity in the United States Since 1938* (New York, 1980); and Richard M. Fried, *Nightmare in Red: The McCarthy Era in Perspective* (New York, 1990). All three books are noteworthy for indicating the decline of overt appeals to racism, traditional nativist themes like anti-Catholicism, and anticommunism within extremism after 1960.

Three recent studies of Depression-era "extremists" also exhibit more empathy with their subject than most previous scholarly works. Alan Brinkley, *Voices of Protest: Huey Long, Father Coughlin, and the Great Depression* (New York, 1982), emphasizes that the radio priest's anti-Semitism developed only after 1938, when he had ceased to be a national figure. But Brinkley also regards these men as neither "leaders of irrational, antidemocratic uprisings" nor "vanguards of a great, progressive social transformation." Rather, Long and Coughlin sought to reestablish "a society in which the individual retained control of his own life and livelihood; in which power resided in visible, accessible institutions; in which wealth was equitably (if not necessarily equally) shared." In *Struggles for Justice: Social Responsibility and the Liberal State* (Cambridge, Mass., 1991), meanwhile, a major reinterpretation of American reform from the 1890s through World War II, Alan Dawley challenges Brinkley's subtle reassertion of liberal-pluralist views. He rejects Brinkley's portrayal of both Long and Coughlin as right-wing populists, akin to European fascists except for their liberalism, emphasizing instead Coughlin's general antiliberal outlook and Long's "leftist ideas" on distributing wealth. Glen Jeansonne, *Gerald L. K. Smith: Minister of Hate* (New Haven, Conn., 1988), is a model biography of a controversial man whose life illustrates "that the career of a person of remarkable talents can be tragic if it is guided by a lust for power and fueled by a bigotry that appeals to latent hatred."

More than other historians, Wayne S. Cole and Justus Doenecke have outlined with sensitivity the struggle of Charles Lindbergh, America First, and other noninterventionists to prevent American participation in World War II, and the reverberations of that campaign after 1945. Cole's studies include *Roosevelt and the Isolationists* (Lincoln, Nebr., 1983); *Charles A. Lindbergh and the Battle Against American Intervention in World War II* (New York, 1974); and "A Tale of Two Isolationists—Told Three Wars Later," *Newsletter* of the Society for Historians of American Foreign Relations, V (March 1974), 2–15. An indefatigable historiographer and author, Doenecke allows members of America First to speak for themselves in *In Danger Undaunted: The Anti-Interventionist Movement of 1940–1941 as Revealed in the Papers of the America First Committee* (Stanford, 1990). In *Not to the Swift: The Old Isolationists in the Cold War Era* (Lewisburg, Pa., 1979), Doenecke traces the postwar careers of many noninterventionists, finding (consistent with the diversity of committee members) many defections to anticommunism as well as much principled opposition to American Cold War globalism. These tensions made for an unstable mix.

These sources may be supplemented by Michele Flynn Stenehjem, *An American First: John T. Flynn and the America First Committee* (New Rochelle, N.Y., 1976); Ronald Radosh, *Prophets on the Right: Profiles of Conservative Critics of American Globalism* (New York, 1975); and Thomas N. Guinsberg, *The Pursuit of Isolationism in the United States Senate from Versailles to Pearl Harbor* (New York, 1982).

Doenecke and John Wiltz provide a solid overview of the decade before Pearl Harbor, together with numerous suggestions for further reading, in *From Isolation to War, 1931–1941* (2nd rev. ed., Arlington Heights, Ill., 1991). Robert Dallek's magisterial *Franklin D. Roosevelt and American Foreign Policy, 1932–1945* (New York, 1979), meanwhile, though in most respects defending FDR's prewar leadership, admits that the President's strategy against noninterventionists bordered on the unethical and set precedents for the imperial presidency that culminated in Watergate. Other important assessments of official treatment of responsible dissent as unlawful conspiracy may be found in Richard W. Steele, "Franklin Roosevelt and His Foreign Policy Critics," *Political Science Quarterly*, XLIV (Spring 1979), 15–32, and several discriminating studies of J. Edgar Hoover and the FBI. More than any other institution of government, the FBI defined the limits of lawful protest within liberal democracy in increasingly narrow—and dubious—ways. See Richard Gid Powers, *Secrecy and Power: The Life of J. Edgar Hoover* (New York, 1987); William W. Keller, *The Liberals and J. Edgar Hoover: The Rise and Fall of a Domestic Intelligence State* (Princeton, N.J., 1988); Kenneth O'Reilly, *Racial Matters: The FBI's Secret File on Black America, 1960–1972* (New York, 1989); Athan Theoharis, *Spying on Americans: Political Surveillance from Hoover to the Huston Plan* (Philadelphia, 1978);

Theoharis and John Stuart Cox, *The Boss: J. Edgar Hoover and the Great American Inquisition* (Philadelphia, 1988); Theoharis, ed., *From the Secret Files of J. Edgar Hoover* (Chicago, 1991); and Curt Gentry, *J. Edgar Hoover: The Man and the Secrets* (New York, 1991).

On questions of racism and anti-Semitism in the Roosevelt White House (and other high places), see Polenberg, *One Nation Divisible*; Christopher Thorne, *Allies of a Kind: The United States, Britain, and the War Against Japan, 1941–1945* (New York, 1978); Henry Feingold, *The Politics of Rescue: The Roosevelt Administration and the Holocaust, 1938–1945* (New Brunswick, N.J., 1971); David Wyman, *Paper Walls: America and the Refugee Crisis, 1938–1941* (Amherst, Mass., 1968); Wyman, *The Abandonment of the Jews: America and the Holocaust* (New York, 1984); and Saul Friedman, *No Haven for the Oppressed* (Detroit, 1973). On the racial basis of the Pacific War and Japanese American relocation, basic perspectives appear in Akira Iriye, *Pacific Estrangement* (Cambridge, Mass., 1972); John Dower, *War Without Mercy: Race and Power in the Pacific War* (New York, 1986); and Roger Daniels, *Concentration Camps North America: Japanese in the United States and Canada During World War II* (Malabar, Fla., 1981).

On the emergence of "vital-center" liberalism after World War II, which had so much to do with the interpreting of extremism before and after Pearl Harbor, I have been influenced by Leo P. Ribuffo's biting " 'Pluralism' and American History," *Dissent*, XVIII (June 1971), 272–278; William L. O'Neill, *A Better World: The Great Schism: Stalinism and the American Intellectuals* (New York, 1982); Richard Pells, *The Liberal Mind in a Conservative Age: American Intellectuals in the 1940s and 1950s* (New York, 1985); Mary Sperling McAuliffe, *Crisis on the Left: Cold War Politics and American Liberals, 1947–1954* (Amherst, Mass., 1978); and, for the ensuing years, Steven M. Gillon, *Politics and Vision: The ADA and American Liberalism, 1947–1985* (New York, 1987). Other helpful works include Howard Brick, *Daniel Bell and the Decline of Intellectual Radicalism: Social Theory and Political Reconciliation in the 1940s* (Madison, Wisc., 1986); Nathan Liebowitz, *Daniel Bell and the Agony of American Liberalism* (New York, 1985); and John P. Diggins, "The Socialization of Authority and the Dilemmas of American Liberalism," *Social Research*, XLVI (Autumn 1979), 454–486. Although overstated in argument, Marian J. Morton, *The Terrors of Ideological Politics: Liberal Historians in a Conservative Mood* (Cleveland, 1972), is suggestive. An important collection that brings together new scholarship on the decline of interest-group liberalism since the late 1930s may be found in Steve Fraser and Gary Gerstle, eds., *The Rise and Fall of the New Deal Order, 1930–1980* (Princeton, N.J., 1989).

On extremism in the 1950s and 1960s, and its place within consensus historiography (and liberal-pluralist policymaking assumptions), the best overview remains Bernard Sternsher, *Consensus, Conflict, and American Historians* (Bloomington, Ind., 1975). My understanding of interest-group liberalism—its triumph and its travails—borrows from Alonzo Hamby, *Beyond the New Deal: Harry Truman and American Liberalism* (New York, 1973); and Hamby, *Liberalism and Its Challengers: F.D.R. to Reagan* (New York, 1985). Liberal-pluralist analyses and denunciations of "extremism" by such scholars as Richard Hofstadter, Daniel Bell, and Seymour Martin Lipset are noted in the bibliographical note to the first edition of *To Save a Nation*. Lipset's *The Politics of Unreason: Right-Wing Extremism in America, 1790–1977* (with Earl Raab, Chicago, 1977), contains an exhaustive bibliography and suggests the journey of many liberal-pluralist social scientists to neoconservatism. Daniel Bell, ed., *The Radical Right: The New American Right, Expanded and Updated* (Garden City, N.Y., 1963), remains the standard liberal-pluralist statement on extremism, while Richard Hofstadter's *The Paranoid Style in American Politics and Other Essays* (New York, 1965), remains the most interesting. A contrasting analysis, which makes use of psychological insight from a critical, left perspective, and which, with Ribuffo's book, is the most important work to emerge on extremism in the last quarter-century, is Michael Rogin, *"Ronald Reagan," the Movie, and Other Episodes in Political Demonology* (Berkeley, 1987). Rogin's use of Freudian insights is particularly interesting, given his earlier critique of liberal-pluralist uses of psychology in explaining McCarthyism. Compare his *The Intellectuals and McCarthy: The Radical Specter* (Cambridge, Mass., 1967).

Liberal concern (some would say, obsession) with the evils of materialism is assessed in different contexts in Barbara Ehrenreich, *Fear of Falling: The Inner Life of the Middle-Class* (New York, 1989); David M. Potter, *People of Plenty: Economic Abundance and the American Character* (Chicago, 1954); John Kenneth Galbraith, *The Affluent Society* (New York, 1958); Carl Degler, *Affluence and Anxiety* (Glenview, Ill., 1968); Alan Wolfe, *America's Impasse: The Rise and Fall of the Politics of Growth* (New York, 1981); Albert O. Hirschman, *Shifting Involvements: Private Interest and Public Action* (Princeton, 1982); Stephen Fox, *The Mirror Makers: A History of American Advertising and Its Creators* (New York, 1963); and Betty Friedan, *The Feminine Mystique* (New York, 1963).

The sea change in American politics in the late 1960s and early 1970s, from both Republican and Democratic perspectives, together with the rise of neoconservatism and the Republican comeback after the Barry Goldwater debacle in 1964, is told in David W. Reinhard, *The Republican Right Since 1945* (Lexington, Ky., 1983); Nicole C. Rae, *The Decline and Fall of the Liberal Republicans from 1952 to the Present* (New York, 1989); Peter Steinfels, *The Neoconservatives: The Men Who Are Changing America's Politics* (New York, 1979); Neil Jumonville, *Critical Crossings: The New York Intellectuals in Postwar America* (Berkeley and Los Angeles, 1991); and Sidney Blumenthal, *The Rise of the Counter-Establishment: From Conservative Ideology to Political Power* (New York, 1986). These sources are complemented by Kevin Phillips, *The Emerging Republican Majority* (New Rochelle, N.Y., 1969); Richard M. Scammon and Ben J. Wattenberg, *The Real Majority* (New York, 1970); Phillips, *Post-Conservative America: People, Politics, and Ideology in a Time of Crisis* (New York, 1982); and Kirkpatrick Sale, *Power Shift: The Rise of the Southern Rim and Its Challenge to the Eastern Establishment* (New York, 1975).

The sociocultural upheaval accompanying the Vietnam War and Watergate, and the unraveling of the liberal consensus and decline of interest-group politics, are analyzed in Todd Gitlin, *The Sixties: Year of Hope, Days of Rage* (1987); Theodore J. Lowi, *The End of Liberalism* (New York, 1979); Allen J. Matusow, *The Unraveling of America: A History of Liberalism in the 1960s* (New York, 1984); and James Miller, *Democracy in the Streets* (New York, 1987). The breakup of the coalition of American blacks and Jews, crucial to the liberal consensus, is discussed in Jonathan Kaufman, *Broken Alliance: The Turbulent Times Between Blacks and Jews in America* (New York, 1988). For the emergence of the issues of "permissiveness" and the threat posed by the New Class, see the essays in Seymour M. Lipset and Philip G. Altbach, eds., *Students in Revolt* (Boston, 1969); Daniel Bell and Irving Kristol, eds., *Confrontation: The Student Rebellion and the Universities* (New York, 1969); John W. Aldridge, *In the Country of the Young* (New York, 1970); Nathan Glazer, *Remembering the Answers: Essays on the American Student Revolt* (New York, 1970); William P. Gerberding and Duane E. Smith, eds., *The Radical Left: The Abuse of Discontent* (Boston, 1970); and B. Bruce Briggs, ed., *The New Class?* (New Brunswick, N.J., 1979). This liberal-pluralist (neoconservative) linkage of student protest with totalitarianism is criticized in Ehrenreich, *Fear of Falling*; Richard Flacks, *Student Power and the New Left: The Role of SDS* (Chicago, 1968); and Philip E. Slater, *The Pursuit of Loneliness: American Culture at the Breaking Point* (3rd rev. ed., Boston, 1990).

For economic and cultural anxiety among the middle class, and its emergence as a political force—especially in behalf of George Wallace and Richard Nixon—see the essays in Murray Friedman, ed., *Overcoming Middle-Class Rage* (Philadelphia, 1971); Louise Kapp Howe, ed., *The White Majority: Between Poverty and Affluence* (New York, 1970); Richard Lemon, *The Troubled American* (New York, 1969); Michael Novak, *The Rise of the Unmeltable Ethnics: Politics and Culture in the Seventies* (New York, 1972); and Ronald P. Formisano, *Boston Against Busing: Race, Class, and Ethnicity in the 1960s and 1970s* (Chapel Hill, 1991).

Neoconservative critiques of Johnson's Great Society, Black Power, the counterculture, feminist challenges to traditional sex/gender arrangements, "distributive justice," and the "equality of condition" may be traced in *Commentary* magazine, with 1970 signifying a key turning point. By 1980 neoconservatives had written numerous books on most aspects of public policy. See, for example, Midge Decter, *The New Chastity and Other Arguments Against Women's Liberation* (New York, 1974); James Q. Wilson, *Thinking About Crime* (New York, 1975); Herman Kahn, *The Next 2000 Years: A Scenario for America and the World* (New York,

1976); Seymour Martin Lipset and Everett Carll Ladd, *The Divided Academy: Professors and Politics* (New York, 1975); Daniel Bell, *The Cultural Contradictions of Capitalism* (2nd ed., London, 1979); Nathan Glazer, *Affirmative Discrimination: Ethnic Inequality and Public Policy* (New York, 1975); Irving Kristol, *Two Cheers for Capitalism* (New York, 1978); and Samuel P. Huntington and Michael Crozier, *The Crisis of Democracy: Report on the Governability of Democracies to the Trilateral Commission* (New York, 1975).

Decter's ongoing critique of the women's movement influenced conservative George Gilder's criticism of changing sex roles and domestic arrangements, as it did Phyllis Schlafly's increasingly effective campaign against the Equal Rights Amendment. See especially Gilder's *Sexual Suicide* (New York, 1973) and *Naked Nomads: Unmarried Men in America* (New York, 1974). On Schlafly in the 1970s, see David Brady and Kent L. Tedin, "Ladies in Pink: Religion and Political Ideology in the Anti-ERA Movement," *Social Science Quarterly*, LVI (March 1976), 564–575; and Carol Felsenthal, *The Sweetheart of the Silent Majority* (Garden City, N.Y., 1981).

Richard Nixon found much to identify with in these accounts. Norman Podhoretz's autobiography, *Making It* (New York, 1967), for instance, juxtaposes well with the President's own self-image as a self-made man. On this point, compare Podhoretz with Garry Wills, *Nixon Agonistes: The Crisis of the Self-Made Man* (Boston, 1970). On Daniel Patrick Moynihan's switch to neoconservatism and his influence on Nixon, see Douglas Schoen, *Pat: A Biography of Daniel Patrick Moynihan* (New York, 1979), especially pp. 144–186.

Nixon's conspiratorial view of his adversaries (which fits Hofstadter's categories in *The Paranoid Style*) is a key theme in Jonathan Schell, *The Time of Illusion* (New York, 1975). Nixon's presidency marked the point of transition in the use of psychology by scholars—from a lever to delegitimize dissent, to a means to analyze presidential performance. See, as early examples, Bruce Mazlish, *In Search of Nixon: A Psychohistorical Inquiry* (New York, 1972); Nancy Geiger Clinch, *The Kennedy Neurosis* (New York, 1973); Fawn M. Brodie, *Richard Nixon: The Shaping of His Character* (New York, 1981); Lloyd de Mause and Henry Ebel, eds., *Jimmy Carter and American Fantasy: Psychological Explanations* (New York, 1977); and, more recently, Rogin, "Ronald Reagan," and John M. Ormon, *Comparing Presidential Behavior: Carter, Reagan, and the Macho Presidential Style* (Westport, Conn., 1987). Concern with presidential personality is also a central concern in political scientist James D. Barber's influential *The Presidential Character: Predicting Performance in the White House* (3rd rev. ed., Englewood Cliffs, N.J., 1985).

The McGovern candidacy and the fateful election campaign of 1972 are dealt with in Theodore H. White, *The Making of the President 1972* (New York, 1973); Eleanor McGovern, with Mary Finch Hoyt, *Uphill: A Personal Story* (Boston, 1974); and Gordon L. Weil, *The Long Shot: George McGovern Runs for President* (New York, 1973), pp. 156–194. James Wooten, *Dasher: The Roots and the Rising of Jimmy Carter* (New York, 1978), is good on Carter's populist background (and the plastic character of that term). Carter's economic policies as a "conservative-liberal" are dealt with fairly in Erwin Hargrove, *Jimmy Carter as President: Leadership and the Politics of the Public Good* (Baton Rouge, La., 1988). Carter's downfall is assessed in Betty Glad, *Jimmy Carter: In Search of the Great White House* (New York, 1980); Hamilton Jordan, *Crisis: The Last Year of the Carter Presidency* (New York, 1982); Clark R. Mollenhoff, *The President Who Failed: Carter Out of Control* (New York, 1980); Gaddis Smith, *Morality, Reason, and Power: American Diplomacy in the Carter Years* (New York, 1986); and Donald S. Spencer, *The Carter Implosion: Jimmy Carter and the Amateur Style of Diplomacy* (New York, 1988).

Jerome Himmelstein and James A. McRae, Jr., argue that by the late 1970s economic questions had supplanted the social issues that dominated political discourse during the late 1960s and early 1970s, but warn that one risks oversimplification by distinguishing them too sharply. See Himmelstein and McRae, "Social Conservatism, New Republicans, and the 1980 Elections," *Public Opinion Quarterly*, XLVIII (Fall 1984), 592–605; and "Social Issues and Socioeconomic Status," *idem.*, LII (Winter 1988), 492–512. Everett Carll Ladd, meanwhile, explores electoral apathy in *Where Have All the Voters Gone? The Fracturing of America's*

Political Parties (New York, 1982), while the Reagan triumph is explored from other perspectives in Jack W. Germond and Jules Witcover, *Blue Smoke and Mirrors: How Reagan Won and Why Carter Lost the Election of 1980* (New York, 1981); Thomas Ferguson and Joel Rogers, *Right Turn: The Decline of the Democrats and the Future of American Politics* (New York, 1986); and the essays in Thomas Ferguson and Joel Rogers, eds., *The Hidden Election* (New York, 1981), especially Walter Dean Burnham, "The 1980 Earthquake: Realignment, Reaction, or What?" pp. 98–140.

Recent updates of political realignments, suggesting the key significance of conspiratorial symbols and abstractions in Republican Party success, include Byron E. Shafer, ed., *The End of Realignment? Interpreting American Electoral Eras* (Madison, Wisc., 1991); James A. Stimson, *Public Opinion in America: Moods, Cycles, and Swings* (Boulder, Colo., 1991); Samuel L. Popkin, *The Reasoning Voter: Communications and Persuasion in Presidential Campaigns* (Chicago, 1991); and Thomas Byrne Edsall, "Willie Horton's Message," *New York Review of Books*, XXXIV (February 13, 1992), 7–11.

For the development of the political New Right of the late 1970s and 1980s, see Michael Kazin, "The Grass-Roots Right: New Histories of U.S. Conservatism in the Twentieth Century," *American Historical Review*, XCVII (February 1992), 136–155; George Nash, *The Conservative Intellectual Movement in America Since 1945* (New York, 1976), persuasive in its argument for sustained conservative growth after 1945; Alan Crawford, *Thunder on the Right: The "New Right" and the Politics of Resentment* (New York, 1980); Michael W. Myles, *The Odyssey of the American Right* (New York, 1980); Richard A. Viguerie, *The New Right: We're Ready to Lead* (Falls Church, Va., 1980); and Viguerie, *The Establishment vs. the People: Is a New Populist Revolt on the Way?* (Chicago, 1981). For the Christian New Right and Moral Majority, see Frances FitzGerald, *Cities on a Hill: A Journey Through Contemporary American Cultures* (New York, 1987), pp. 121–202; Jeffrey K. Hadden and Charles E. Swann, *Prime Time Preachers: The Rising Power of Televangelism* (Reading, Mass., 1981); and Robert C. Liebman and Robert Wuthnow, eds., *The New Christian Right: Mobilization and Legitimation* (Hawthorne, N.Y., 1983). These sources may be supplemented by William G. McLoughlin, *Revivals, Awakenings, and Reform: An Essay on Religion and Social Change in America, 1607–1977* (Chicago, 1978), pp. 179–216; Leo P. Ribuffo, "Liberals and That Old Time Religion," *The Nation*, CCXXXI (November 29, 1980), 570–573; Garry Wills, *Under God: Religion and American Politics* (New York, 1990); and Robert Wuthnow, *The Restructuring of American Religion Since World War II* (Princeton, 1988), especially pp. 200–214.

The Jacksonian distinction between "producers" and "nonproducers," so crucial to New Right, free-market ideology and conspiratorial notions, is explained in Marvin Meyers, *The Jacksonian Persuasion: Politics and Belief* (Stanford, 1957), pp. 11–23. Ongoing critiques of "permissiveness" and its equation with the New Class, the media, and poverty include William A. Rusher, *The Making of the New Majority Party* (New York, 1975); Kevin Phillips, *Mediacracy* (Garden City, N.Y., 1975); Burton Yale Pines, *Back to Basics: The Traditionalist Movement That Is Sweeping America* (New York, 1982); George Gilder, *Wealth and Poverty* (New York, 1981); Charles Murray, *Losing Ground: American Social Policy, 1950–1980* (New York, 1984); and R. Emmett Tyrell, *The Liberal Crack-Up* (New York, 1984).

For critiques of New Right and Reagan administration programs, see Richard A. Cloward, Barbara Ehrenreich, and Frances Fox Piven, *The Mean Season: The Attack on the Welfare State* (New York, 1987), especially pp. 45–108; and Ehrenreich, *Fear of Falling*, especially pp. 183–195. John D'Emilio and Estelle Freedman denote the contradiction between the Right's condemnation of pornography and its extolling of the free market that has done so much to accelerate the sexualization of commerce and the commerce of sexuality. See *Intimate Matters: A History of Sexuality in America* (New York, 1988), especially pp. 326–330, 345–354. For the weakening of the New Right during the 1980s, see Sidney Blumenthal, *Our Long National Daydream: A Political Pageant of the Reagan Era* (New York, 1988); Blumenthal, *Pledging Allegiance: The Last Campaign of the Cold War* (New York, 1990); and Haynes Johnson, *Sleepwalking Through History: America in the Reagan Years* (New York, 1991).

The debate over populism continues. For critiques of the New Right's appropriation of the term, see Blumenthal, *National Daydream*; Harry C. Boyte and Frank Riessman, eds., *The New Populism: The Politics of Empowerment* (New York, 1986); Lawrence Goodwyn, "The New Populism," *The Progressive*, XLVIII (June 1984), 18–20; and John T. Saloma III, *Ominous Politics: The New Conservative Labyrinth* (New York, 1984), especially pp. 38–49.

For definitions of "center extremism," which exhibits intolerance toward blacks, poor, the wealthy, and social planners, see Donald Warren, *The Radical Center and the Politics of Alienation* (South Bend, Ind., 1976); Eugene Litwack, Nancy Hooyman, and Donald Warren, "Ideological Complexity and Middle-American Rationality," *Public Opinion Quarterly*, XXXVII (Fall 1973), 317–332; and Samuel T. Francis, "Message from MARS: The Social Politics of the New Right," in Robert W. Whitaker, ed., *The New Right Papers* (New York, 1982), especially pp. 68–69). For examples of contemporary hate groups, see David Hamlin, *The Nazi-Skokie Conflict: A Civil Liberties Battle* (Boston, 1980); Philip Finch, *Gods, Guts, and Guns* (New York, 1983); and Dennis King, *Lyndon La Rouche and the New American Fascism* (New York, 1989). On recent anti-Semitism, suggesting the moderate right's role in protecting Jewish interests and the consistency of that protection with the Jewish community's emphasis upon the equality of opportunity, not condition, see Nathan Perlmutter and Ruth Ann Perlmutter, *The Real Anti-Semitism in America* (New York, 1982); and David A. Gerber, ed., *Anti-Semitism in American History* (Urbana, Ill., and Chicago, 1986).

Current criticism of "political correctness" reverberates with overtones of liberal-pluralist condemnations of McCarthyism and the radical right during the 1950s and 1960s and neoconservative censure of student radicals during the late 1960s and early 1970s. This campus-centered conflict reflects anger at those who would challenge the central place of the traditions of Western, white, male civilization in curricula, as well as the symbolic tension between demands for ethnic pluralism and multiculturalism, and perhaps the strongest myth in American history—the myth of the melting pot. See Allan Bloom, *The Closing of the American Mind* (New York, 1987); Dinesh D'Souza, *Illiberal Education: The Politics of Race and Sex on Campus* (New York, 1991); Roger Kimball, *Tenured Radicals: How Politics Has Corrupted Our Higher Education* (New York, 1990); and C. Vann Woodward, "Freedom and the Universities," *New York Review of Books*, XXXVIII (July 18, 1991), 32–37. For rejoinders to Vann Woodward and other critics of political correctness, see "Illiberal Education: An Exchange," *idem.*, XXXVIII (September 26, 1991), 74–76; and the essays by various authors in *The Women's Review of Books*, IX (February 1992), 13–35.

Index